SATYENDRA PAKHALÉ
Culture of Creation

nai010 publishers

CULTURE OF CREATION
Jane Szita

Satyendra Pakhalé, born in 1967, India, trained both in his native country and in Switzerland. For the past two decades, he has been working globally from his studio in Amsterdam. His design work is an act of unity going beyond any binary such as high- and low-tech, industrial production and traditional crafts, functionality and poetic significance. You might say that he stands at the crossroads of the diverse currents shaping contemporary design.

Satyendra Pakhalé: Culture of Creation, the first comprehensive monograph devoted to his work, explores the way that the designer navigates these currents on multiple levels. The notion of a 'culture of creation' refers simply to the ancient and innate impulse behind human making. It engages with the very roots of the human need to create, to design, to make, to build and bring something into reality.

Over the last twenty years or so, Pakhalé has cultivated a design practice that focuses on the culture of creation, from mass-produced industrial products to experimental one-offs, always with the aim of returning to objects and their environment the sensorial qualities that have so often been lost due to the excesses of industrialization and consumerism. A sensorial object resonates with humanity's broadest needs. It is charged with those qualities that connect people to the object itself. Therefore, we are unlikely to discard it.

Any design monograph is necessarily visual, and this one is no exception. Yet it is also much more than that. Over the years, intellectual curiosity has been a constant feature of Pakhalé's design practice. Besides his own research, he has been in dialogue with professionals from various fields including architects, writers, curators, academics, and prominent figures in the design industry, several of whom have contributed to this book.

Themes such as the culture of making, poetic analogy, perception, sensorial design, atmosphere, social modernity, secular humanism, craftsmanship, technology and more, in which his thinking and his work are rooted are addressed in twelve critical essays by authors like architect and architectural-design thinker Juhani Pallasmaa, Helsinki; Paola Antonelli, Sr., curator MoMA, New York; René Spitz, scholar on HfG Ulm, Cologne; Aric Chen, curator at large of M+ Museum, Hong Kong; Jacques Barsac, director of the Fondation Charlotte Perriand, Paris; Tiziana Proietti, architect and professor, University of Oklahoma, Norman and Stefano Marzano, former CEO Philips Design, Eindhoven.

Through these essays, the monograph illustrates the designer's world view and intellectual position, and the theoretical heritage underpinning the cultivation of a 'culture of creation'. The essays put his design projects into a wider, deeper context, offering the kind of food for thought on which he himself thrives.

The monograph structure consists of three overlapping layers, namely a project layer, documentary (studio practice) layer and research (critical essays) layer. The essays are interwoven with the project layer and documentary layer that give an insight into Pakhalé's studio practice, and with accounts from his industrial partners such as Alberto Alessi, Giulio Cappellini, Cristiano Crosetta, and Vittorio Livi. The project layer meanwhile zooms in on specific processes and approaches called 'project clusters' that are presented in the monograph with a dense graphical layout. Over the years there have been several topical design explorations carried out at Pakhalé's studio. Some of the results went into industrial production; some became limited edition gallery pieces and others remained ideas. Theory, practice and production – concepts, words, photos, sketches, watercolours, models, prototypes and more – are linked throughout these pages. Concluding the book is Satyendra Pakhalé's Chronology of Works, introduced by Ingeborg de Roode, curator of Industrial Design, Stedelijk Museum, Amsterdam, which provides an overview of his body of work.

Satyendra Pakhalé: Culture of Creation illustrates the designer's journey by placing his work in the cultural, artistic and intellectual context to which it belongs, and to which it always returns. At the same time, it anticipates what is yet to come.

CONTENT

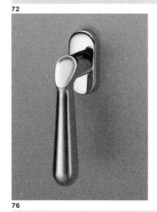

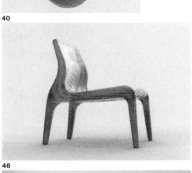

CONTENT

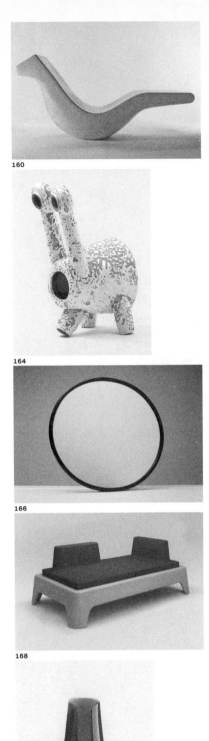

218

250

282

224

256

288

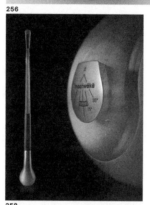

228

258

292

230

260

296

232

264

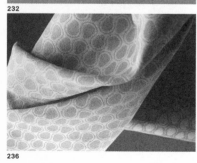

236

268

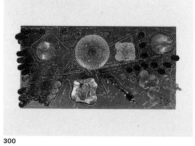

298

300

CONTENT

302

314

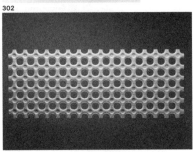

322

326

330

332

346

352

354

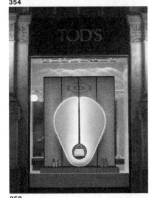

358

360

378

382

388

392

396

398

CULTURAL CONTEXT

CULTURAL CONNECTIONS

Pakhalé with his deep curiosities on a wide range of topics cultivated over the years sees the world as one place of our common human condition. Intellectual curiosity has been a constant feature of Pakhalé's design practice, leading to various themes and projects that provide a wider, deeper context and cultural connections across the book. The 'Culture of Creation' is the thinking and the research that inspires Pakhalé's everyday studio activity. It aims at exploring why we as human beings do what we do and how the things we create nurture our sensorial and social nature. Contextualizing Pakhalé's multi-facetted, culturally diverse and technologically rigorous design practice, the monograph sheds light on his design approach, way of creation, studio practice, background, critical thinking, world view and intellectual position. The monograph is designed in the form of layers such as the essay layer as reflections on the works, the documentary layer as an insight into the studio practice and the project cluster layer as a specific project process that resulted in a diverse design output. Links are provided between various layers and sections connecting concepts, ideas and projects to historic places and people across time and space. The book thus offers food for thought to cultivate further cultural connections.

01

DESIGN
BY HEART

The best contemporary
objects are those

which express
consciousness

by showing the reasons
why they were made,

and the process
that led to their making.

Paola Antonelli

A

B

C

D

DESIGN BY HEART
Paola Antonelli

Stereotypes stick to some designers like glue. In the star-system of design, Marc Newson will forever be the Australian surfer, Starck is Pierrot le Fou, Jasper Morrison the reclusive British minimalist. Even though they are not always welcomed by the designers themselves, these stereotypes can be useful ways to (initially) carve a personal space in the memory of journalists, manufacturers and buyers. Stereotypes open the door, and once the door is open, the real fullness of a designer's universe can finally be explored.

Satyendra Pakhalé, as the name, appearance, and some of the products testify, is Indian. Yet he is not your romantic idea of an 'Indian designer'. He is a creature of the world, a 'cultural nomad', as he defines himself. His education began at the IDC (Industrial Design Centre) at IIT, the renowned Indian Institute of Technology, Bombay. The IDC was founded on the model of the legendary HfG Ulm School of Design, translated into the Indian context. His studies continued at the Art Center College of Design Europe, in Switzerland.

The next stop was Philips, the Dutch appliances manufacturer, where he was a senior product designer until 1998. His current practice is based in Amsterdam, The Netherlands, but also comprises several trips around the world and long stopovers in India each year. If a stereotype is really needed, Pakhalé can be brought in as an example of the balance between nationalism and globalism, between product design and craftsmanship, between high and low technology. In other words, he is an exquisitely contemporary designer.

Local Culture, Global Priorities

Contemporary design thrives on eclecticism and diversity. The emancipation from the old-fashioned concept of 'absolute style' was timely and unavoidable, and it is certainly one of the biggest achievements of the past century. One of its best consequences is a resurgence of regional and national cultures, which has brought the public to appreciate local authenticity and to seek it as a way to acquire knowledge and to experience the world. Since the 1970s, local culture has proved to be, both for design and for architecture, the safest and most convincing way to move beyond modernism without giving up the great qualities of modern design.

A   IIT-B Indian Institute of Technology Bombay is recognized worldwide for its engineering education and research. The institution was founded in 1958 at Powai, Mumbai, India. The IIT-B campus is situated between the Vihar and Powai lakes and is divided into clusters of 584 main buildings with a combined area of around 2.2 square kilometres. Courtesy: Industrial Design Center, IIT-B, IN.

B   IDC Industrial Design Centre at IIT-B campus was founded on the Ulm model in an Indian context in 1969. Courtesy: Industrial Design Center, IIT-B, IN.

C   Art Center Europe, (1986-1996) was a sister campus of Art Center College of Design, Pasadena, California. It was located in Le Château de Sully, La Tour-de-Peilz, Switzerland. Courtesy: © Steven A. Heller, Art Center College of Design, USA.

D   Farm building at the Art Center Europe campus. Workshops, classrooms and studio spaces for students and instructors. Courtesy: © Steven A. Heller, Art Center College of Design, USA.

Pakhalé's work exemplifies how crafts and industrial design can come together

in the dimension of human nature.

Paola Antonelli

E

F

G

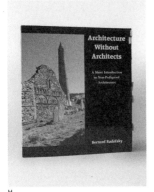

H

In 1964, Bernard Rudofsky, one of the greatest champions of local culture in architecture and design, organized the brilliant *Architecture Without Architects* exhibition at The Museum of Modern Art in New York. In the exhibition and in the catalogue, Rudofsky celebrated 'vernacular, anonymous, spontaneous, indigenous, rural, as the case may be' architecture from all over the world. Rudofsky's declaration carried to a dramatic expression a sensible trend that had already started to happen. Architects and designers in many parts of the world were mitigating the modernist rule by interpreting it in their own dialect. And today, they mitigate the homogenizing power of technology by returning a human dimension to it.

Architects and designers all over the world seem capable of recognizing the most contemporary priorities: it is a global necessity to look at the built environment with an economical and respectful consciousness, and to thus establish global standards and criteria as common goals; while at the same time there is a need to salvage the legacy of local culture as a meaningful tool to achieve such common goals. Satyendra Pakhalé is a champion of this unique evolutionary trend, and his objects add to our experience of the world.

High and Low Technologies

Pakhalé is fluent in the international language of product design, as exemplified by his collaboration with Renault while at Philips, around 1997. At the same time, by delving into the material culture of the country that generated him, he is able to add a new human and spiritual dimension to design. With his Bell Metal lost-wax casting objects, especially his B.M. Horse and Playing with Clay family of objects – the symbolic totemic ceramics chairs he produced while at the European Ceramic Work Centre, so close to the technique and language of Indian craftsmen – he has added depth to his works, even of the industrial kind. His design has evolved into contemporary objects and industrial products for leading design clients such as Cappellini❶, FIAM❷, Bosa❸, Poltrona Frau❹ and Tubes❺, in which the sensorial qualities are cultivated and innovated into more current materials and more universal forms, without losing their essence.

Pakhalé's low-tech tendency, which is more an acquired training than a direct by-product of his cultural background, also

E–G Bernard Rudofsky, *Architecture Without Architects* installation views of the exhibition by Bernard Rudofsky. The Museum of Modern Art Archives, New York. November 11, 1964 – February 7, 1965. Courtesy: © 2019. Digital image The Museum of Modern Art, New York, USA / Scala, Florence, IT.

H Bernard Rudofsky, *Architecture Without Architects*, University of New Mexico Press, USA, 1987. Courtesy: Satyendra Pakhalé Archives, Amsterdam, NL.

If a stereotype is really needed, Pakhalé can be an example in a discussion about

the balance between nationalism and globalism,

between product design and craftsmanship, between high and low technology.

In other words, he is an exquisitely contemporary designer.

Paola Antonelli

positions him at the forefront of contemporary design research. Contemporary design is in fact an extremely interesting composition of high and low technologies that offers designers a new, exhilarating freedom. Many advanced materials, especially fibres and composites, can be customized and adapted by the designers themselves, and some actually demand manual intervention, as do many low-tech recycled materials. It so happens that those designers who are not only conversant with materials, but also especially knowledgeable in hands-on techniques, have a cultural advantage in their approach to both crafts and industrial design.

The Expression of Consciousness
In both art and design, materials are chosen not only for their physical properties, but also for their metaphorical ones. Natural substances like wax, wood and mud can allude to creation at its most elemental level, while highly artificial or industrial ones like fibreglass and aluminium set a more contemporary and progressive tone. Moreover, materials old and new can be tweaked and changed to signify new directions and old rebellions. The designer's relationship with materials, on the other hand, which is traditionally tight, dialectic, and passionate, has also evolved dramatically during the past forty years. New materials have been introduced, along with new processes that have empowered designers and pushed them towards experimentation. Many design landmarks of the past four decades display the designer's surprise and delight in response to the unexpected creative freedom that new materials and techniques make possible.

Pakhalé's work exemplifies how crafts and industrial design can come together in the dimension of human nature. His work shows that the best contemporary objects are those whose presence expresses history and contemporaneity; those which exude the humours of the material culture that generated them, while at the same time speaking a global language; those which carry a memory as well as an intelligence of the future; those which are like great movies in that they either spark a sense of belonging in the world — in these exciting times full of cultural and technical possibilities — while also managing to carry us to places we have never visited before. The best contemporary objects are those which express consciousness by showing the reasons why they were made, and the process that led to their making.

ɪ   Full scale model of the B.M. Stool being made at the maker's studio, Nagpur, IN. Courtesy: Satyendra Pakhalé Archives, Amsterdam, NL.

ᴊ   Third generation B.M. Objects model being made at Pakhalé's studio, Amsterdam, NL. Courtesy: Satyendra Pakhalé Archives, Amsterdam, NL.

ᴋ   Test wax models of the third generation of B.M. Objects being made at the foundry near Milan, IT. Courtesy: Satyendra Pakhalé Archives, Amsterdam, NL.

Pakhalé's low-tech tendency, which is more an acquired training than a direct by-product of his cultural background,

positions him at the forefront of contemporary design research.

Paola Antonelli

CONTENT

FISH CHAIR — An easy chair enabling a comfortable, reclined posture, it can be used as a solo piece or in large groups, in domestic or public spaces, and in both indoor and outdoor settings. Made with rotational moulding, Fish Chair has a special insert making it a bi-colour object. It is produced in seven different colours, always with the white inside. Fish Chair was the first chair designed by Satyendra Pakhalé. He recalls: 'I never designed a chair before Fish Chair, and it is one of those projects which led me to really understand the meaning of prototypes. It went through several prototypes before becoming a product. Looking back, I can feel how important it was to the product-manufacturing process to resolve all the issues through the prototypes.'

Satyendra Pakhalé is a poet of form and materials. Even when his designs are industrial products, like the Fish Chair, which we spotted in Milan and put into production in 2005, or the Add-On Radiator ❶, they still have an appeal connected to form and materials. This has roots in his country of origin and he expresses it in a contemporary way. He is one of those rare designers who can mix this cultural DNA with a present-day sensibility.

I find him extremely intriguing and I still think of him as a 'young' designer, as he looks at the world through the eyes of a child. He expresses great curiosity about form, materials and their expressions and meanings without betraying their origins. What I appreciate most about Satyendra's way of working is that it is always highly contemporary.

Some of his early ceramic pieces, such as the Flower Offering Chair ❷ and Roll Carbon Ceramic Chair ❸, and the B.M. Horse in bronze, start from the investigation of a traditional craft culture, rooted in his Indian heritage. Yet these pieces are absolutely contemporary and international in their interpretation of crafts and ways of making.

I think it is important for a designer to create while looking to the future, but without killing history. It is evident from Satyendra Pakhalé's various design works that his curiosities are projected into the future, yet with full awareness of the past.

Another important facet of his multi-disciplinary design practice is his respect for materials. He loves working with many different materials – natural and artificial. Before starting the design of a product, he wants to know all about the possibilities and expressions of a given material. For design, it is important to make people smile and dream, and he does that with his projects. Experiencing his work is a joy.

— Giulio Cappellini

One of the design icons of the third millennium, imagined by one of the few authors capable of truly speaking another language. He is determined to combine the never placated ideal of reaching big numbers, through true industrial production in order to improve people's lives with a healthy drive towards the expressive pleasure of making a mark on one's time with objects and gestures that are far from silent, never banal and always original in terms of form.

— Beppe Finessi and Marva Griffin Wilshire

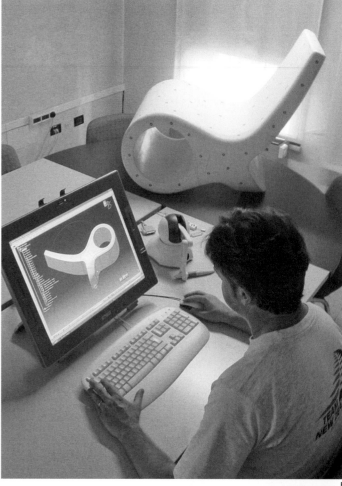

A   First full scale fibreglass prototype of Fish Chair at the maker's studio, Nagpur, IN.

B   The full-scale model being 3D-scanned and rebuilt using parametric software to achieve a controlled surface at Vicenza, IT.

C   Prototype being studied for making a mould at Cappellini, Mariano Comense, IT.

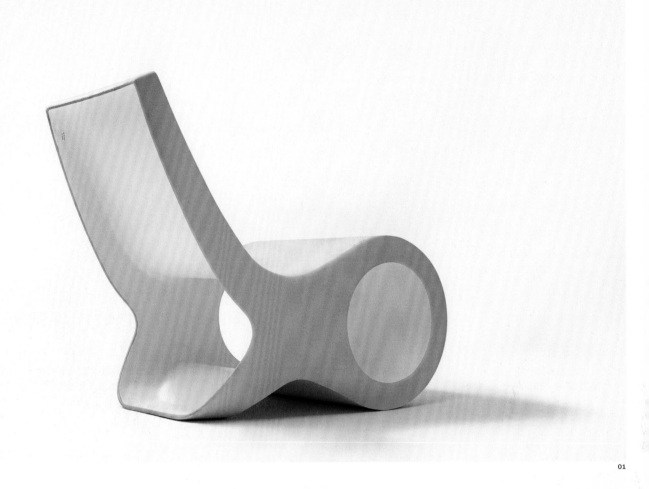

01 First batch production in fibreglass painted in a soft touch coating. Soft touch paint is derived from coatings used in aerospace applications such as fuselage cabin and structures that have to be extremely tough and durable with latest aesthetics.
02 Fish Chair in rotational moulding plastics with sturdy cross-section for long durability. It has a special insert making it a bi-colour object and is produced in seven different colours, always with the white inside.

03

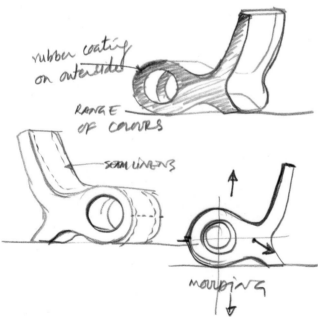

rubber coating on outerside

RANGE OF COLOURS

SEAM LINENS

MOULDING

04

03   Industrially produced Red Fish Chair in rotational moulding plastics with the white inside.
04   Design sketch made during product development illustrating the mould opening and surface coating ideas.
05   The articulate rear foot detail creating surface continuity.

D

E

F

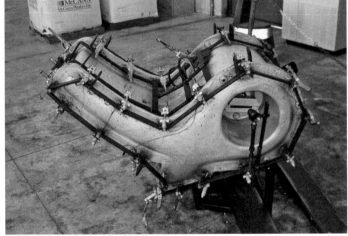

G

H

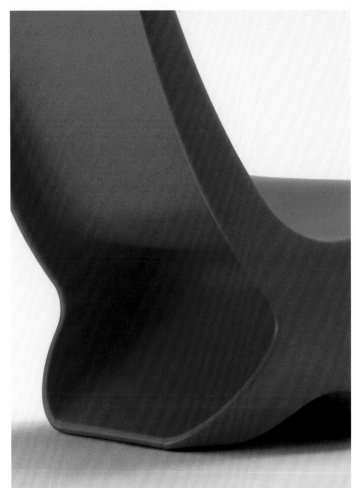

05

D, E First fibreglass model being weighed for shipping from Nagpur, India to Milan, IT. Pakhalé checking the first physical full-scale model.

F, G Pakhalé controlling the final 3D CAD mathematical model before making the moulds at Cappellini, Mariano Comense, IT.

H Fish Chair being launched by Cappellini during the Milan Design Week 2005, IT.

IN-BETWEEN — The average person uses over 700 pounds of paper products every year, which is ten times more than a century ago, and almost twice the per capita consumption of the 1970s. There are a number of things we can do to reduce our consumption of paper. We can apply the 3R motto - Reduce, Reuse and Recycle. But the best possibility would be to solve this over-consumption problem in a sustainable manner. Too often, paper is printed on one side only and then trashed. The other side of the page could be used for all sorts of purposes, such as brainstorming and noting down thoughts and ideas. Responding to the current crisis, Pakhalé created a new typology of objects called 'In-Between' that can be placed in-between spaces. The utility of these stools and side tables is to encourage the reuse of one-sided printed A4, A3 and A2 paper.

The objects are designed to act as a reuse bin in the form of a stool and a table that accommodate paper formats A4, A3 and A2. Applying the moulded pulp container manufacturing process that is currently used for making egg packaging in an innovative manner, In-Between objects are produced in a sustainable way. Looking at the bigger picture, Pakhalé believes 'Consumption is a treatable disease. It can be treated with multiple design approaches, and one of those strategies is creating objects which are made of recycled paper and encourage users not to trash but to reuse one-sided printed paper.' These In-Between objects for the office and home encourage users to reuse, reduce and recycle office paper and hopefully affect a behavioural change.

01

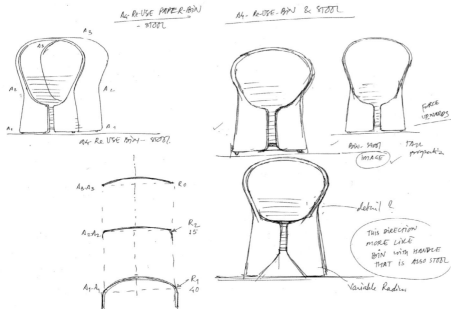

02

01   In-Between A3 Centre Table as a reuse bin for the office or home. It has a space to hold used or single-side printed A3 paper with a recycled chipboard base.
02   Design sketch of a stool-cum-A4-paper-reuse-bin as an In-Between object. Convenient for a quick meeting with a team-mate at the office.
03   In-Between stool with A4 paper reuse bin that is made with the moulded pulp container manufacturing process familiar from egg packaging.

BELL METAL OBJECT MAKING

In Satyendra Pakhalé's view, industrial design products, with their built-in obsolescence, lack 'symbolic content and cultural significance.' In an attempt to find alternatives to this sterility in mass manufactured goods, he aims to create 'sensorial qualities in industrial design – such as the texture and warmth we recognize in age-old objects, yet without passively accepting traditions.'

Pakhalé believes that 'manual work is an integral part of every design process, in industrial design just as much as craft. Working with the hands is a way of thinking and keeping in touch with the kind of making that expresses universal values that are understandable everywhere.'

As a means of reclaiming sensoriality, Pakhalé cast a fresh eye on a technique that has been practiced for many hundreds of years in central India: the art of cire perdue - lost wax metal casting. Once ubiquitous, the ancient craft is still practiced in bell metal by the Muria community in the Bastar region of central India. Pakhalé first visited this area in 1996 and recalls being 'captivated by the Muria people and their ancient yet progressive system of living. Their process of making lost-wax cast objects is completely pre-industrial and was rooted in their way of living.'

The Muria are one of India's oldest indigenous peoples. Pakhalé was 'fascinated by their democratic social structure and the dance-loving socio-ethical educational system of Ghotul: a social institution, a training resource centre and recreational club for young people based on equality, simplicity and freedom.'

He also admired their 'homes that are wonderful examples of earth architecture, and a way of life in harmony with nature that rests on sharing resources democratically. The Muria afford the same rights to women as to men. Every Muria individual wears different clothing, and an amazing level of creativity seems to go into their dress and other everyday items. The culture of object-making is at the heart of their way of life.'

Pakhalé makes it a basic principle to avoid 'the codified forms and style of traditional craftsmanship, along with the works of traditional artisans that have no practical utility.' Nevertheless, he strives to 'observe traditional cultures objectively, reflecting on their meaning and relevance in the contemporary context.' His objective is always to create contemporary works with universal reach and the sensorial qualities that he so values. The Muria craft techniques that he discovered in the 1990s offered the perfect opportunity to do exactly that. Working together with Muria craftsmen, Pakhalé's early experiments evolved into the first generation of Bell Metal objects.

A   Traditionally rough moulds are made. Pakhalé suggested having a potter make them instead, that is not the practice as the two communities usually do not work together, but he convinced them of the benefit of collaboration.

B   The dried clay mould is rubbed with local tree leaves to make the surface smooth and clean. The craftsmen have developed a refined sensitivity to objects created with ecological means.

C–F   Natural wax is collected from trees, melted and strained through a fine cloth, keeping it clean and free of impurities. Then it is squeezed through a sieve to create wax wires.

F

G

H

I

Three periods of lost-wax casting experimentation in bell metal can be identified in Pakhalé's studio practice. Spanning over fifteen years and resulting in the family of the first, second and third generations of the B.M. Objects ❶. The three phases date from 1996–1998; 2006–2008; and 2010–2012 respectively. Each generation has its own distinct identity.

They are differentiated not only by the objects' sizes, proportions and formal language, but also the object-making process and technique that evolved with each generation of B.M. Objects.

By training Indian craftsmen in new design approaches, by creating bigger, more complex objects using this technique, and by mixing craftsmanship, industrial technique, engineering and material research, Pakhalé pushed the boundaries, resulting in the biggest B.M. Object so far: the totemic B.M. Horse ❷. By refining and renewing a traditional process, he created truly contemporary design objects.

The Muria Lost-Wax Process
First, the Muria make a core with a mixture of fine clean sand and clay. Traditionally, goat's dung is then soaked in water, ground and mixed with clay in equal proportions. This soft mixture forms the base mould. Once dried, it forms the basis for the wax pattern. A specially filtered natural beeswax is melted over an open fire and strained through a fine cloth into a basin of cold water where it becomes solid. Care has to be taken to keep the wax absolutely clean and free of impurities. Next, it is squeezed through a sieve and recovered in the form of wax 'wires' (as thick or thin as desired). Each of these wires is wrapped around the core, one after another, until the whole surface is covered. Originally, the artisan would have sat in the sun to let the clay core and the wax coating warm up uniformly. The whole form is finally covered in a mixture of clay, sand and cow dung in equal parts, and then fired. Base metals – brass, bronze, copper, tin – are melted together and poured into the fired-clay mould to form the metal object, the wax being lost in the process. Pakhalé applied this process to the first generation B.M. Objects while refining it. Later, he developed a unique updated process by making a PVC cord of special density and flexibility and using silicone moulds to achieve results which are refined and more challenging to cast in a seamless manner.

B.M. Objects – First Generation 1996–1998
These are the first B.M. Objects made with the traditional lost-wax technique practiced by the Muria community in central India with its long tradition of making ritual figurative objects and a specific culture

G, H Each wax thread is wound once around the core, one after another, until the whole surface is covered. The craftsman sits in the sun to let the clay core and wax coating warm up uniformly.

I After carefully doing the wax thread work, a handle pattern is cut out with the help of a simple template, improving the quality of the final cast object. Such basic techniques are hardly Used due to the limited educational possibilities.

of creation. The first generation of objects was made using natural beeswax and a mould made of fine clay that is broken after casting. That means a new beeswax model has to be made for each casting. The forms are relatively small in size at around 10 × 15 × 25 cm. All share a central departure point and are symmetrical in shape. These are totally handmade objects, meaning each step of the process has to be repeated from the beginning if something goes wrong or if the results are not as expected. The process is perhaps the total opposite of industrial or semi-industrial ways of making an object. ❸

B.M. Objects – Second Generation 2006–2008
Between 2006–2008, Pakhalé developed a second generation of objects in Europe using an evolved version of the lost-wax method. The second generation of B.M. Objects benefit from the development of a special, spaghetti-like, flexible PVC cord with a specific flexibility and density. This replaces the traditional beeswax spaghetti. In various diameters, the new PVC cord was used for all the objects of the second and third generation. In addition, Pakhalé further developed the traditional process by making a silicone mould to replace the clay mould, therefore allowing for serial production. The second generation objects are bigger in form than the earlier versions, although still made with a central departure point and a symmetrical shape. The second generation of B.M. Objects was produced in a small series. ❹

B.M. Objects – Third Generation 2010–2012
The most recent series of B.M. Objects was developed in a similar manner to the second generation using silicone moulds, but with greater formal complexity owing to the off-centre starting point. This asymmetrical departure point results in two types, one that keeps the form symmetrical on both axes, and another with an asymmetrical form on at least one axis. This process leads to a unique opening at the top of the object which has a distinct form, creating an effect that makes us think about how this object was made.

This very specific process results in a new language for the third generation of B.M. Objects, with their controlled geometric forms and strong totemic presence. Despite the advanced-level application of current state-of-the-art software at Pakhalés studio, such geometry resulting in a distinct opening form at the top of the object could not have been achieved without the continuous evolution of B.M. Objects making process over the extended period of time. Pakhalé recalls, 'we could not achieve the desired results by modeling these objects with 3D CAD; they

J   A Muria craftsman works on a scale model of the B.M. Horse Chaise.

K, L   After being covered with a thick layer of a mixture of clay, sand and cow dung, the model is ready for firing.

M, N   Pieces of scrap brass, bronze and copper are melted together and poured into the fired clay mould to form the first generation One-Off Bell Metal Objects, the result of a sustainable process of making.

M

N

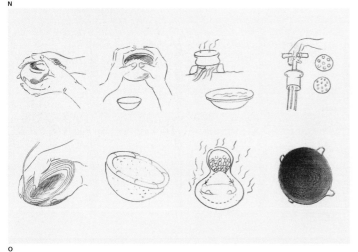

O

o   Drawing illustrating the bell metal making process described above.

can be remodelled after making them with the high level of craftsmanship that we evolved over the years, but that does not help design the objects, it is simply redrawing them in three dimensions.' He therefore calls these pieces 'post-3D CAD objects'. The third-generation objects are all relatively larger in size than their predecessors, at around 30 × 35 × 45 cm. All of them were produced in limited editions. ❺

The Steps of the Bell Metal Making Process
Making the clay mould: Traditionally Muria craftsmen make moulds by hand. However, Pakhalé could convince the craftsmen to make articulate clay moulds on a potter's wheel.

Refining the clay mould: After drying, the clay mould is rubbed with local tree leaves to make the surface smooth and even out the roughness of the mould. The craftsmen have developed a refined sensitivity to objects created with ecological means. Subsequently, when the mould is dried, it becomes a base for the wax pattern.

Making wax wires: A natural wax collected from trees in abundant quantity on jungle terrain is melted over an open fire and strained through a fine cloth into a basin of cold water, where it becomes solid. Great care is taken to keep the wax absolutely clean and free of impurities. Then it is squeezed through a sieve syringe and formed into thick or thin wax wires.

Wax work: Each wax thread is wound once around the core, one after another, until the whole surface is covered. The highly skilled craftsman sits in the sun to let the clay core and wax coating warm up uniformly to avoid uneven deformation.

Covering with clay: Once the entire model is covered with a thick layer of a mixture of equal parts of clay, sand and cow dung the model becomes ready for firing.

Lost-wax casting: The clay covered models are then fired in an open pit oven until the wax is burned and the clay mould becomes a mould cavity. Then, pieces of scrap brass, bronze, and copper are melted together and poured into the fired clay mould to form the bell metal object.

Mould opening and finishing: After the casting, as the temperature of the mould falls to room temperature, it is broken open to access the bell metal object. The entire process is carried out diligently. If all stages went well the object does not have any holes or air gaps. The object is then brushed to take off the burrs. The Muria people metaphorically associate this entire bell metal making process with life.

01

B.M. OBJECT FAMILY — The first generation of B.M. Objects was made using the lost-wax technique of the Muria community. The forms share a central departure point and are symmetrical in shape. The mould is made of clay and destroyed after casting, which means a new beeswax model is needed for each cast object. After carefully observing the craft, Pakhalé started thinking about how to create contemporary objects by refining the entire process, but without losing its handmade charm. This proved difficult, but the designer trained the craft practitioners to learn his slightly improved process, before focusing on creating everyday table-top objects including a spoon, vase, bowl, fruit bowl, and hanger.

 ➔ 190–193 ➔ 196–203 ➔ 282–287

01   A spoon with an integral handle. This object was realized to achieve a singularly consistent work in the chosen process of bell metal casting.
02   B.M. Bowl with integrated single handle.
03   B.M. Bowl with integrated side opening detail. It is made with such refined craftsmanship that the wax texture is retained on the inside as well as the outside of the object. This is a unique achievement, as to avoid airlocks and defects in the lost-wax casting process generally one surface is smoothed out, as in the image above. Such an object could be made only by highly skilled artisans with acute sensibilities and a thorough understanding of the lost-wax casting process.

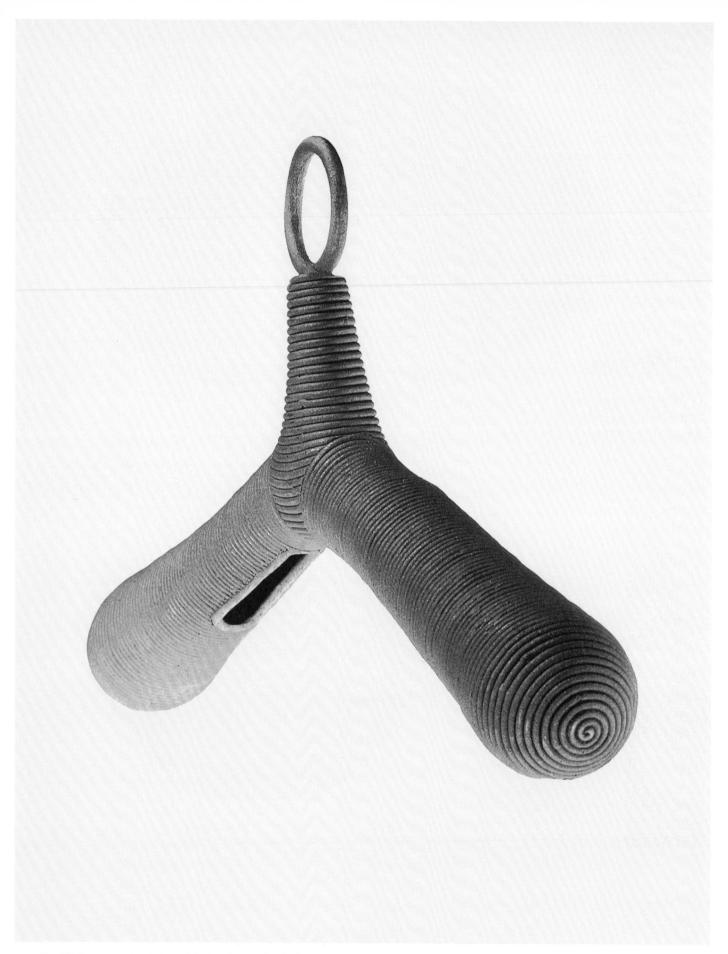

04 The B.M. Hanger is a singularly consistent work cast using the first generation Bell Metal process.
05 The B.M. Fruit Bowl set has two parts, a lower and an upper basket. A bowl with a single integrated handle and base with three integrated legs, it can be used for various purposes.
06 Working drawing for the Muria craftsmen made during the making of the first generation of B.M. Objects.

B.M. OBJECT FAMILY

B

C

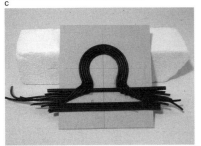

D

E

F

05

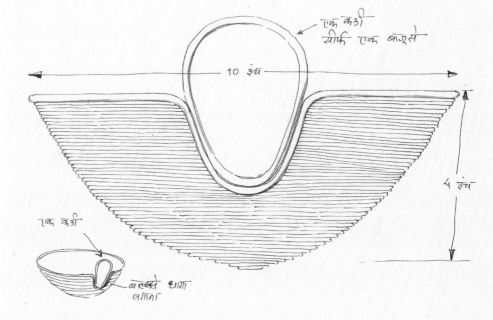

06

A   The second generation B.M. Objects evolved through the development of the spaghetti technique when beeswax was replaced with black flexible PVC cord.

B, C   Pakhalé briefing his team and developing the process further. The flexible PVC cord was designed especially for the making of the second generation B.M. Objects when the clay mould was replaced by a silicone mould.

D–F   Second generation B.M. Objects: handle details being studied at the studio with black flexible PVC cord. Model of a basket and a vase being cast into a silicone mould.

07

G

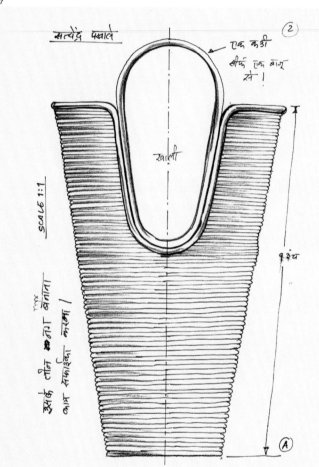

H

I

08

07 A set of three vases with three types of integrated handles.
08 Models based on the sketches and working drawings craftsmen. After initial difficulties and tryouts, Pakhalé did manage to make relatively complex forms and created highly crafted first generation B.M. Objects.
09 A bracelet made using the bell-metal lost-wax casting technique.

J

K

L

M

N

09

G–I The second generation B.M. Objects cast in bronze are chiseled and sandblasted. A 3D printed (stereo-lithography) model of a basket allows the surface tactile quality to be studied.

J–L A base study model before black flexible PVC cord modeling. A completed vase model after PVC cord modeling and test silicone mould with plaster case around it.

M,N The second generation B.M. Objects are finished with a soft grain sandblasted surface finish.

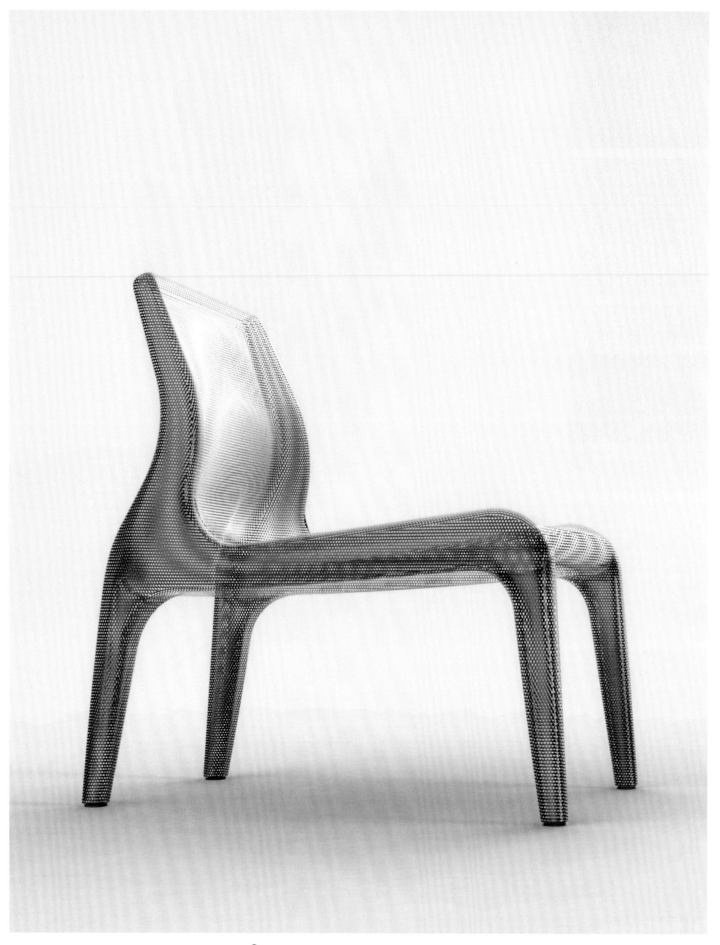

LITTLE PANTHER — After creating the Panther multi-chair ❶, the idea was to evolve an industrially produced easy chair in a similar language for both indoor and outdoor settings using injection moulded polycarbonate with a metal wire-mesh insert. As Pakhalé explains, 'I am interested in bringing an unexpected aspect to industrial manu-facturing processes that could evoke another perceptual and experiential quality in an industrial design object.' At the end of the chair's life-cycle, a thermo-electric shock on the wire mesh helps to separate metal and plastics for recycling.

A

B

C

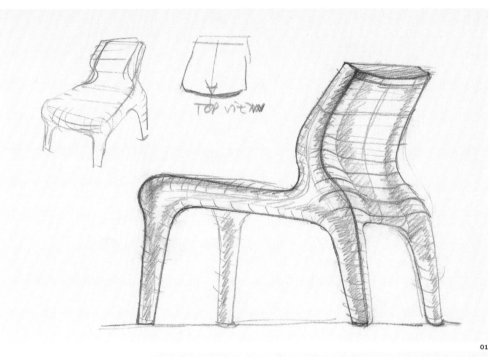

01

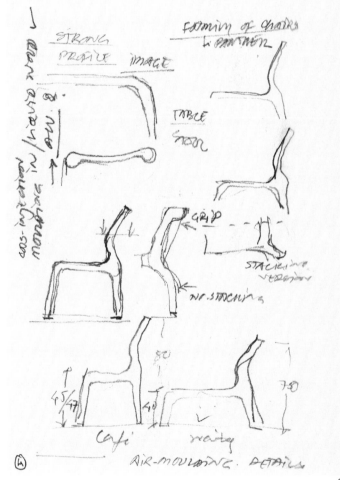

02

A–C   Various study scale models in styrofoam and cardboard.

01   Design sketch illustrating model surface contours.
02   Design sketch illustrating model cross sections and thicknesses.

02
ACT OF UNITY

True beauty exists in the realm where there is no distinction between the beautiful and the ugly,

a realm that is described as 'prior to beauty and ugliness' or as a state

where 'beauty and ugliness are as yet unseparated'.

There can be no true beauty, then, outside that realm where beauty and ugliness have not yet begun to conflict with each other.

Soetsu Yanagi

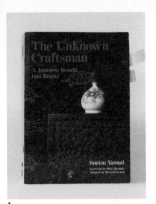

A

B

ACT OF UNITY
Tiziana Proietti

We tend to believe that the world we live in is composed of opposites and dualities – beautiful or ugly, affluent or impoverished, innovative or traditional, east or west, rational or emotional, high-tech or low-tech. Everything we experience is touched by the idea of an opposite element or concept that works as a filter for us to assign a value to the experienced object. Something expensive is mostly perceived as *not poor* and therefore good – perhaps because it is made from precious materials, by refined processes or carries a famous name. We spontaneously ascribe values to things and the environment surrounding us due to our preconceived notion of opposites, which we carefully build into a stratified system of thinking. However, the powerful essence of what we experience discloses itself only in the field between the two extremes of opposition – and therefore in a place equally distant from them both, where the definition of extremes does not exist at all. That middle way is the most fascinating and powerful realm of intuitive perception – or the 'intuitive eye' to use Soetsu Yanagi's words – as the source of the most sensorial experience of the surrounding reality.

As Yanagi says, 'True beauty exists in the realm where there is no distinction between the beautiful and the ugly, a realm that is described as "prior to beauty and ugliness" or as a state where "beauty and ugliness are as yet unseparated". There can be no true beauty, then, outside that realm where beauty and ugliness have not yet begun to conflict with each other'[1]. Deeply rooted in the early secular Buddhist philosophy[2] that focuses on the human perception and cognition of external reality, this search beyond dualities fully trusts in the senses, but with the insight of considering the mind as a sense just like the other senses.

The Middle Path
The artists and designers committed to the genuine act of making do not choose beauty to eliminate ugliness, and they do not fight against certain concepts to achieve or conquer their opposites. They are the ones disclosing that field in between, where the extremes become parts of a dialogue where one is essential to the existence of the other. This is the realm where the emotional and the rational blend, and where the mind joins the other senses as a

A, B   Calligraphy by Soetsu Yanagi, 'Beyond beauty and uglines' and 'Today the sky is clear', *The Unknown Craftsman. A Japanese Insight into Beauty*, Tokyo, New York: Kodansha International, 1989. Courtesy: Satyendra Pakhalé Archives, Amsterdam, NL.

1   Soetsu Yanagi, *The Unknown Craftsman. A Japanese Insight into Beauty*, Tokyo, JP; New York, USA: Kodansha International, 1989, p. 130.
2   The secular Buddhist philosophy was born in India, named in Pali as *Jhāna*, translated into Sanskrit as *Dhyāna* and transmitted to China, Vietnam and Korea as *Ch'an*, *Thien*, *Sŏn* and *Zen* respectively, and finally to Japan.

51   ACT OF UNITY   TIZIANA PROIETTI

In real existence there is only unity.

Rumi

C

D

sense in itself. The process of making, through which human beings modify the natural world to make it accessible to the senses and to inhabit it, is the strongest manifestation of this encounter.

Today, we often interpret the rational solution to a given design problem as embodying functionality and efficiency. But we often tend to forget that there is no rationality without emotion, and any necessity, rationally addressed, asks also for a sensorial solution. As human beings we acquire knowledge of the world from sensorial inputs that reach our brain, cultivating our senses. This act of knowing through experience is far from being merely rational. It is a mix that happens all at once in the process of perceiving. Similarly, the act of designing is an embodied multi-sensorial act where all the senses work silently together, just like riding a bicycle, to mention an action familiar to most of us. While sitting on the bicycle, positioning the feet and starting to pedal, we are simultaneously activating our sense of navigation, balance and location as well as our physical and most sensorial aptitudes by grasping the brakes, moving the legs in rhythm, looking around to keep the context connected to our movements, and more. All of this happens naturally after a process of learning and coordinating all those senses. Design practice, or 'sensorial cultivation', is similarly a perfectly balanced merger between the senses. The cultivation of this middle path between rational and emotional is vital to Pakhalé's design practice.

Only Unity

The poet Rumi said, 'in real existence there is only unity'[3]. Pakhalé's everyday activity and studio practice is committed to the edification of design culture as a creative act beyond dualism: beyond tradition as opposed to innovation; handmade as opposed to digital; or high-tech as opposed to low-tech. Design for him is not about making one component of the existent duality win over another. Only by going beyond this contention it is possible to look at materials, techniques and their expressions along with design processes and search for magical encounters. With this insight, the projects are developed in the day-to-day design practice at the studio. For Pakhalé, 'design is an act of unity.'

When, in 2002, Pakhalé was commissioned by Tubes Radiatori Italy to design a radiator, he rethought the way we make our space comfortable in winter by making it warmer. While designing

C, D Jalal al-Din Rumi, *Masnavi*, illustrated manuscript. This epic poetic masterpiece in Persian by Rumi consists of six books of poetry that together amount to about 25,000 couplets. Ink, watercolour and gold on paper with leather binding, gift of Alexander Smith Cochran, 1913. Courtesy: Metropolitan Museum of Art, New York, USA.

3   Jalal-al Din Rumi, *Masnavi*, book four, 3829–3853, 1207–1273.

The cultivation of the
middle path between
rational and emotional

is vital to Pakhalé's
design practice.

Tiziana Proietti

E

F

the Add-On Radiator ❶, his objective was to conserve energy, minimize waste and optimize usability by rethinking the way the traditional radiator is mounted on a wall. The Add-On Radiator was conceptualized as an autonomous wall, with air passing through it, and both sides warming the space. At the same time, it creates a sensorial, comforting architectural space within a space; a new ambience and atmosphere. It is perfectly designed to address a basic human need in an innovative way. It is rationally thought out and comes from a tireless investigation into technology and materials, and at the same time is a piece charged with sensorial qualities, designed by engaging a thorough understanding of human senses. Such a design could only be created by going beyond dualities and preconceptions. Only by looking beyond conventions and current conditions could Pakhalé create an object like the Add-On Radiator.

Equal Validity

At Pakhalé's studio, techniques are not romanticized or approached with any bias or preconceived notions. It is clear that *handmade* cannot be understood as opposite to *digital*, just as it cannot be idealized or dressed up in nostalgia. Human making has developed over centuries by means of numerous techniques in which both hand and tool play a role in the creation of the final object. A chisel, and even the material sculpted, collaborates with the hand in order to create a specific form. Even when we use digital tools, there is still a collaboration between hand and tool. Every tool has a specific merit in the way it contributes to the process and all tools are equally valid. Handmade and digital tools are available to the contemporary world and by using them wisely, objects can be made that address our broadest needs and are utilitarian, physical, sensorial, and intellectual. The resulting objects embody a sense of human warmth without compromising utility. In the same way there is no stratification of values to be assigned to materials, poor or rich, humble or precious. Every material is noble and valid as long as it is not toxic. The value comes from the expressiveness of the object that successfully meets the properties of the material and the applied techniques.

The design challenges are far too complex and deeply existential to be dealt with solely in a conceptualized, rational manner. It is subtly sophisticated emotion, interwoven with rational thought and action, that creates deeply sensorial work.

E,F   Add-On Radiator that can be either mounted on the wall or recessed in the wall, creating a space divider and allowing air to pass through it for more effective heating. Courtesy: Tubes Radiatori, IT.

It is subtly sophisticated emotion, interwoven with

rational thought and action,

that creates deeply sensorial work.

Tiziana Proietti

CONTENT

AGMA TOY TROLLEY — Agma Toy Trolley is a playful object for children aged two to six. It has a utilitarian side as a way of storing toys and returning them to the child's room. Through play, it helps children to cultivate the good habit of tidying up after playing. However, the object also appeals to the child's highly developed sense of fantasy, as Pakhalé explains: 'I provided an integral handle for the toy trolley so one child can sit and hold the handle while another child pulls the draw bar − suddenly making it a car, train or a plane in their imagination − or a ship, an elephant, space shuttle or anything else.'

01

01 Agma Toy Trolley has a round handle designed to fit into the steering bar. It has a protruding curved shape that allows a child to lift it easily when it is on the floor. In the child's imagination, the steering bar could become the aileron of an aeroplane, the helm of a ship, the steering wheel of a car, or a space shuttle's orbiter. Gas-injection moulding results in a soft-touch surface that is easier to grip.

02   Agma Toy Trolley wheels are two component injection-moulded with a soft layer on top to prevent injury and to reduce noise when used on hard surface. A generous
      gap is provided between the body of the toy trolley and the attachment detail so children's fingers cannot get stuck in between.
03   Agma Toy Trolley facilitates children's highly developed sense of fantasy with an integral handle, so that one child can sit and hold the handle bar while another child
      pulls the draw bar.

WIRE MESH FAMILY — Wire Mesh Chair is the result of Satyendra Pakhalé's fascination with Charles Pollock's Penelope Chair: 'Few pieces in the history of design stand out for their cultural contribution as this one does,' he says. 'The Penelope Chair is one of those innovative objects which synthesized a new way of making an industrial object, leading to a specific aesthetic. I wanted to create a contemporary café chair using a similar industrial manufacturing process, and so the Wire Mesh Family was born.' The chair has a basic aluminium extrusion profile that holds a wire mesh shell, giving it structural strength. An elegant chair, it can nevertheless be produced in high volumes. The wire mesh is formed using a simple mould made out of synthetic resin or wood and coated with an epoxy paint to retain the three-dimensional shape. It also

prevents corrosion and rusting and makes for an aesthetic surface finish. Wire Mesh Chair is versatile, suitable for outdoor as well as indoor use. A whole range of products can be fairly economically achieved from just one aluminium extrusion profile, including a family of chairs, easy chairs, chaise longues, stools, café tables, central tables and side tables. The Wire Mesh Chair and other objects are characterized by the transparency of the material, which evokes a feeling of lightness.

01

02

PAGE-1 Ⓑ maximum pump area.

THE FILLET
GRADUALLY INCREASES FROM
THIS POINT ONWARDS.

FRONT-VIEW Satyendra
WIRE-MESH-CHAIR
DESIGN: Satyendra Pakhalé

03

01–03 Wire Mesh Chairs, 3D-scanned surface from full-scale styrofoam model.
04 The series' café table and set of stools have a fresh, light atmosphere.
05 The centre table in the series is suitable for both indoor and outdoor use.

A

B

C

04

D

05

A, B Full-scale styrofoam model of the chair with integrated armrest.

C Product development meetings.

D Wire Mesh Chair full-scale styrofoam model being assembled.

CONVERSATION SOFA — Hästens of Sweden, a heritage company making high-end beds, invited Satyendra Pakhalé to invent a new typology of object using Hästens' natural materials and manufacturing process. After carefully studying them, Pakhalé designed a utilitarian sofa that makes use of the company's patented twin-spring technology. This sofa has an upright and compact posture. It is not for lounging, but for conversation – hence its name. Conversation Sofa uses carefully sourced, all-natural materials including horsehair, cotton, wool, flax, pine, steel, and down for comfort and durability.

➡ 218–223

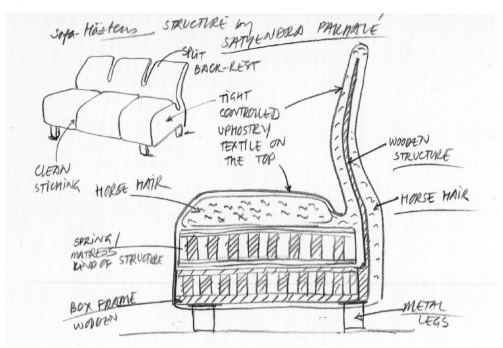

01

A

B

02

C

D

01 Design sketch by Pakhalé in which he reinterprets the patented bed-spring technology and adapts it to create a sofa with an upright and compact structure.
02-04 Conversation Sofa set: the three-seater, two-seater, chaise longue and ottoman in steelcut and Hästens Blue Check textile.

E

F

G

H

I

03

04

A   Horsehair comes with its own extremely effective, built-in ventilation system, making it perfect for a sofa.

B   Pure new wool is used as stuffing. Because it can both warm and cool, it works as the sofa's natural climate control unit.

C, D   A highly skilled team of craftsmen and women worked on this project, as shown.

E, F   Building the prototypes at Hästens, Sweden R&D department.

G, H   Developing the upholstery solution.

I   A chaise longue completes the Conversation Sofa set.

SURYA SUNDIAL CALENDAR — With our current non-physical experience of digital devices, the sundial as an everyday object has become almost lost in antiquity. Pakhalé, who worked on handheld digital communication devices in the mid-1990s, created SURYA, a sundial and calendar, to counteract our obsession with such devices in 1999. Pakhalé wanted to bring back the mathematical beauty of the sundial and rethink the ancient calendar as a physical object that encourages play, like a puzzle as a table-top object. He integrated a CE – Common Era – calendar and NEWS coordinates (north, east, west, south) along with sundial mathematics for specific latitudes in a single gesture, creating a meaningful contemporary object.

01

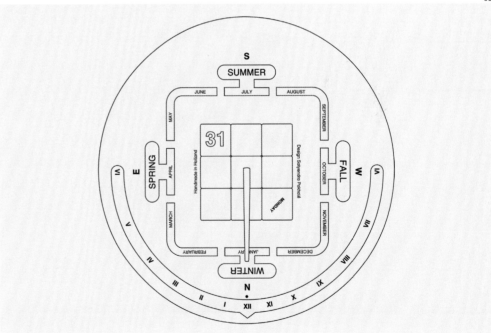

02

01   SURYA was designed and prototyped for *Work 'n' Play*, one of Satyendra Pakhalé's first exhibitions in Milan, 2001. It is made of anodized aluminium with laser etching and engraved Corian.

02   The core concept of the object is the integration of a sundial and calendar as shown in the diagram. The objective is to help people experience the daily ritual of maintaining a calendar while understanding the sundial.

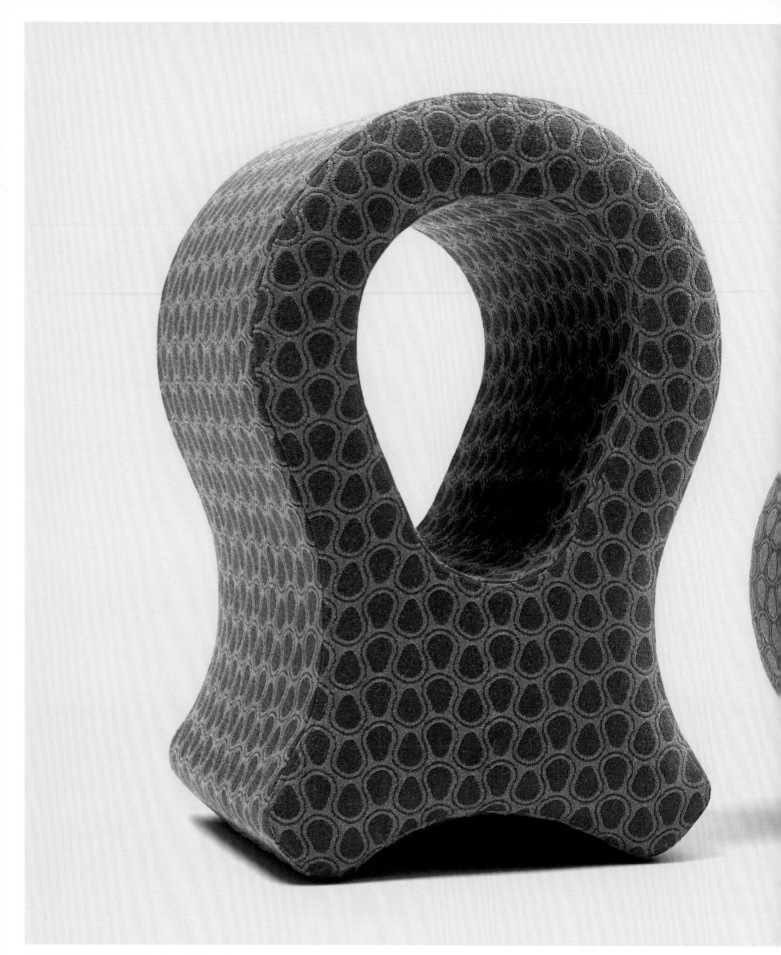

MEANDER STACKABLE STOOL — This upholstered stool is a seating object designed for intuitive, active use in collaborative spaces, making it ideal for spontaneous meetings and conferences. The stool can be used and stacked in two different ways – vertically or horizontally – creating a fascinating landscape in an interior space. The stacked stools can become a colourful backdrop or partition wall separating work and meeting spaces in open office areas and providing a good sound-absorbing wall. Pakhalé: 'The main feature of this object that I have observed is that it evokes a ludic response in users. They pick up the stool from the stacked wall, use it for sitting however they like, and place it back in the stacked position.' The stacked stools occupy little space.

01

01   The geometry of the stackable stool makes it tessalate perfectly in both upright and horizontal positions.
02   Meander prototypes being tested for horizontal stacking stability.
03   Sketch of the Meander concept by Pakhalé.

A

B

C

D

02

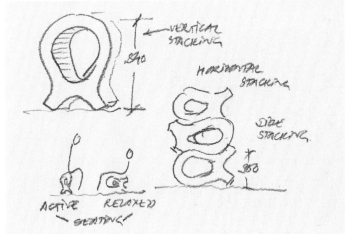

03

A   Meander study models at Pakhalé's studio, Amsterdam, NL.   B, C   The first prototypes in use.   D   The stools being used at Pakhalé's studio, Amsterdam, NL.

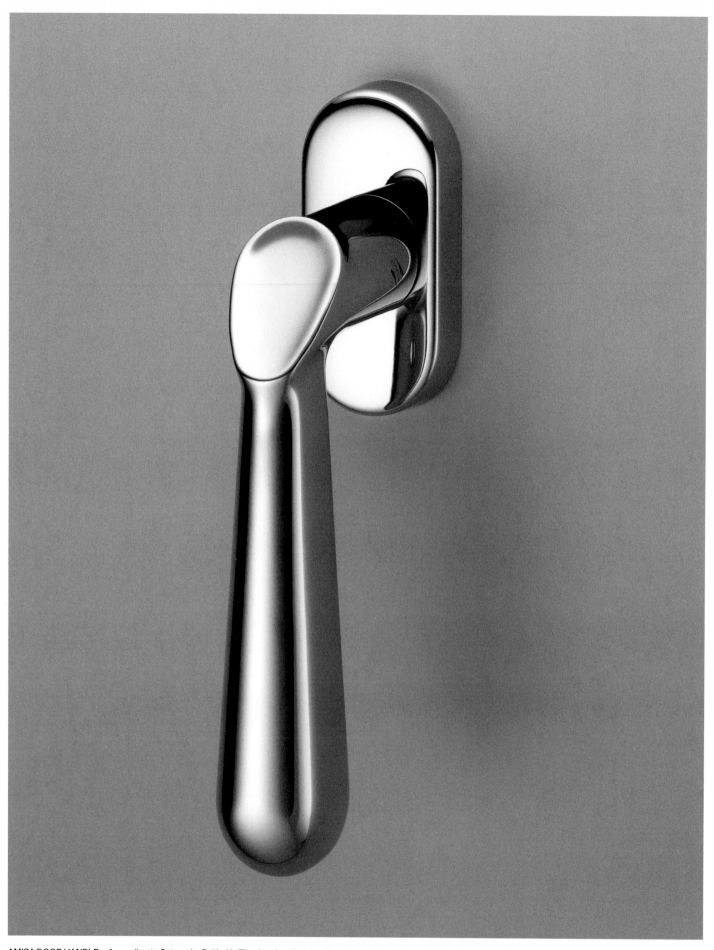

AMISA DOOR HANDLE — According to Satyendra Pakhalé, 'The door handle is the first handshake with a work of architecture so it ought to be welcoming and enthused with human warmth.' The objective of the Amisa door handle is therefore to convey 'a sort of personality while in the hand'. It is a controlled, yet delicately contoured form which sits in the grasp 'with all its sensorial honesty' while performing the everyday act of opening or closing a door. It has a special ergonomic feature – a contoured element on which to rest the thumb when opening the door. While designing it, the designer thought of the following quote by Jean-Paul Sartre (in Nausea) 'Just now, when I was on the point of coming into my room, I stopped short because I felt in my hand a cold object which attracted my attention by means of a sort of personality. I opened my hand and looked: I was simply holding the door-knob.'

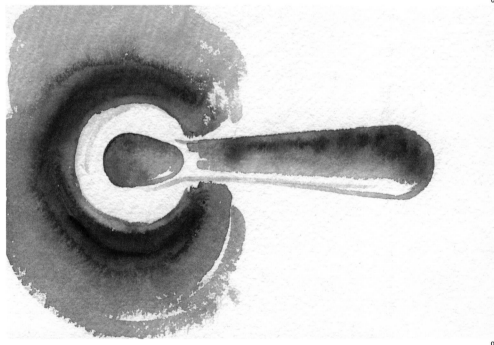

01   Amisa is manufactured in die-cast brass with an anodized surface coating and brushed finish.
02   Concept watercolour sketch by Pakhalé.

INDUSTRIAL DESIGN   77

PANNA SPECTACLES — Observing how people wear and handle spectacles, specially the wear and tear to the hinges, Pakhalé created an integral spring effect using pressure die-cast manufacturing with the properties of the chosen metal alloy. This not only facilitates the handling of the spectacles, but also reduces the potential damage to the hinge mechanism.

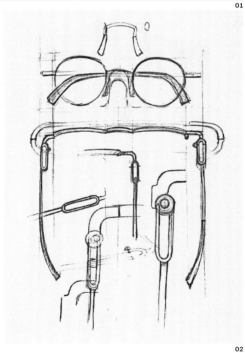

01   Panna spectacles are made of an aluminium-magnesium alloy which is ultra-light and perspiration-corrosion resistant, allowing a wide range of colours and surface finishes.
02   Sketch study of the integral spring mechanism by Pakhalé.

03

AFTER 'ULM AND AFTER'

Pakhalé cultivates a design approach that does not reject rationality,

but that invariably takes it a stage further,

pushing the boundaries to create truly human, multi-sensory designs.

René Spitz

A

B

C

D

All sorts of different currents, movements and initiatives – in the most diverse and even contradictory idioms – are described as 'modernist'. Yet as heterogeneous as they may be, they have certain fundamentals in common. Among them is a determination to live in the present, based on the conviction that today is more important than yesterday. It is not that modernists deem the past to be utterly irrelevant, worthy only of history's proverbial dustbin. After all, looking back can explain how we arrived at where we are now, and so expose those strong roots that may yet serve us as guidelines. But the past lends no legitimacy to the everyday life of the present, nor can it, given that conventions and traditions no longer carry any authoritative weight.

This radical commitment to the present is a defining feature of modernists. Some feel it to be an unreasonable demand that has led many despondent souls to feel alienated and lost. This in turn has made them easy prey for power-hungry demagogues with their anodyne promises of a life as simple, orderly and predictable as it was in the past, or so they claim. Hence the tendency among modernists to disdain traditionalists, who in their eyes cling onto the empty husks of obsolete practices and rituals that have long since been drained of all meaning. Modernists want to shape the future, a better future that will be brought about not by keeping the past firmly within our sights, but only by looking ahead.

Humane, Habitable, Hospitable

The question of how designers might further the development of society so as to prevent any repetition of the destructive insanity of fascism was central to the Ulm School of Design as it was to no other. The foundation of the Hochschule für Gestaltung (HfG), in the German city of Ulm, was motivated not by the desire to make the world more beautiful, but rather a perceived need to make it more humane, habitable and hospitable. So uncompromisingly radical were the school's key players, first and foremost among them Otl Aicher and Tomás Maldonado, that they happily left beauty to the domain of art, regarding it as neither a paramount nor even a primary concern of design. Design problems should be solved intellectually, they argued, and in this crucial respect set

A, B   Architecture Max Bill, Hochschule für Gestaltung Ulm, DE, 1953–1955. The school was open for students till late in the evening. Courtesy: HfG Archive Ulm, DE.

C   Austere Interior of the HfG Ulm, unpainted concrete, untreated natural timber, brick infill painted white, good lighting , glass boxes of student work – everything very simple and an effective illustration of the 'Ulm Standard' and unconscious education. On the right a passage to the main entrance and along the walls all the information lined up with push pins for students in lower case. Courtesy: Michael Penck, AU.

D   Design Degree Show – the class of S. Nadkarni and M. Penck, HfG Ulm. The work produced over the year in metal, wood, plastic, plaster, typography and photography was exhibited and evaluated by the tutors over several days to decide who met the 'Ulm Standard', the end-of-year exhibition 1962–1963. Courtesy: Michael Penck, AU.

themselves apart from the Bauhaus, a school of art whose teachers were themselves artists for the most part and hence approached design from an artistic angle. The Ulm School of Design took a very different stance, regarding the form and aesthetics of the end result as just one aspect among many that design as a discipline had to take account of – and not the dominant one at that.

The design perspective propagated at the HfG viewed the individual as part of a larger social context. Thus understood, design endeavours to strike a balance between the wishes and needs of the individual on the one hand, and the contingencies and demands of society on the other. Ulm School students learned to identify these complex correlations by analysing their tasks in the light of a range of factors, such as material science and manufacturing methods as well as economic, environmental, cultural, sociological, philosophical and political considerations. This enumeration of the various lines of inquiry underpinning each new design is alone enough to show that, at the HfG, form and aesthetics were regarded as just one influential factor among many.

Secular Humanism

The HfG ethos rested on the belief that since the world can be grasped objectively, it can also be changed for the better, for and by each and every individual in it – a conviction perhaps best described as secular humanism. The role of design, therefore, was to further the development of 'social modernism' – 'social' not in the sense of 'charitable', but rather 'conducive to social cohesion'. The ideal thus referenced is also expressed in the concept of the 'common good', meaning whatever is best for most people and for their harmonious co-existence in the long run.

There is something utopian about an approach to design that claims to be as inclusive and enduringly influential as this. In this respect, the Ulm School was in excellent company and takes its place alongside older, but similarly idealistic reform movements such as the Arts and Crafts movement in Britain, and on the continent Jugendstil/Art Nouveau, the Deutscher Werkbund, the Dutch De Stijl movement and of course the Bauhaus. Design in each case was understood as an activity that oversteps the bounds of the old disciplines in order to integrate all objectively required findings.

E   Prof. Hans Gugelot, Architect from Zurich with Dutch origins, teaching at HfG Ulm, DE. One of the HfG Ulm's leading lights, Gugelot mentored Sudhakar Nadkarni, encouraging him to found IDC, IIT-B in Mumbai, IN. Courtesy: Michael Penck, AU.

F   Prof. Tomás Maldonado, Argentine painter, designer and thinker in the HfG Ulm typesetting studio. During his tenure at HfG Ulm from 1954 to 1967, he developed the legendary 'Ulm model'. Courtesy: Michael Penck, AU.

Shared Values

The German word *gestalt* lends expression to this same holistic ideal. According to *gestalt* theory, human perception does not consist in the accumulation of isolated stimuli. Instead, we apprehend our surroundings in terms of overall impact. The German verb *gestalten*, generally translated as 'to design', is thus the holistic practice of lending shape to something.

This was the conviction underlying modernism's appreciation of those shared, transcendent values that bind all people together. After all, the lesson the modernists learned from the devastating experience of the Second World War was that emphasizing the unique and the peculiar tends to be divisive and ultimately has the effect of pitting people against each other. Hence modern design's aspiration to universal validity.

Such a view pushes culturally specific aspects to the sidelines, which should not be taken to mean that they are unimportant. Applied over a period of several decades, however, such a principle inevitably gave rise to styles of architecture and design that were felt by the majority of the population to be anonymous and interchangeable, or were experienced as foreign bodies imposed on them by some arrogantly remote hand. Such is the impact of these forbidding grey blocks on their neighbourhoods that their specific cultural diversity is wrecked beyond repair. Abstract, know-it-all modernism has not won any friends in this way, which perhaps helps explain the success of silly, irrational, upbeat Postmodernism.

Universal and Specific

Yet modernism's universalist approach has lost none of its appeal. Its heyday, specifically the two decades between the mid-1950s and the mid-1970s, saw the founding of India's National Institute of Design (NID) in Ahmedabad in 1961, for example. It was no accident that the most important inspiration for the NID – alongside Charles and Ray Eames – was one of the HfG Ulm's leading lights, the lecturer Hans Gugelot. Right from the start it was clear that in India, at any rate, any brand of modernism that failed to take account of key cultural factors would be unfit for purpose. The integration of aspects both universal and specific thus counts among the primary motives behind the NID's efforts to develop a social modernism in line with the times.

G   Prof. Hans Gugelot explaining the 'Ulm model' over tea during one of the visits to NID – National Institute of Design, Ahmedabad, IN. Courtesy: Gugelot Archieve, Hamburg, DE.

H   Prof. Hans Gugelot with students at NID. He was one of the most important inspirations for the NID alongside Charles Eames. Courtesy: National Institute of Design Ahmadabad Archive, IN.

AFTER 'ULM AND AFTER' RENÉ SPITZ

At the heart of Pakhalé's
work are two key concerns:

his conviction that
cultural influences have
to be factored in,

and his perception of the
rational, the emotional and
the multi-sensory as one.

René Spitz

The work of Satyendra Pakhalé stands out against this backdrop as an approach that articulates the values, ideas and convictions of a social modernism fit for the 21st century. Pakhalé trained as a designer under Professor Sudhakar Nadkarni at the Industrial Design Centre (IDC) of the Indian Institute of Technology Bombay (IIT-B) in Mumbai, India. Nadkarni had been a student at Ulm, where his tutor and mentor was Hans Gugelot. The two men became close friends during Nadkarni's four years in Ulm and it was Gugelot who encouraged his Indian protégé to go back to India and launch a design school there. On his return, Nadkarni started teaching a design program at the NID – Gugelot having recommended him to its director, Gira Sarabhai – and the following year, 1969, he founded the IDC at the IIT-B in Mumbai. Pakhalé, having studied at the IDC, is directly connected with the work of the HfG Ulm and Hans Gugelot.

Multi-Sensory Design

Pakhalé began his studies in 1989, the centre's 20th anniversary, which it celebrated with an international conference called 'Ulm and After'. That opportunity to meet so many HfG alumni in person – and not just from Germany, France and Japan but from all over the world – was a great boost to Pakhalé's young, aspiring mind and made a lasting impression on him during those crucial formative years.

Pakhalé cultivates a design approach that does not reject rationality, but that invariably takes it a stage further, pushing the boundaries to create truly human, multi-sensory designs. Taking the cultural context into account, he creates designs based on a sense of responsibility that is rooted in his experience and world view. His commitment to secular humanism results in designs that connect humanity and that aspire to be universal. At the heart of his work are two key concerns. The first of these is his conviction that cultural influences have to be factored in, which leads to design solutions that draw on past forms of expression without succumbing to either nostalgia or traditionalism, since only then can their positive value be protected and used. The second is his perception of the rational, the emotional and the multi-sensory as one.

By revisiting and then synthesizing these two aspects, Pakhalé has developed a brand of social modernism rooted in social cohesion that is at once contemporary and forward-looking.

I   IDC – *Industrial Design Centre*, late night working culture, all workshops accessible to students for 24 hours and 7 days a week. Courtesy: Satyendra Pakhalé Archives, Amsterdam, NL.

J   Amphitheatre at the rear of the IDC for informal discussions and meetings for students and faculty. Courtesy: Satyendra Pakhalé Archives, Amsterdam, NL.

K   *Ulm and After* – 20 Years of the IDC. International Design Conference, 1989. Courtesy: IDC Archive, IIT-B, IN.

L   IDC visiting faculty Kohei Sugiura, a designer Japan with Prof. Nadkarni walking through the Infinite Corridor that connects all departments at IDC, IIT-B campus. Kohei Sugiura taught visual communication at HfG Ulm in the 1960s. Courtesy: Sudhakar Nadkarni, IN.

AFTER 'ULM AND AFTER'   RENÉ SPITZ

His work recalls a special moment in the history of the HfG Ulm, specifically the visit of Walter Gropius, who was invited to speak at the inauguration of the HfG's new building on the Kuhberg in Ulm on 2 October 1955. Gropius used his address to caution against the glorification of reason and rationality and to urge the students and lecturers present not to forget what he called 'the magical' just because it eludes our cognitive faculties.

Such a vision calls for staying power and persistence. Yet it is worth the effort, for only when design strikes the right balance between the rational and the magical is it truly human.

CONTENT

KALPA VASE BOWL — On the invitation of Gijs Bakker, the art director of Cor Unum in 2002, and in response to the theme 'Clay and Beyond', Satyendra Pakhalé created a vase and bowl in a single object called Kalpa. Standing upright, it can be used as a vase; turned upside down, it can serve as a fruit bowl. Made using the slip casting technique, Kalpa starts out as several identical white clay pots – glazed white outside and coloured inside – which are fired separately. After firing, the pots are assembled together in a mould with a two-component adhesive. This object also makes a passing reference to the old Delftware tulip vase in classic blue and white. *Kalpa* means poetic imagination.

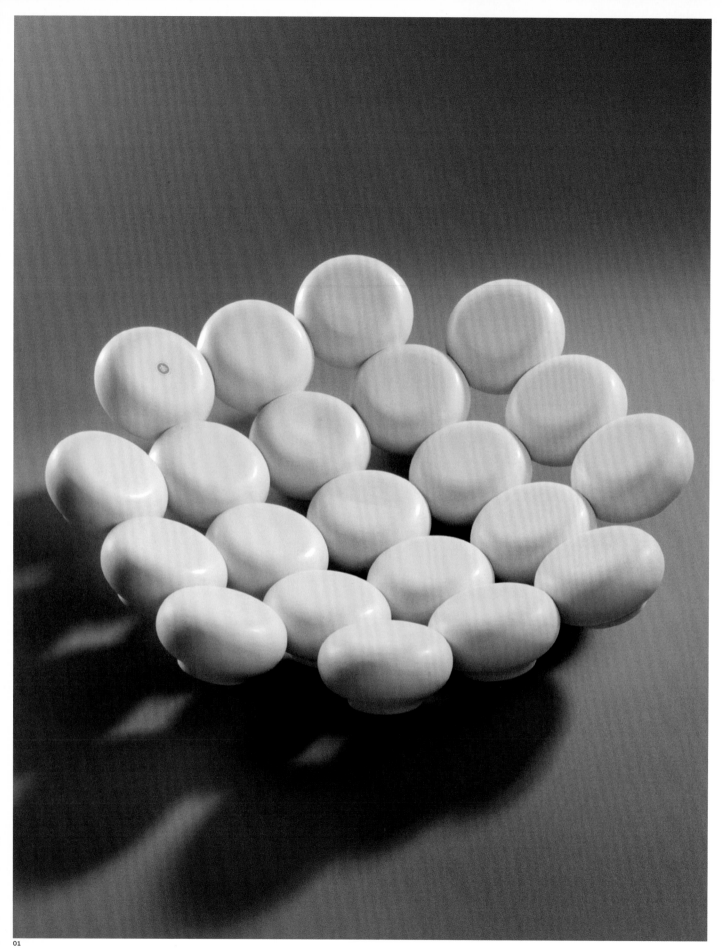

01   Standing upright, Kalpa can be used as a vase; turned upside down, it can serve as a fruit bowl. Such dual functionality can be observed in various projects. Pakhalé: 'Around the world the space for living is getting smaller and smaller, especially in urban areas. I think how nice it would be to have more than one utility for an object, so places are not cluttered.'

02   Concept sketch illustrating how the piece should be made.

                  KALPA VASE BOWL

A

B

C

D

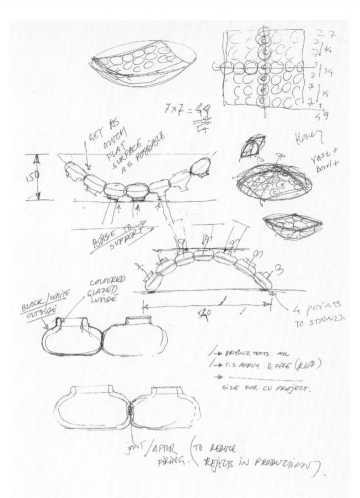

02

A Several identical clay pots – glazed white outside and coloured inside – are fired separately. After firing, the pots are assembled together in a mould with a two-component adhesive.

B First hand-thrown ceramic prototype proving that the pots could be assembled together in a specific geometry.

C Test model studied at EKWC **1** during the residency.

SQUARE MEAL — This piece in ceramic is a steam cooking utensil designed for the Good Food project of the Design Biennale Saint-Étienne, France, 2006. The brief from the curator Céline Savoye was to take an age-old utensil from the designer's cultural background and create a new contemporary object for cooking or serving food. Pakhalé wanted to evoke the notion of the good-old 'square meal' and what it means to us today. He explains: 'Looking at the panorama of cooking utensils from India, there is a lot to choose from. I selected this wonderful steam cooking technique from Kerala, India. They call it puttu; it has vertical proportions and is traditionally made of bamboo. Taking the basic idea of steam cooking, we developed it into a contemporary vessel for preparing good food.'

   102–105   140–143

01

01 Square Meal is made in slip-cast ceramic with a high-gloss white glaze.
02 The base pot and sieve together.
03 Exploded view. The lower pot contains water for steam cooking; the upper elements hold the food.
04 Design sketch by Satyendra Pakhalé.

02

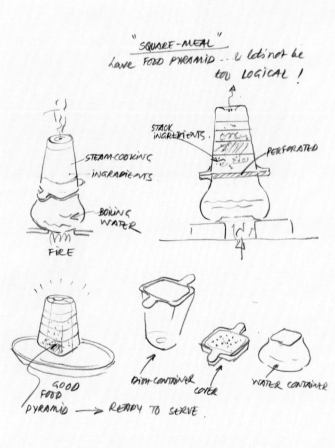

"SQUARE-MEAL"
Long FOOD PYRAMID ... & let's not be
too LOGICAL!

STEAM-COOKING
INGRADIENTS

BOILING
WATER

FIRE

STACK
INGREDIENTS

PERFORATED

GOOD
FOOD
PYRAMID → READY TO SERVE.

DISH-CONTAINER   COVER   WATER CONTAINER

03

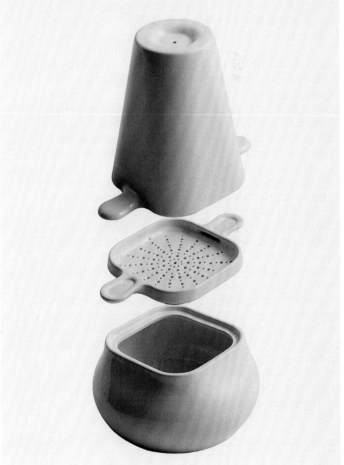

04

In 2001, Satyendra Pakhalé was invited for a residency at the European Ceramic Work Centre (EKWC) in the Netherlands. During that period, the centre encouraged professionals with hardly any prior ceramics experience, including architects and designers to join a residency in order for them to act as a catalyst for innovation. Pakhalé had already worked with ceramics on a smaller scale, experimenting with artisans at the Bhadrawati ceramic centre in India. EKWC was an opportunity for him to further develop his interest. 'I am fascinated by ceramics, an age-old, yet high-tech material,' he says.

'Not being a ceramist,' he adds, 'You cannot know the limitations, so you're willing to try out new things, which allows you to go further. I have a lot of respect for this material, perhaps one of the most magical and ancient innovations of humankind. Ceramics is a material with a long history; as long as the Earth has existed, ceramics have been around. But it is also a very high-tech material. This is the paradox I was working with.'

Pakhalé worked at EKWC on two different occasions, separated by a year. His first residency involved working with skilled artisans and EKWC's technical staff to develop test models for one singular piece - a chair; the second period was focused more on developing the technical joint between the backrest and the body of the chair to make it work at full scale. Part of his goal was always to create something that could be produced at least in limited numbers. 'The object has to be multiplied to become a valid object,' he explains. 'Only then is it a valid object in terms of producibility. As an industrial designer, my goal is serial production.'

His approach to ceramics was novel: traditionally, ceramics has never been associated with structural objects like chairs. 'When I began, I was not sure how to proceed,' Pakhalé recalls. 'I imagined creating hollow clay volumes in order to assemble a chair-like object. I wanted to create a piece of furniture as a symbolic object. Personally, I have no nostalgic or traditional values regarding ceramics.'

For pragmatic reasons, he chose to work with the hand-thrown pottery process in order to get faster results. He found artisans and assistants who had pottery-making skills, and a skilled artisan who had developed a particular method of hand-throwing using mirror reflections to achieve perfectly symmetrical forms. Pakhalé would run his studio for a good part of the day and then rush to EKWC in the evening, working late into the night drawing and visualizing the

A   Full-scale hand-thrown volume being prepared for joining in wet condition.

B   The drying process was one of the critical steps to avoid cracks while making these ceramic pieces. Here the drying process being monitored by Pakhalé.

c, d   The dried ceramic pieces were skillfully stacked in the EKWC's large kilns using a forklift truck.

E

F

G

pieces which eventually became the Flower Offering Chair ❶ and Roll Carbon Ceramic Chair ❷.

'Turning a shape on the wheel is a technique that requires amazing hand to eye coordination and it is one of those skills that takes years to master,' Pakhalé explains. While making use of this process, he attempted to do something completely new: to make a chair by joining parts and pots together to achieve unexpected results. From the beginning, he was clear that this would be no traditional seat. 'It is not a chair to sit on in front of the computer for eight hours a day,' he says. 'The Flower Offering Chair is more of a ceremonial object to welcome people. Something like a universal statement, offering flowers as a friendly gesture. Design, for me, is not only functional. There are psychological and social aspects as well.'

Pakhalé began with the basics: throwing a pot. He undertook research into a wide range of materials, searching for a clay mixture that would tolerate high-temperature firing in the kiln. Unlike metal or plastic, ceramic is an unpredictable material with an element of surprise. In the firing process, anything can happen. The piece can deform, or worse still crack or break or even explode inside the kiln. During the first period, several models of various sizes were made, clays were mixed and remixed, wall thicknesses were adjusted to allow for the natural shrinkage of the drying clay, and pieces were fired, sometimes coming out beautifully, other times cracking or becoming distorted. Then, back to the wheel and more pots were thrown based on Pakhalé's sketches, which covered the walls of the studio space at EKWC. Once all these tests were completed, the technical staff and Pakhalé moved on to full-scale prototyping. Not only did the clay composition have to be just right, but because of different thicknesses in each piece, firing had to be carefully calibrated. The joining of the back pieces to the seat was a big challenge. 'At first, we put them together and then fired them,' Pakhalé recalls. 'But this made them susceptible to cracking and exploding. So I designed a special ceramic joint.

We made the parts separately and connected them after firing with the joint and a two-component polyurethane glue. The piece was placed on a shrinkage slab to enable equal shrinkage during drying and firing in order to avoid deformation or splitting.' After several failed attempts, successful scale prototypes were eventually realized. Based on these, full-scale ceramic chair-like objects could be made. Once these full-scale pieces were successful, the new design opportunities were developed further in collaboration with industry or in a skilled workshop in which the project could be produced in a limited edition.

E   Pakhalé worked with a skilled craftswoman who had developed a method of hand-throwing using mirror reflections to achieve perfectly symmetrical forms.

F   Before finding the skilled artisan, Pakhalé had previously worked with an assistant who could not hand-throw objects taller than 30 cm, despite seven years of throwing practice at the local art school.

G   A joint in wet clay was tried out with mixed results. These trials bore fruit in later projects.

The Process

To begin with, several tests were made to achieve the right mix of clay. Various clays (earthenware and stoneware) and grog were mixed in different proportions to obtain an open structure. This also improved the clay quality, especially during firing, by reducing the tension. Several scale models were made to test various ideas, like joining the clay and then firing it at 1200°C. After these tests, the real task of making a full-scale prototype began. Creating the large forms with joints and connecting them while still wet was a real endeavour.

The consistent drying of the relatively complex ceramic structure was essential and took 15 to 20 days. The exact drying time depends on the clay body (mixture), scale, complexity and thickness. Getting the product through the different stages of drying from plastic to dry was another hurdle.

After building the initial clay prototypes, firing the entire chair structure proved problematic as some prototypes cracked. Developing the joint created new possibilities for industrial realization. This new ceramic joint was developed as a separate parts and fired independently to be connected afterwards with two-component PU glue.

Experimenting with the material presented the opportunity to produce the ceramic chair on an industrial level. With this technical development it was possible to produce the chair with the help of moulds for slip casting, similar to the moulds used in the bathroom industry. For this relatively new production method, currently used exclusively for the production of ceramic bathtubs, the form and size of the ceramic chair needed to be adapted. Adding materials such as vitreous china – perfect for large ceramic objects and with the possibility of connecting separate parts after firing – fuelled new design opportunities. These needed to be developed further in collaboration with an industrial workshop. Pakhalé launched a search for such a ceramic workshop and after visiting a few he settled for the family-owned ceramic manufacturer, based in the north of Venice, Italy.

The next phase, critical to the chair's ultimate viability, was to find a way to produce the piece in some non-handmade quantity. Pakhalé: 'It took quite some time to find a ceramic workshop that could make the special moulds for the seat and the backrest with a special metal fixture to turn them during the slip casting process.'

While Pakhalé would never expect to make thousands of these chairs, being able to make and use dozens is important to him. He wants an object that, while ceremonial, still lives in the real world.

H

I

J

H–J Scale models of ceramic audio speakers. Pakhalé experimented and played with the idea of developing ceramic speakers in the early phase of his EKWC residency.

K Experimental piece during the first phase of the residency.

K

L

M

N

Therefore, he points out. The Flower Offering Chair is therefore extremely sturdy and can also be used both indoors and outdoors.

Although Pakhalé pushed the boundaries of ceramics and traditional processes into untested and innovative areas, the clay resisted, asserting its natural properties. 'The ceramic material itself is very surprising and fascinating. It's very hard to control,' Pakhalé explains. 'A person like me, a control freak, needs to control every single detail of the project. I have a very clear picture in my mind, and with every industrial design project, I know how it all fits together. When you have a concrete idea, you can get it made immediately in 3D CAD, or as a precisely crafted model, exactly as you want. With ceramic, you can't do that.' As satisfying as the final product is, with all its whimsical, symbolic, ancient, contemporary, high-tech, low-tech, and tactile associations mixed together, Pakhalé wanted to take what he had learned from it into new applications, materials and new products. The intensely productive period at EKWC led to many other design works with a similar, ceramics-like finish (although they are not made in ceramics) such as the Add-On Radiator ❸ and Kangeri Nomadic Radiator ❹.

L   Fruit bowl with Ananda Totem engraved with glaze ❺.

M   A successful wet clay structural study with a joint.

N   A scale model study with a joint in wet clay tried out during the early phase of the residency.

FLOWER OFFERING CHAIR — In 2001, during a residency at the European Ceramic Work Centre (EKWC) in the Netherlands, Satyendra Pakhalé decided to use ceramics to create a structural piece – a chair-like object. Pakhalé: 'In every culture we offer flowers, so I created a Flower Offering Chair.' It is an innovative piece, structurally strong enough to sit on, and with two removable vases in its backrest to hold flowers. Underlining the symbolic, 'welcoming' aspect of the piece, Pakhalé envisioned the chair from the start as being at home 'in a lobby, or at the front desk of a hotel'.

A

B

C

01

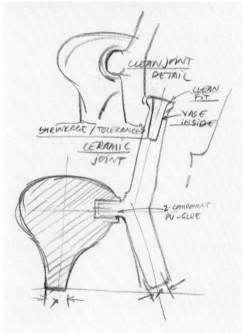

02

A–C Serial production in the slip casting technique called for special moulds for the seat and the backrest. Pakhalé checking the proportions and dimensions of the first serially produced piece.

01 First joint test at EKWC. A new idea for a ceramic joint was developed to allow the parts to be created independently and fired separately and connected afterwards with two-component PU glue.

02 A joint study sketch by Pakhalé, also illustrating the removable vase.

03

03 Finding the right finish was critical to the project's success. Normal glazes were ruled out because of their shiny, 'plastic-like' appearance. Instead, terra sigillata was used – an ancient technique that applies a very thin layer of clay slip to the surface with a brush. This gives a satiny, glowing finish. Subsequently a platinum and Bosco green glazes were developed.

04 Flowering Offering Chair watercolour sketch showing that Pakhalé envisaged it as 'an object to welcome people - a ceremonial object, something like a universal, friendly gesture.'

FLOWER OFFERING CHAIR

D

E

D Pakhalé found a small, family-owned Italian ceramics workshop to take on the challenge of producing the Flower Offering Chairs.

E A removable vase that sits in the backrest for holding flowers.

MINI ROLL CERAMIC CHAIR — This totemic table-top object is evolved from the limited-edition piece Roll Carbon Ceramic Chair ❶ from Satyendra Pakhalé's early experimental work in ceramics at the European Ceramic Work Centre (later developed with a family-run ceramic workshop north of Venice). This evocative symbolic table-top object for day-dreaming can also be used as a vase. Mini Roll Ceramic Chair uses the slip casting ceramic process. It is glazed in deep cosmic blue outside with a fresh white glaze inside.

01   Mini Flower Offering Chair is a symbolic object creating a positive ambience through its cheerful nature. It can be used as a vase for a single flower or to place something precious. It evolved from the limited-edition piece Flower Offering Chair ❷. It is glazed in deep red, yellow, green and several other vibrant colours.

AKASMA CENTREPIECE — The Akasma baskets (low and high) and centrepiece tray are bent-glass objects. They revisit an ancient typology of baskets and trays with an innovative making process, resulting in a set of distinctive contemporary objects. In this project, architectural glass is reused from the highly technological production of an industrial-glass manufacturer. This makes these products eminently sustainable, as – being glass – they are also completely recyclable in themselves. In industrial manufacturing, bent glass is one of the most challenging materials to work with. It requires great control to achieve the desired form. This project demanded such a high level of technical precision that it almost became an industrial craft process. A lot of work went into precisely calculating the profile of the glass with the required tolerances.

First, the tempered glass had to be cut into a precise profile. Then a mechanized heating and bending process had to create the desired form with a very precise, clean line between the two parts. Finally the two identical parts were assembled into a single object. Pakhalé: 'After carefully considering the material and manufacturing process, I wanted to create a series of glass objects which reveal how they were made. In doing so, I wanted to take the bent-glass process to its limits.' *Akasma* means a sudden happening. This name was chosen for these glass objects to reflect the fact that they look as though they were born with ease and almost by chance. However, the actual making of the objects was very challenging.

01

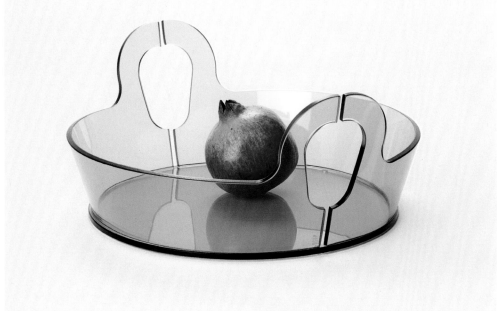

02

 01   The Akasma centrepiece is a relatively large object, hence challenging to make.
02   The smallest of the three pieces in the collection is the Akasma Low, which can be used for fruit.
03   Handle detail. The controlled parallel gap between the two identical parts is a defining feature of the object.

A

B

C

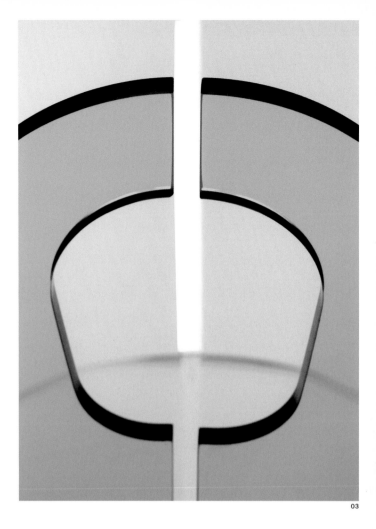

A   Study model in cardboard made at Pakhalé's studio.

B   At the factory the glass is cut with a water jet to the pre-calculated profile, including tolerances, and mounted with the fixture on the mould.

C   The glass is bent and tempered to remove all the stresses in the material in the high-temperature furnaces.

04

DESIGN AND PLURALISM

In the new global and geopolitical condition

there are at the very least multiple centres and peripheries.

Or taking it further, everywhere is both at the centre and the periphery at the same time.

Aric Chen

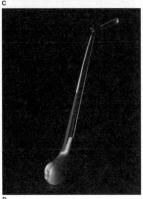

DESIGN AND PLURALISM
Aric Chen

It didn't escape me, when I first met Satyendra Pakhalé at his studio in Amsterdam in 2014, that anyone listening in on our conversation might have seen a tangled logic at work. As Pakhalé adamantly resisted being labelled an 'Indian designer', while showing me work that was full of Indian inferences, I was speaking on behalf of a Hong Kong-based museum that aimed to redefine 'global' in an Asian, yet not *'Asian'*, sense. The contradictions seemed all too rich. Except they weren't contradictions.

The burdens of history are never easy to offload, yet Pakhalé's work offers a way of rethinking how we construct design narratives. On a biographical level, Pakhalé – born and raised in India, educated there and in Europe, and now living and working from the Netherlands – is very much a product of globalization. In this sense, he is not alone.

However, Pakhalé stands out especially for his ability to navigate multiple identities as a designer – Indian, global, European, industrial, conceptual, craft-driven, whatnot – in a way that doesn't so much reconcile them as embrace their seemingly dissonant co-existences. Whether expanding design's cultural and interpretive possibilities, or discarding its disciplinary boundaries, he approaches the field with an equanimity that draws no hierarchical distinctions between hand-crafted tradition and emerging technologies, high-tech and low-tech, ceremonial and utilitarian – whether expressed in ritual offering vases❶ and concept cars❷, or bell metal sculptures and speculative walking sticks for the moon❸. To look within his body of work, and at his work in the broader landscape, is to see an argument for design as a more pluralistic enterprise.

Network of Narratives
Pakhalé is emblematic of a discursive moment that has seen, in fits and starts, the undoing of binary logics – between East and West, functional and decorative, modern and traditional. At the same time, design and design history – long dominated by the largely Euro-American narratives at its centre, with most everything else at the periphery – has opened up to a new global and geopolitical condition, in which there are (at the very least) multiple

A   Roll Carbon Ceramic Chair, ammann // gallery at Design Miami/ Basel, CH, 2007. Courtesy: Satyendra Pakhalé Archives, Amsterdam, NL.

B   B.M. Objects III, ammann // gallery at Design Miami/ Basel, CH, 2018. Courtesy: Ammann Gallery, DE.

C   Pangéa concept car at Geneva Motor Show, 1997. Courtesy: Philips Design, NL.

D   Moonwākā, first hiking gauge for the Moon at the Moon Life Concept Store, Amsterdam, NL, 2011. Courtesy: Danny Hollander, NL.

To look within Satyendra Pakhalé's body of work

is to see an argument for design as a more pluralistic enterprise.

Aric Chen

E

F

centres and peripheries. Or taking it further, everywhere is both at the centre and the periphery at the same time.

In this context, Pakhalé was among the first designers we sought out as we began forming the permanent design and architecture collection of M+, the museum in Hong Kong. At the time, using a rather blunt, and knowingly problematic, shorthand we described M+ as 'a global museum from an Asian perspective'. This was a way of emphasizing, in response to lingering assumptions to the contrary (within and also beyond Asia), that a museum could be simultaneously 'Asian' and 'global' at once.

Of course, 'Asia' is itself a troublesome term. But we used it not only out of convenience, but also with the idea that what we were describing was not some predefined notion of 'Asianness' or Asian identity or, for that matter, 'Chineseness,' 'Hong Kongness,' or 'Indianness.' Instead, we were referring to the complex mechanisms of cultural production that wend their way across time and geographies to create networks of narratives – of which cultural identities are a part – that densify based on where one is situated.

Opposites Reconciled

Put simply, we were Asian because we were in Asia, and we were global because we were in the world, and the two are not in opposition. From this starting point, we saw a resonance with Pakhalé's designs, which root themselves in specific contexts while also moving fluidly among them. While there was much throughout his work that attracted us, we homed in on his Roll Carbon Ceramic Chair, whose ceramic form, wrapped in carbon fibre, presented its didactic purpose all too well.

The chair's technical challenges are not insubstantial. But it is the co-existence of its two seemingly diametrically opposed materials and making processes, sculpted into a form whose ritualistic nature supersedes any other ostensible function, that makes the point. While conflating high- and low-tech, the design bears a ceremonial aura that can certainly be traced to Pakhalé's own work, research and background in India – but also tangentially to the Italian designer Ettore Sottsass Jr. (a great influence on Pakhalé), whose own debt to India, beginning with his visits there in the 1960s, is becoming more fully understood. In its singular way, the Roll Carbon Ceramic Chair contains multiple readings and narratives that move and intersect across geographies.

E   Ettore Sottsass Jr. at Sottsass Associati, Milan, 2003. Courtesy: Satyendra Pakhalé Archives, Amsterdam, NL.

F   Ettore Sottsass Jr. letter to Pakhalé, *'Thank you for the beautiful rock-cut architecture'*, 1996. Courtesy: Satyendra Pakhalé Archives, Amsterdam, NL.

DESIGN AND PLURALISM ARIC CHEN

Pakhalé is deeply aware
of his own historicity.

He is Indian, and
he is a designer.

However, he has always insisted
that to read his work through
some perception

of what might be construed
as 'Indian' would be limiting
and inaccurate.

Aric Chen

Cultural Nomadism

Many non-Euro-American designers of Pakhalé's generation, and those before them, were often left to choose between being a designer in the broader sense and being an 'Indian', or 'Japanese', or *other*, designer.

Pakhalé is deeply aware of his own historicity. He is Indian, and he is a designer. However, he has always insisted that to read his work through some perception of what might be construed as 'Indian' would be limiting and inaccurate. As he puts it, he doesn't mind being called a 'designer with Indian origins' or a 'designer from India', but 'cultural nomad' covers it just as well.

Now, only five years after my first meeting with Pakhalé, the idea of a 'global Asian museum' is less difficult to explain – but, somewhat ironically, the world has meanwhile become more fragmented, divided and polarized. Considering this fact, if design is a means by which we articulate the human realm, and our interactions with it and each other, then it seems even more urgent to look at the work of Pakhalé and other like-minded designers through the world views - plural - that inform them.

Pakhalé approaches design with an equanimity that draws no hierarchical distinctions

between hand-crafted tradition and emerging technologies,

high-tech and low-tech, ceremonial and utilitarian.

Aric Chen

CONTENT

BLACK WHITE SWAN — Pakhalé embarked on this project in summer 2005, creating a basic clay model in his summer atelier in central India. After experimenting with various materials, White Swan was produced in white Carrara marble from Italy and Black Swan in Nero Marquina marble from Spain. The piece marks the first use of marble, 'One of the most ancient meaning-impregnated materials on our planet capable of creating a sensorial feeling', as he calls it.

01

A

B

C

D

A   First clay model of the project in summer 2005 at the maker's studio, Nagpur, IN.

B   A full-scale model of Swan is 3D-scanned and reverse engineered to achieve its precise geometry and surface quality using parametric software, Vicenza, IT.

C, D   The marble block is first cut to the profile and then machined using a robotic arm fed with the precise 3D CAD. Later it is hand-polished skilled artisans.

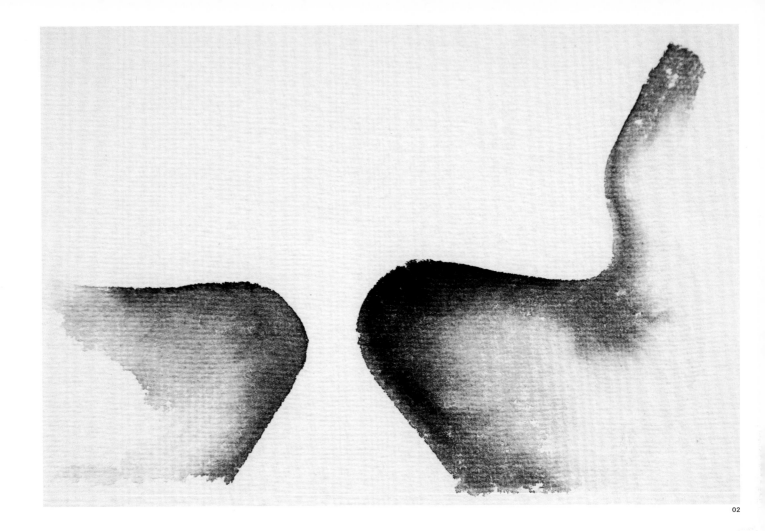

01   Black Swan in Nero Marquina marble from Spain. Pakhalé: 'For me objects are like companions and I am fascinated by the possibility to bring life, elegance and even
dignity into them.'
02   A watercolour sketch by Pakhalé conveys the essence of the piece.

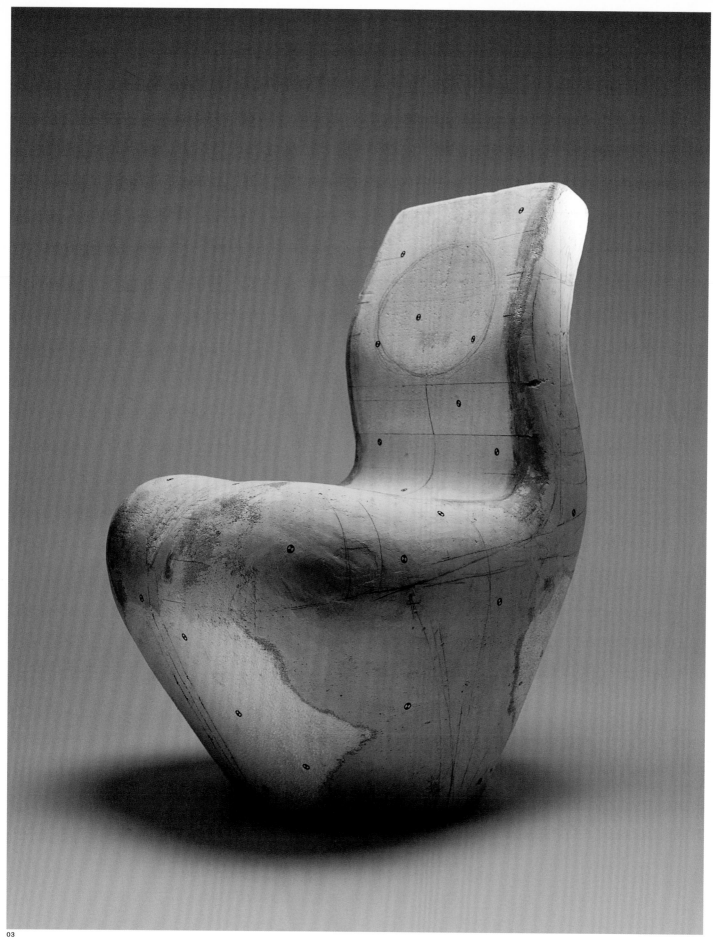

03

03   From the first sketches a 3D CAD model was built. A styrofoam model was then made using CNC. To achieve the desired proportions and ergonomics, it was then further modified. This modified model was then scanned to achieve the final result by reverse engineering. Pakhalé: 'When it comes to achieving precise geometry in an object, often one spends hours or weeks on computers and it still falls short of what one has in mind. So we developed a process by quickly getting a soft model machined from the initial 3D CAD and modified it manually to the desired geometry and proportions before reverse engineering it. This is made a lot faster through eye-to-hand coordination.'

04

05

04   White Swan with drainage details that are almost invisible on the seat and foot rest. This allows the pieces to be placed outdoors as well as indoors.
05   Black Swan drainage feature that opens up gradually to become large in diameter, helping water to drain out smoothly.

POTTERY CHAIR — During a residency at the European Ceramic Work Centre (EKWC), Pakhalé experimented with various ways to create objects by putting together hollow ceramic forms. Several experimental prototypes were designed and built to create a symbolic chair. Pottery Chair is a three-dimensional form in which two big ceramic pots are interlocked to form the piece. Technically, it was a challenge to trim the respective pots to the correct size and shape and assemble them in a wet-clay condition in an ingenious way, creating a suggestion of the infinity sign at both front and back of the chair.

A

B

C

D

E

A, B   Hand-throwing was used to create the forms relatively quickly, without spending time on making models and moulds.

C   It was a real-time 3D visualization task to trim the pots to the correct size and shape and assemble them as an interlocking form in a wet-clay condition.

D, E   To avoid uneven shrinkage, the pieces needed to dry on a ceramic shrinkage slab made of the same clay composition. The kiln being loaded by EKWC staff with the help of a forklift truck ready to be fired up to 1200°C.

STEELWAVE

Alberto Alessi got to know Satyendra Pakhalé's Bell Metal (B.M.) Objects at the *Design Beyond Europe* exhibition curated by Paola Antonelli, Giulio Cappellini and Vanni Pasca at Abitare il Tempo Verona, 1999. Alessi was fascinated by the B.M. Objects – which had been well received for their contemporary interpretation of the age-old lost wax casting process. With their unique craftsmanship rooted in a specific culture and revived as a way of creating objects, they generated interest in Pakhalé's design works. The president of the iconic Italian dream factory invited Pakhalé to design a collection of objects and so began a long investigation into numerous typologies in stainless steel for Alessi.

The idea behind the Steel Wave project was to explore in stainless steel the sensorial qualities embodied in the B.M. Objects. After early meetings between Alberto Alessi and Satyendra Pakhalé, the idea was to prototype his designs in stainless steel. The continuous research and development undertaken by Alessi in collaboration with Pakhalé resulted in several prototypes. It turned out to be long process of design and product development, starting with Steel Wave Vase and later moving on to sets of serving bowls, plates, fruit bowls, trays, a candlestick, eggcup, incense stick holder and so on. Numerous prototypes were developed between 2000 and 2005.

The Steel Wave Family project was once again revised during 2011–2012. New typologies of objects, such as a tea strainer, were designed and developed. After another round of meetings with Alberto Alessi and Satyendra Pakhalé, it was decided he should focus on making a smaller object in order to develop an additive manufacturing process. The tea strainer was the first prototype made by Alessi's technical office in 2012, based on Pakhalé's design concept. The idea was to make a tea set. This would not only help to communicate the concept behind the project, but also create a small family of objects that could grow into a collection. For various reasons the initial objective, to bring the sensorial qualities and the tactility of the B.M. Objects to the Steelwave Family, did not succeed. Nevertheless, the project is still in development and is likely to see the light of the day at some future date. Meanwhile the Steelwave Family prototypes became part of the ongoing exhibition, *Alessi IN-possible*, and of the collection of Museo Alessi.

A   Steelwave studies for a set of bowls with variations in wave formation in stainless steel.

B   Two bowl studies with two variations of base details.

C, D   Prototypes of baskets and saucer.

E

F

G

H

E   Incense stick holder study with integral feet detail.

F, G   Refined study of bowl and tray in stainless steel.

H   Prototype of basket with handle.

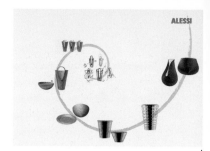

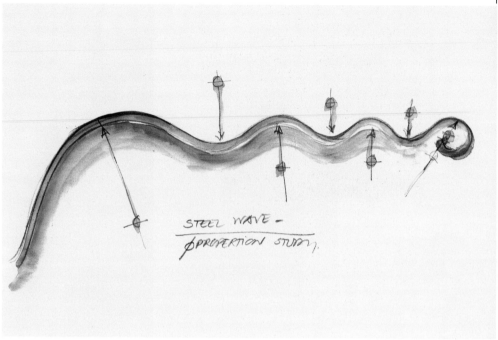

STEEL WAVE –
$PROPORTION STUDY.

I Illustration showing the journey from the first generation B.M. Objects to the prototype Steelwave objects and from there to the third generation B.M. Objects and further developments of the Steelwave Family.

J,K Evolution of of the steel wave idea, inspired by the ripple effect when a pebble is dropped into water, as shown in the design sketch and model cross-section.

L Prototype set of three trays.

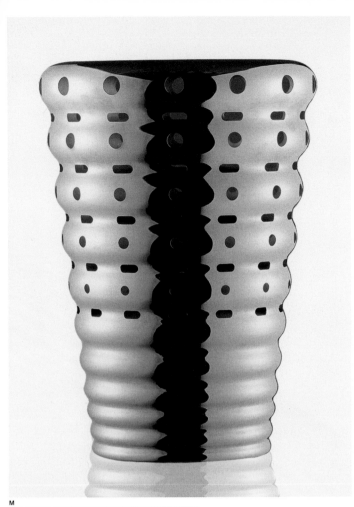

M

N

O

M   The Steelwave Vase with incremental
pattern.

N   A set of two ceramic serving bowls with
stainless steel lid and small tray.

O   A set of sugar and creamer prototype
ceramic sugar and creamer set with stainless
steel base.

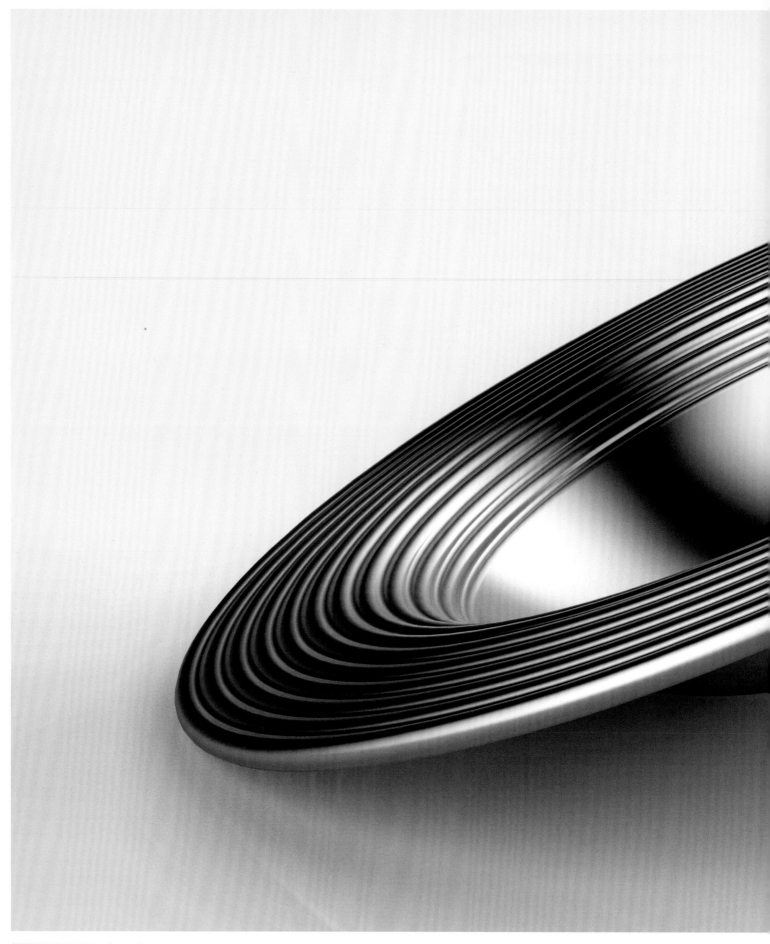

STEELWAVE FAMILY — Saturn Fruit Bowl whose rim is inspired by the rings of Saturn creating a wonderfully wobbling effect. The Steelwave Family was developed as an evolution of the early B.M. Objects ❶ ❷ made using the lost-wax casting process. The family of objects consists of diverse types of table-top objects which vary in size from a large Steelwave Vase to a small Steelwave Tea Strainer and more.

01

A

B

C

D

A Pakhalé reviewing and studying all the prototypes developed by Alessi's technical office over a decade.

B Steelwave objects presented at Satyendra Pakhalé's solo exhibition *Design by Heart*, Gallery Otto, Bologna, IT, 2003.

C, D teelwave objects by Pakhalé on show at the exhibition *Alessi IN-Possible* at the Triennale Design Museum, Milan, IT, 2016.

STEELWAVE FAMILY

01   Steelwave Salad serving set.
02   The tea strainer was the first prototype in an additive process made by Alessi's technical office based on Pakhale's idea of a tea set: 'This would not only help commu-
      nicate the idea behind the project, but also create a small family of objects that can grow into a collection for contemporary tea-drinking culture,' says the designer.
03   Prototyped in metal electro-deposit technology, the tea strainer, evokes the memory of the B.M. Objects made using the lost-wax casting process.

Dear Satyendra,

Since I first met you many years ago in the Alessi factory in Crusinallo, I have been extremely interested in your way of practising design by exploring the sensorial qualities of an object, rethinking them in a new manner yet deeply rooted in your Indian ethos. Since I believe that good design is always an expression of the cultural background of a designer, your case is a very good example of that conviction. I recall when we started with transforming and evolving your early experimental B.M. Objects into stainless steel, calling it the Steelwave Family. Do you remember how many prototypes we made, trying to make one or more products for our catalogue from your drawings? It has been a long, passionate journey. I still have in my office a kind of porcelain vase, or maybe it is a steamer, that you conceived for the *Good Food* exhibition at the Biennale of Design 2006 in Saint-Étienne, France ❶.

I regret we have not yet been able to translate your poetry into Alessi products – despite our common efforts. But sometimes life works like that: it asks time to make a dream real!

—Alberto Alessi

E

F

G

H

E–H   While discussing the prototypes developed over a decade with Alessi's technical office, Pakhalé came up with the idea of Steelwave Watch for Alessi.

04

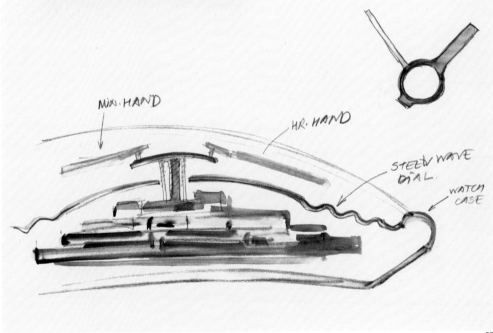

05

04   Steelwave Watch was born of the Steelwave trays. The dial takes the form of the steel wave, as shown in the sketch. The brand name is integrated into the hour hand, creating a unique identity within Alessi watches. Steelwave Watch hands have a special feature – the centre is hollow – giving the watch a subtle yet distinct character. The 42 mm diameter watch features a stainless steel case and moulded leather band.

05   Watercolour sketch sketch of a cross-section of of the Steelwave Watch by Pakhalé.

NEKA NON-ELECTRIC KITCHEN APPLIANCES — In the NEKA project, Pakhalé revisits the hand-operated kitchen appliance, applying recent developments in materials and manufacturing techniques. The human effort required to use NEKA objects is significantly less than that needed for traditional hand-operated kitchen appliances. The project offers a sensorial and efficient way of preparing food, with minimum components that are easy to clean. NEKA addresses the current awareness about healthy living and the environment. It is designed to encourage cooking as social cohesion – as a basic act of living, with an awareness of healthy food preparation and preservation as a family activity that instills an element of self-sufficiency.

NEKA NON-ELECTRIC KITCHEN APPLIANCES

01

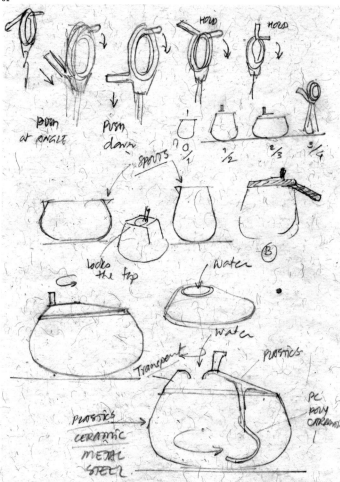

02

01   NEKA Mixer with rotational and random movement.
02   Design sketch of NEKA by Pakhalé. The set of three NEKA objects is designed for whisking, blending and mixing. Blending uses rotational movement, whisking uses
      random movement and mixing uses both rotational and random movement.
03   Cross-section illustrating polymer assembly and the efficient mechanism with mixing patterns for ease of use.
04   Design study exploring various configurations of the handle grip and the rotating crank mechanism.

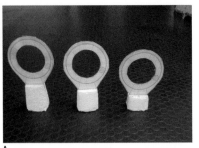

A

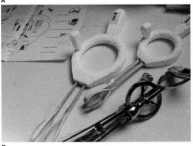

B

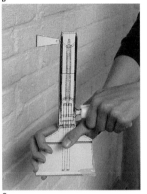

C

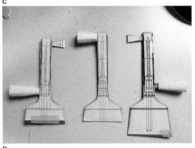

D

03

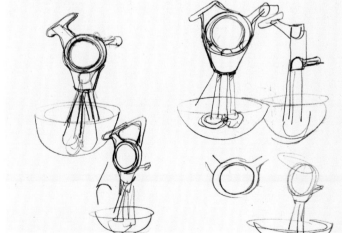

04

A   NEKA handle and grip study.

B   Studying and learning from the ageold non-electric kitchen tool.

C, D   NEKA is designed to enhance the pleasure of cooking with taste and touch, making it a sensorial experience.

05

THE REALM
OF POETICS

Analogical thinking is deeply rooted in human perception.

Satyendra Pakhalé's objects open up the realm of poetic analogy

by reflecting larger imaginative entities beyond themselves.

Tiziana Proietti

THE REALM OF POETICS
Tiziana Proietti

Our minds are constantly in search of easily graspable images. From babyhood, we look at the world and begin discerning, simplifying, categorizing and typifying shapes to build the structure of our knowledge through experience. Indeed, our brain's main task is to gain knowledge of the surrounding world. However, the matter of perception is far from simple, and the brain's task is not an easy one. It has to transform external, unlimited information, which is complex and extremely differentiated, and make it accessible to our limited sensorial and cognitive abilities. In doing so, it searches for the relevant generic features of a given, perceived object, and stores the information gained.

The brain is constantly seeking the essence. While perceiving, we are in search of universal common denominators, constancies, enduring forms, or constant elements that are the constituent parts of uncountable forms, and that our mind can process, associate and even expand upon. We are selective in our way of perceiving, and we leave aside any information not related to those universal, essential features meant to summon up the object of perception in the vast realm of analogies activated by our mind. Indeed, thinking through analogies is like breathing: humans do not need to rationalize it. This aptitude, which we can define as 'analogical thinking', is deeply rooted in human perception.

Instinctive Perception

Shapes are captured and crystallized by our brain just before being confined in any object specificity, leaving them floating in the realm of analogies. When art acts like the brain, the object produced resonates powerfully with instinctive human perception by favouring the analogical thinking that is the ground for an act of self-identification: an empathic relationship brought into being between observer and object. Human memories, broadest needs and sensorial aptitudes are projected upon the object by activating the vast realm of poetic forms, so appropriately defined by Philip Rawson in his analysis of Indian sculpture as 'poetic analogies'. Indeed, in Indian sculpture 'the different realms of life and thought are represented and summarized'[1].

A   Dietrich Seckel, *Before and Beyond the Image* (1976), argues that the 'most crucial spiritual insights lie beyond the power of human imagination to describe or depict; the visual arts can allude to them only obliquely, through omission or the use of non-iconic figures'. Courtesy: Satyendra Pakhalé Archives, Amsterdam, NL.

1   Philip Rawson, *Indian Sculpture*, London: Studio Vista, UK, 1996, p. 34.

Rawson elaborates: 'The "meaning" of forms is thus seen to reside in their suggestions of similar forms seen and remembered from other contexts. And if the forms in question are not merely the strict geometrical forms of analysis, but consist each of a subtle combination of geometrical classes which refer directly back to particular referents in real experience they will have a 'poetic significance', quite distinct from the prose sense of straightforward analysis and far more powerful in its emotional effects'.[2]

From antiquity, sensorial existence was the cornerstone of the Indian art tradition. Artists searched for forms and images to convey the enigma of human sensorial perception. Simple primal forms were used, resulting in abstraction, archaism and plasticity. The well-known sense of suavity belonging to the great tradition of Indian secular art, which dates back to the reign of Ashoka from 270 to 232 BCE,[3] comes from the morphological properties of objects as connected to the sensorial qualities they embody and convey.

The Tone of Existence

Looking at the earliest rock-cut architecture and sculpture from India, still standing in World Heritage sites like Ajanta, Bhaje, Karle and Sanchi, it is easy to note how the primary means of expression comes from irreducible units that cannot be broken down further into equally essential and concise units. As Rawson points out, by using only pointed and flat chisels and the method of strip-cutting, or 'cutting the stone in a series of facets, each of which runs like a continuous band from top to bottom of the figure, and corresponds to one outline of the silhouette', sculptors, in a highly sophisticated manner, delved into the very essence of each unit of form. This ability to catch the essence of things, or what we might call the 'tone of existence', comes from the Indian mind that 'was captivated by its vision of the immense, the infinite ground of Being'.[4]

All the sculpture techniques used by Indian sculptors emphasized the roundness and even the thickness of volumes, inviting spectators to experience and look at objects from the inside, rather than from the outside. The meaningful inner structure, manipulated and conveyed by sculptural methods and techniques, at the same time strictly rational and purely expressive, is the real raw material of Indian secular art. The geometry of convexities and the mathematics of pointed lines running around the rounded volumes are shaped to produce impressive sensorial objects.

B   Rock-cut architecture at the UNESCO World Heritage site of Ajanta. Here: cell no. 9, view of stupa, 1st cent. CE. Courtesy: Satyendra Pakhalé Archives, Amsterdam, NL.

C   The couple at Karla, Maharashtra, is the oldest surviving example of rock-cut Buddhist architecture, dating from ca. 160 BCE. The carving represents the egalitarian traditions in the Buddhist era when new social energies, entrepreneurial roles and cultural innovations burst forth in India. Courtesy: Kevin Standage, UK.

D   A group of 22 rock-cut cells in Bhaja. Earliest example of a chaitya on an ancient trade route running from the Arabian Sea eastward into the Deccan Plateau (the division between North India and South India), 2nd BCE. Courtesy: Kevin Standage, UK.

2   Philip Rawson, 'The Methods of Indian Sculpture', in *Oriental Arts*, 1957, p. 142.
3   The Indian secular art referred to in this passage belongs to the period from around the 2nd century BCE (Before Common Era) to the 5th century CE (Common Era).
4   Philip Rawson, *Indian Sculpture*, London: Studio Vista, 1996, p. 60.

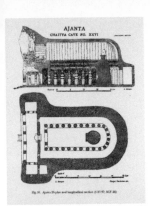

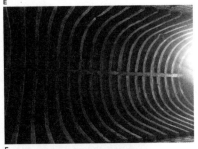

E   Walter M. Spink, Ajanta 26 plan and lon-
gitudinal Section of a Chaitya from Ajanta:
*History and Development, Volume Four,
Painting, Sculpture, Architecture Year by Year*,
Koninklijke Brill NV, Leiden, NL, 2009. Courtesy:
Brill Publishers, NL.

F   A group of 30 rock-cut cells in Ajanta.
Example of a chaitya with a vaulted horseshoe
ceiling, 2nd BCE. Courtesy: Satyendra Pakhalé
Archives, Amsterdam, NL.

G   Torana Gate Sanchi, life in Uruvelā. A
sculptural detail depicting scene of everyday
village life, where women pound rice, winnow it,
crush spices, roll out dough, fetch water from
the river in which water buffaloes laze and
empty seat that serves as a marker for the
presence of the Buddha. A remarkable feature
of these oldest surviving examples of narrative
art from India. By depicting Buddha with only
aniconic symbols, this phenomenon can hardly be explained as the result of general absence of images. The artistic creation of the
Buddha image begins with the non-image –
seemingly paradox, but quite in keeping with
the teachings of the enlightened Buddha.
Sanchi architectural complex is one of the important architectural specimens by the emper-
or Ashoka – India's founding father, he es-
poused non-violence and the utterly novel
concept of conquest by moral force alone, establishing a welfare state in 2nd century BCE.
Courtesy: ASI Archaeological Survey of India.

Poetic Analogies

The aptitude for projecting the image of our functions upon the outside world and reading external reality on our own terms is ancient and profound. It is the primal way of interpreting the world through an act of self-identification. It is a way of humanizing the world through 'poetic analogies'.

Satyendra Pakhalé's objects similarly open up the realm of poetic analogy by reflecting larger imaginative entities beyond themselves. The Fish Chair (2005)❶, or the B.M. Horse (2000)❷, Black-White Swan (2012)❸ and Panther (2002)❹ offer a continuous invitation to self-identification by allowing the mind to think analogically and matching the acquired knowledge with memory and imagination. The meaning of each Pakhalé object does not lie in the object itself, but in our experience of it, or better yet in the 'reception' charged with emotional and sensorial values and the ability to animate the inanimate. The perceived object becomes simultaneously a carrier of emotions, functions and analogies, triggering all the human senses, including the 'sense of mind'.

A Step Beyond All Forms

The convexly curved forms of Pakhalé's body of work are designed, progressively refined and controlled to expand the realm of analogies to evoke unlimited images that arouse meanings rather than representing anything. As in the earliest secular Buddhist sculpture, the convexity of shape becomes the container of a sense of being to be interpreted and expanded in the act of perceiving.

The common denominators and unbreakable units that animate Pakhalé's design come from patiently and sensitively working beyond the boundaries of form. Indeed, he is aware that, to use Dietrich Seckel's words, 'the more abstract a visual sign is, the truer and more effective it is. An image fulfills its purpose all the more if it reaches the boundary of all form, and allows the step into the realm beyond all form [...] Beyond all images, even the most sublime ones, there is always one more step'.[5]

Self-Expressiveness of Forms

Pakhalé is constantly pursuing that 'one more step' — by pushing the limits of the representative character of symbols and making them capable of opening the broadest field of self-identification

5   Dietrich Seckel, *Before and Beyond the Image. Aniconic Symbolism in Buddhist Art*, London: Paul Holberton Publishing, UK, 2008, pp. 56–57.

The convexly curved forms
of Pakhalé's works are
designed, progressively
refined and controlled

to expand the realm
of analogies to evoke
unlimited images

that arouse meanings rather
than representing anything.

Tiziana Proietti

in the vast, human, pluralistic ways of being and expression. Indeed, analogical thinking is rooted in the act of associating and bringing into being a scenario that may change according to the lines of association followed. This means that the final form, or units of form, may have a symbolic value without being confined to specific figures. This is the power of representing the essence of forms, as experienced so strongly in Pakhalé's designs, in their natural state of openness, captured just before they are confined to a specific symbol that does not need to be associated with any specific meaning.

Any attempt to capture the specific meanings of symbols in Pakhalé's design objects is useless. Effectively, it is not necessary that symbols symbolize something. No explicit or implicit shared knowledge allows the precise and unique interpretation of symbols. In Pakhalé's projects, symbols are the objects of special knowledge, sometimes easily accessible, sometimes reserved to experts, sometimes forgotten today, although it existed in the past. This multiplicity of achievable interpretations results from the absence of a code. These copious symbolic associations converge in multi-sensorial objects that show their own compelling 'self-expressiveness'.

H   Fish Chair Viola at *Satyendra Pakhalé: Design at Fairchild*, Fairchild Tropical Botanical Gardens, Miami, USA, 2014. Courtesy: Celia D. Luna, USA.

I   B.M. Chaise Longue at *Satyendra Pakhalé: OriginS*, solo exhibition at ammann // gallery, Cologne, DE, 2008. Courtesy: Satyendra Pakhalé Archives, Amsterdam, NL.

J   Panther at *Satyendra Pakhalé: From Projects to Products*, solo exhibition, Stedelijk Museum, Amsterdam, NL, 2002. Courtesy: Satyendra Pakhalé Archives, Amsterdam, NL.

Effectively, it is not necessary that symbols symbolize something.

Tiziana Proietti

CONTENT

KANGERI NOMADIC RADIATOR — After years of research and development, Satyendra Pakhalé and TUBES Radiatori launched the innovative Kangeri Nomadic Radiator. This mobile radiator warms up the space around the user – a welcome alternative to wasteful central heating systems. Made of steel, oak wood and aluminium, Kangeri rolls freely on three wheels through the domestic or office space, creating a comfortable zone of warmth wherever needed. Kangeri is a new typology of radiator with sensorial qualities; effectively, it becomes the user's companion. The name Kangeri references the *kanger*, a pot filled with hot embers used by Kashmiri people in Northern India beneath their traditional clothing to keep themselves warm. It is an object with great cultural importance. Pakhalé: 'a wonderfully poetic answer to a basic need'.

01

01 A finely crafted top in oak with an integral handle enables the user to move around the nomadic radiator easily and to operate it with just one switch.
02 The integral wooden handle of the Kangeri Nomadic Radiator being tested.
03 Kangeri Nomadic Radiator integral wooden handle design sketch by Pakhalé.

A

B

C

02

D

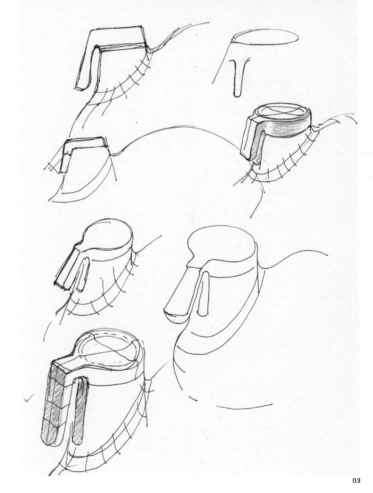

03

A First sketch model for the nomadic radiator being made at Pakhalé's studio.

B Pakhalé refining the scale model and briefing his assistant at his studio.

C,D Pakhalé at his studio working out the object proportions with his team in the conception phase of the project and trying out the handle study models.

04

E

F

G

H

I

E, F Full-scale foam models of the nomadic radiator being made at the Pakhalé studio.

G, H Pakhalé receives the prototype of the nomadic radiator, sent by TUBES technical office. Pakhalé observes how users are likely to handle the object.

I Prototype being tested at the studio.

KANGERI NOMADIC RADIATOR

04 Watercolour sketch of the Kangeri Nomadic Radiator by Pakhalé.
05 Kangeri Nomadic Radiator with extended electric cable. Pakhalé: 'I wanted to create a contemporary object for warming up the space around the user that applies the technology of today and brings poetic imagination back to a utilitarian object – that's how Kangeri was born.'

KUBU — This piece is a chaise longue for open spaces. It is made of basswood, combining a high-tech process with an artisanal, handmade finish. In an idiosyncratic manner, it appears to be simply floating on the surface. This is achieved by creating a fine balance between ergonomics, mass equilibrium and the overall form of the piece. Kubu is the result of a combination of high-tech five-axis CNC machining and highly skilled woodworking. Pakhalé: 'Until Kubu, I had never used wood in such an elaborate manner. I wanted to create a chaise longue with correct ergonomics and a perfect equilibrium, without compromising the overall aesthetics of the piece.' Kubu chaise longue is assembled out of smaller pieces of basswood. The Austronesian name Kubu was intended 'to create awareness about natural resources in the tropical region of our

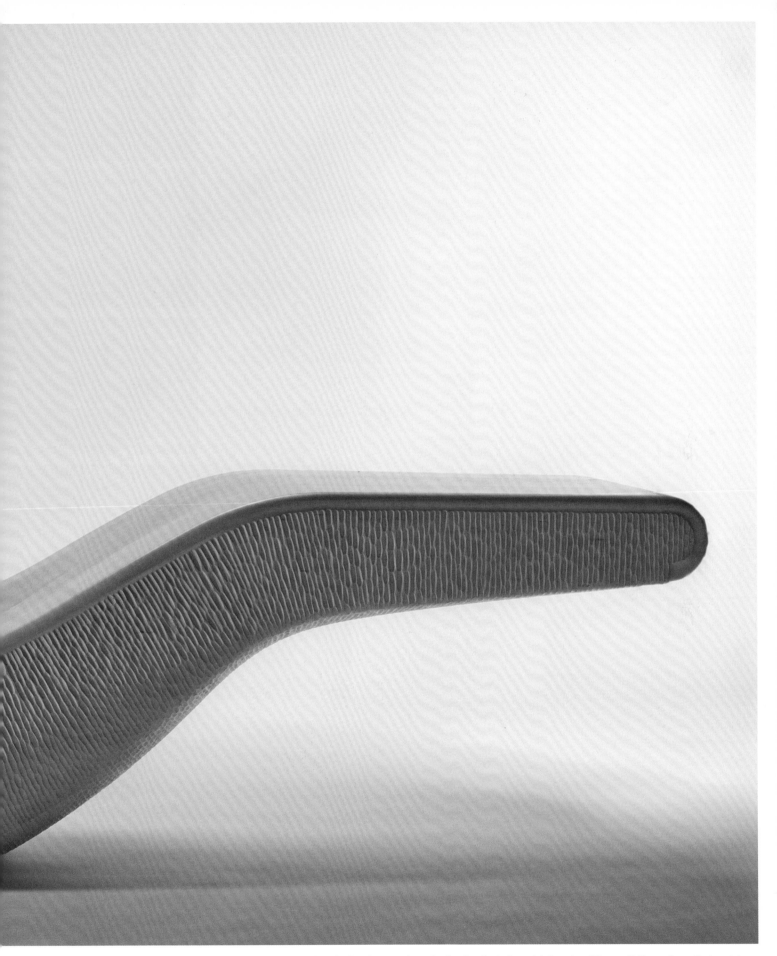

planet although Kubu is not made of any of those resources.' It took a lot of prototyping using handmade study models to arrive at the result. The mathematical model was used to make a precisely machined piece using a five-axis milling machine in the Veneto region. Having done the highly technical machining of the wood, the next step was to find a skilled wood craftsman who could lend it a tactile surface. Pakhalé found sixth-generation wood carvers in the mountains of Bolzano who achieved the desired results with what Pakhalé calls 'a simple yet incredibly meditative act of woodworking'.

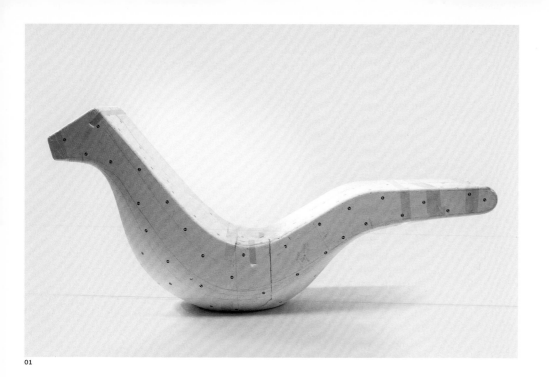

01

A

B

C

D

A–E   Pakhalé carried out research to achieve the correct ergonomics and equilibrium resulting in the final form of the Kubu prototype after several study models.

F–H   A precise 3D CAD model was built from the 3D-scanned surfaces. A Meticulous planning was carried out to achieve unidirectional grains in the piece with smaller basswood blocks.

I   After the CNC machining, the piece was taken to another laboratory for the hand-sculpted texture specified by Pakhalé and carved by an artisan living in the Italian Dolomites.

E

F

G

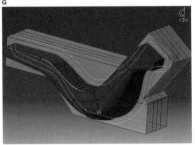

H

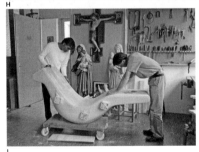

I

02

01   Full-scale, articulate model made at Pakhalé's studio ready for 3D scanning - the process of reverse engineering to build a controlled 3D CAD model based on the scanned surface geometry.
02   The tactile surface that follows the geometry of the piece is the result of highly skilled yet basic wood carving to achieve the desired sensoriality.

KID CERAMIC CHAIR — This piece in ceramic is one of the outcomes of the designer's 'Playing with Clay' residency ❶ at the European Ceramic Work Centre (EKWC) in the Netherlands. Illustrating a similar approach to that used in Pottery Chair and Roll Carbon Ceramic Chair and applying hollow forms, this project set out to explore a design language that would fire a child's imagination. Kid Ceramic Chair provides a wonderful inside space for children. They can play with it, look through it and store toys in it. A special experimental glaze gives a deep sensorial quality to the object.

A

B

C

D

01

A, B   The Kid Ceramic Chair drying on a ceramic slab and coated with an experimental glaze before firing.

C, D   After firing the piece is tested.

01   The hollow space encourages children to play and store toys.

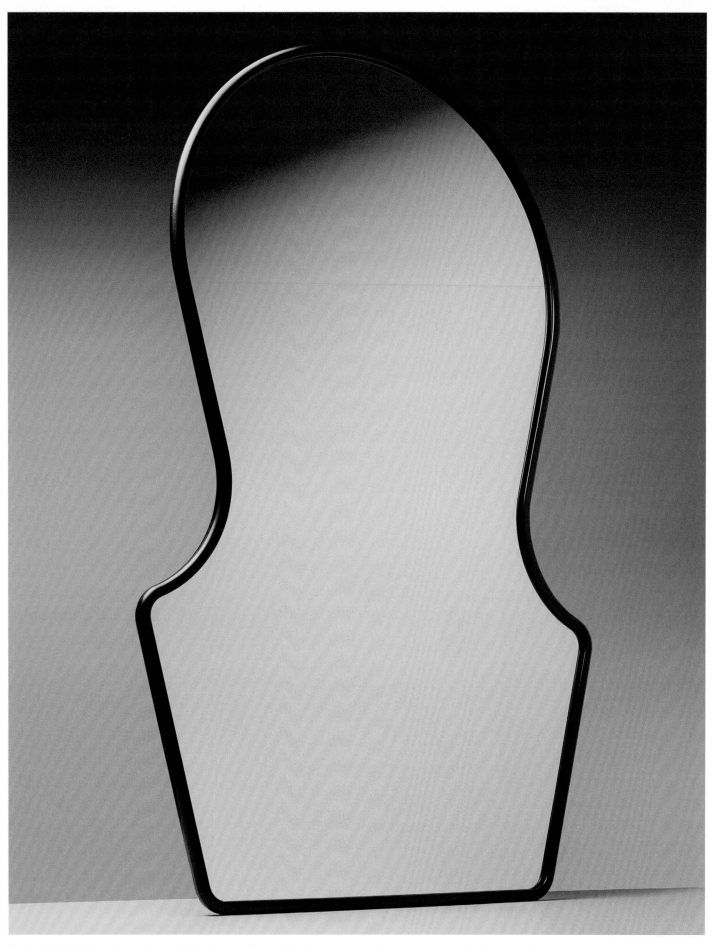

MIRROR FAMILY — A set of three mirrors with injection-moulded flexible polymer that not only protects the mirror rim, but also ventilates and keeps the mirrors moisture-free. The forms are inspired by a memory of an ancient architectural window. The circular mirror form is animated by the sun's profile during sunset with a wonderful geometry that is neither circular nor elliptical but somewhere between the two. All the mirrors can be oriented in both directions, as the fixture is designed in such a manner that it can be hung upside down.

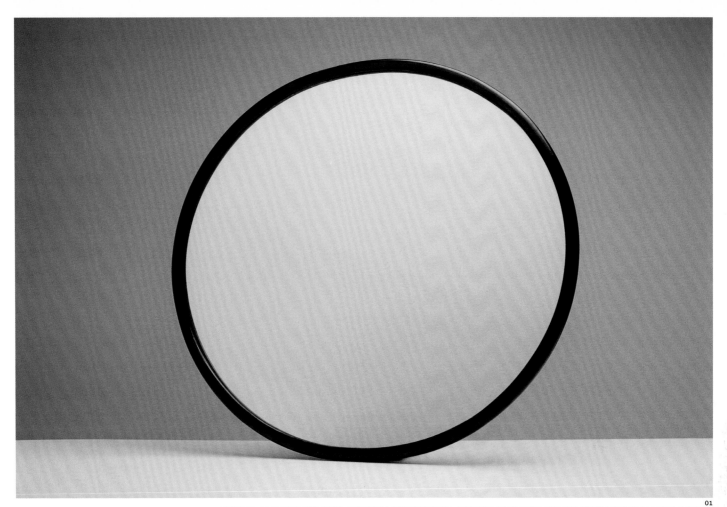

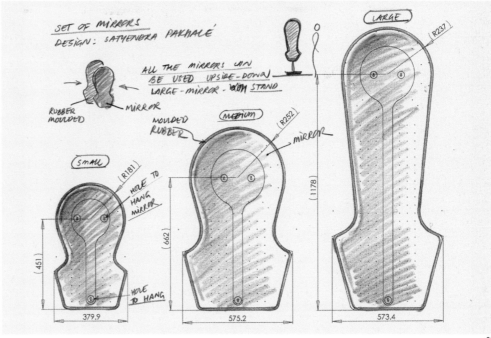

01   The circular mirror form makes a reference to the sun's profile during sunset, a precise geometry between elliptical and circular.

02   Design drawing of the mirror family by Satyendra Pakhalé, in which the forms are inspired by a memory of the beautifully carved windows that allow the breeze to blow through the summer palace Hawa Mahal, Jaipur, IN.

KID DAY BED — This child's bed is conceived for daycare centres as well as for home use as an extra bed when a friend comes to sleep over. It has two modular mattresses that can be used on both sides. The mattress has a backrest on one side, making it a sofa or a playful spatial combination evoking fantasy and play. When the mattress is placed flat, it becomes a bed for an afternoon nap or for sleeping at night. At the daycare centre, several beds can be stacked and stored away. The bed and the mattresses are designed to be light so that two children can move them around easily and can arrange and rearrange the mattresses and make several configurations to play the way their imagination takes them. Made of rotational moulded polyethylene with a waterproof textile for the mattresses, it can be used both outdoors and indoors. To make the

piece light and effective in manufacturing, unnecessary material is removed from the base. When the bed is turned upside down, there is a wonderful feature to discover: it suddenly becomes a game board.

01

02

A

B

C

D

01,02 The mattress has a backrest on one side making it a sofa or a playful spatial combination evoking fantasy and play. Two children can arrange and rearrange the mattresses, indulging their imaginations.
03   When the mattress is placed flat, it becomes a bed for an afternoon nap or sleeping at night.
04   At the daycare centre, several beds can be stacked and stored away. Concept sketch of Kid Day Bed by Pakhalé.

KID DAY BED

04

03

A–E Prototype being tested for various spatial combinations creating diverse imaginative possibilities for children to play with.

F To make the piece light and effective in manufacturing, unnecessary material is removed from the base.

G Pakhalé checking the mattress module prototype.

SALAKA — This large vase with its bowl-like base is a generous form that suggests giving. The base flows into a clearly defined shoulder that leads into a long neck. The vertical cut in the neck is a sensual feature that lends itself to arranging flowers in various ways, underlining the offering gesture. The Salaka vase is made of two layers of Murano glass, a coloured layer outside and a white opaque layer inside, giving depth to the material. 'I was curious about Murano glass and the age-old skills and sensitivities that are cultivated uniquely on this wonderful island,' the designer explains. 'It is exciting to create an object using the fascinating process of mouth blowing that has remained almost unchanged to this day. Glass is a precious sensorial material impregnated with meaning that offers the possibility of creating a delicate object almost instantaneously.' The vase is an ancient

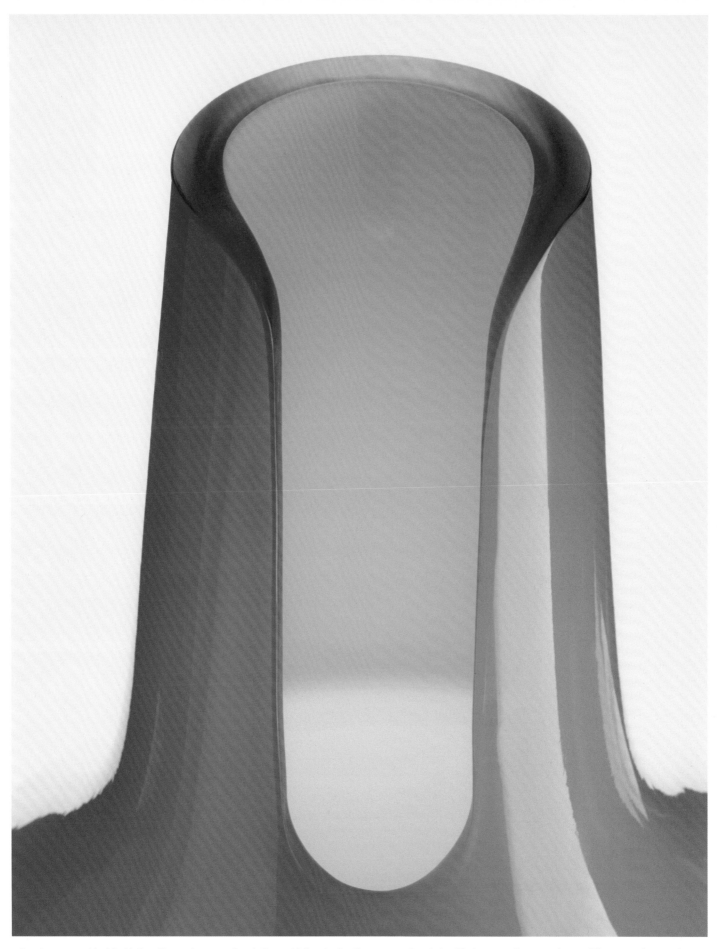

yet contemporary object that is found in nearly every culture in the world. It embodies the essence of our being. Placing a vase in a space is one of those everyday acts that can lift our mood. The Salaka vase in Murano glass creates an atmosphere that not only fills space, but shapes it through the act of daily rituals that the object itself invites us to perform.

01

A

B

C

D

E

01   The vertical cut in the neck is a sensuous feature that lends itself to arranging flowers in various ways. Achieving a controlled vertical cut calls for great skill as it could break the entire piece if not carried out properly.
02   The Salaka vase with the wooden mould.
03   Salaka working drawing in watercolour by Pakhalé.

                SALAKA

F

G

H

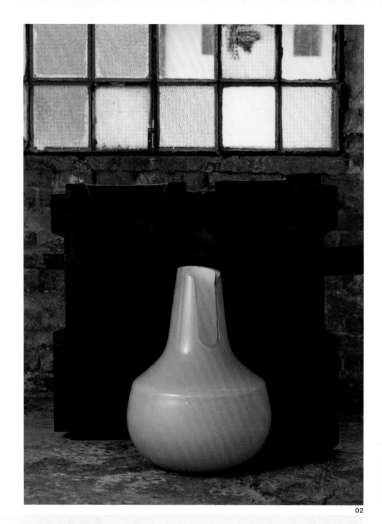

02

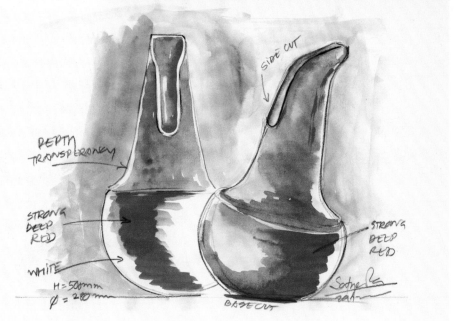

03

A-F The highly culture-specific Murano glass-making process: conserving the wooden mould in water, preparing the glass for blowing larger objects in stages and blowing glass to achieve the final result.

G Master glass craftsman blowing the final piece.

H Pakhalé marking the vertical cut on the pieces.

06

SENSING WITH THE MIND

We cannot mentally survive in a world devoid of historicity, sensuality, and human meaning.

Meaningful design places our bodies and minds harmoniously in the flesh of the world.

Juhani Pallasmaa

SENSING WITH THE MIND
Juhani Pallasmaa

It is commonly understood that we relate to the world through our five senses, which were defined by Aristotle: sight, hearing, smell, taste and touch. This view is supported by the simple fact that we have a specific organ for each one of these five sensory capacities. The ancient Greek philosopher also established the hierarchy of the human senses, from the privileged sense of sight down to touch, and we continue to regard vision as our most important sense. 'Clear vision' is also a strong metaphor in language, and is regarded as equivalent to truth. As a consequence of this tradition, architecture, design and the visual arts are understood as predominantly visual. Yet all our senses are functional specializations of skin tissue and, consequently, are all modes of touch. In fact, touch could well be considered our most important sense, due to its directly protective function.

Recent writings suggest that we interact with the world through twenty to thirty-three sensory systems. In addition to the five senses, others have been suggested such as balance, gravity, proprioception, duration, continuity, scale, sense of effort, and sense of agency. To further complicate the definition of a sense, even our endocrine glands, which are regarded as a closed system sealed inside the body and only indirectly linked with the outside world, have been found to influence virtually everything the body does. Experiments show that these chemical regulators, which include odoriferous glands, scattered about animal bodies, work directly on the body chemistry of other organisms. Even more recent research has revealed the significance of the bacterial universe in our intestines, which has been called our 'second brain'. We are beginning to understand that our sensory systems are far more complicated than we believed, and as a consequence, the qualitative requirements for humanistic design also go far beyond vision.

Flesh of the World
As Maurice Merleau-Ponty suggests, we live in 'the flesh of the world',[1] and the mind, senses and world constitute a continuum. The senses expand us into the surrounding space through the mind and imagination, and we are even able to project ourselves beyond the earth into outer space: 'Through vision we touch the

---

[1] Maurice Merleau-Ponty, 'The Intertwining – The Chiasm', *The Visible and the Invisible,* Evanston, IL: Northwestern University Press, 1992.

Sensory experience is unstable, and alien to natural perception,

which we achieve with our whole body all at once,

and which opens on a world of interacting senses.

Maurice Merleau-Ponty

A

B

C

sun and the stars,' as philosopher Martin Jay poetically suggests.[2] Architecture and design continue to be taught and practised primarily as visual arts, and, even more specifically, as arts of the focused eye. Yet all the senses actively survey the world to determine the situations and conditions which are favourable for us. We tend to think of our senses in isolation, but Merleau-Ponty points out their essential collaboration: 'My perception is not a sum of visual, tactile and audible givens. I perceive in a total way with my whole being: I grasp a unique structure of the things, a unique way of being, which speaks to all my senses at once,'[3] and he writes, adding: 'Sensory experience is unstable, and alien to natural perception, which we achieve with our whole body all at once, and which opens on a world of interacting senses.'[4]

This synthetic and 'symphonic' way of sensing should surely be the architect's, designer's and artist's way of encountering the world and his work. Merleau-Ponty asks: 'How could the artist or the poet express anything else but his encounter with the world?'[5] And he suggests that Paul Cézanne's paintings 'make visible how the world touches us.'[6] The philosopher's thinking makes the human body the centre of our experiential and existential world: 'We choose our world through our bodies as living centres of intentionality, and that is how the world chooses us.'[7] He defines this body-centred view powerfully: 'Our own body is in the world as the heart is in the organism: it keeps the visible spectacle constantly alive, it breathes life into it and sustains it inwardly, and with it forms a system.'[8]

Sense of Being

I would like to suggest that, in the field of architecture and design, the most important sense is not vision, as the synthesizing sense seems to be our existential sense, the sense of being. The existential sense fuses all the sensations with the sense of being and gives them coherence, continuity and meaning. In my view, this existential sense is close to the notion of the earliest Buddhist 'sense of mind' that Pakhalé refers to. Indeed in all respects, the Eastern traditions of thinking have grasped the complex essence of human experience and consciousness, as well as the interactions of the material and the mental, better than our current scientific view. They avoid the categorical divide between the lived and the scientific worlds.

A   Louis Kahn, Architecture IIM-A - Indian Institute of Management in Ahmedabad, IN, built with wisely used basic materials like exposed brick and light. The campus hosts classrooms, hostels, a library, academic facilities and vast corridors that act as a passive cooling system, all gathered around a big courtyard, shaping an area of more than 60 acres. It is a seminal example of Kahn's architecture, 1962-1974. Courtesy: Satyendra Pakhalé Archives, Amsterdam, NL.

B   Alvar Aalto, experimental wood relief. Aalto started experimenting with laminated bent wood in 1929. These reliefs were part of an important process of solving the technical challenges related to his furniture developments as well as a method for Aalto to experiment with bent wood in a playful, artistic way. Courtesy: Satyendra Pakhalé Archives, Amsterdam, NL.

C   Howz, a symmetrical axis pool in the courtyard of the Sidi Saiyyed Mosque, famed for its Tree of Life latticework, in the World Heritage city of Ahmedabad, IN, 1573. Courtesy: Satyendra Pakhalé Archives, Amsterdam, NL.

2   Martin Jay, as quoted in David Michael Levin, 'Introduction', *Modernity and the Hegemony of Vision*, University of California Press, Berkeley: University of California Press, 1993, p. 14.
3   Maurice Merleau-Ponty, 'The Film and the New Psychology', *Sense and Non-Sense*, Evanston: Northwestern University Press, IL, 1964, p. 48.
4   Maurice Merleau-Ponty, *Phenomenology of Perception*, London: Routledge, UK, 1992, p. 225.

Design needs to frame the world, provide it with meaning,

and to grant us our existential foothold in reality.

This foothold has its practical, material and performative,

as well as perceptual, sensory and metaphysical dimensions.

Juhani Pallasmaa

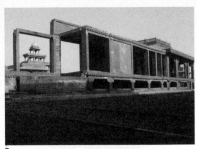

D

E

F

The task of architecture and design is not only to create visual order and beauty. Design needs to frame the world, provide it with meaning, and to grant us our existential foothold in reality. This foothold has its practical, material and performative, as well as perceptual, sensory and metaphysical dimensions. A significant aspect of this task is the re-mythicization and re-eroticization of our relationship with the world. We cannot mentally survive in a world devoid of historicity, sensuality, and human meaning. Meaningful design places our bodies and minds harmoniously in the flesh of the world.

Satyendra Pakhalé's designs suggest a haptic skin-relationship through their sensorial forms, poetic associations and tactile surfaces; they invite the user and stimulate sensations of intimacy and nearness. The shapes present invitations to our body sense, rather than merely displaying retinal images.

D   Fatehpur Sikri, city of victory. The capital of the Mogul empire from 1571 to 1585, built by Akbar the Great, 37 km west of the city of Agra, India. It is believed that the city expresses the personality and principles of Akbar. He had a natural inclination towards industrial crafts and concern for technological innovation. He was so devoted to architecture that he sometimes quarried stones himself along with the workmen. Akbar built a workshop near his palace at Fatehpur Sikri with studios and workrooms for the finer and more reputable arts, such as painting, goldsmith work, tapestry-making, carpet and curtain-making, reports the Jesuit father Francis Henriques, 1580. Courtesy: Satyendra Pakhalé Archives, Amsterdam, NL.

E   Aaram Baugh, meaning 'Garden of Rest', Agra, IN, 1528, is one of the early surviving gardens of the Mughal dynasty in India, located on the banks of the Yamuna river in Agra, a few kilometres away from the Taj Mahal, built by Emperor Babur. It is a Persian garden constructed in red stone and constituted by three descending terraces crossed by a network of canals, fountains, cascades and pools. Courtesy: Satyendra Pakhalé Archives, Amsterdam, NL.

F   The Alhambra is an Arabic fortress located on Sabika Hill in Granada, ES. The first palace of the walled city of Alhambra was named after Muhammad ibn Nasr and built in red brick. In 1492, after the Catholic monarchs' reconquest of Granada, the Alhambra became the royal palace of the kings of Spain and was completed with Renaissance architecture. Courtesy: Satyendra Pakhalé Archives, Amsterdam, NL.

5   Maurice Merleau-Ponty as quoted in Richard Kearney, 'Maurice Merleau-Ponty', *Modern Movements in European Philosophy*, Manchester-New York: Manchester University Press, USA, 1994, p. 82.
6   Maurice Merleau-Ponty, 'Cézanne's Doubt', *Sense and Non-Sense*, op. cit., p. 19.
7   Quoted in Kearney, op. cit., p. 74.
8   Maurice Merleau-Ponty, *Phenomenology of Perception*, op. cit., p. 203.

Satyendra Pakhalé's designs suggest a haptic skin-relationship through their sensorial forms,

poetic associations and tactile surfaces; they invite the user and stimulate sensations of intimacy and nearness.

The shapes present invitations to our body sense, rather than merely displaying retinal images.

Juhani Pallasmaa

CONTENT

RCCC - ROLL CARBON CERAMIC CHAIR — Is it high-tech or low-tech? 'I never see materials as high-tech or low-tech,' says Satyendra Pakhalé. 'I don't even want to see various technologies as high or low-tech. I always want to use what is appropriate in a given situation. However, observing this senseless debate about high- and low-tech as a provocation, I created Roll Carbon Ceramic Chair.' This piece combines two unexpected materials in a seamless manner: supposedly high-tech carbon fibre, and supposedly low-tech ceramic. The Roll Carbon Ceramic Chair is a one-off piece. Thanks to Pakhalé's close relationship with the Italian artisans who took on such an adventurous project and shared the risks, it was possible to achieve the RCCC as a unique structural piece in ceramics with an articulate, crafted surface finish in carbon fibre.

01   RCCC is a piece with a technically resolved joint where the backrest and rear leg units are sensuously joined to the open cylindrical form. The result is a new design language with an evocative symbolic form. RCCC developed from the initial Roll Ceramic Chair pieces made at EKWC during Pakhalé's residency ❶.

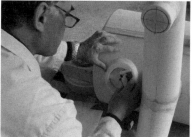

02

A   A full-scale plaster model is built for mould making in the Italian workshop.

B   After getting the joint right, the moulds were produced to make the final parts of the chair.

C   The structural joint being studied in the plaster model.

ROLL CARBON CERAMIC CHAIR

02   Roll Ceramic Chair top detail, made with tubular forms thrown on a wheel, cut and joined in the wet-clay condition.

03   After two cracked prototypes, Pakhalé developed a system for laying the wet clay in a horizontal cylindrical form so that the back parts could be assembled. This in-genious solution led to the development of a special joint between backrest and rear leg units.

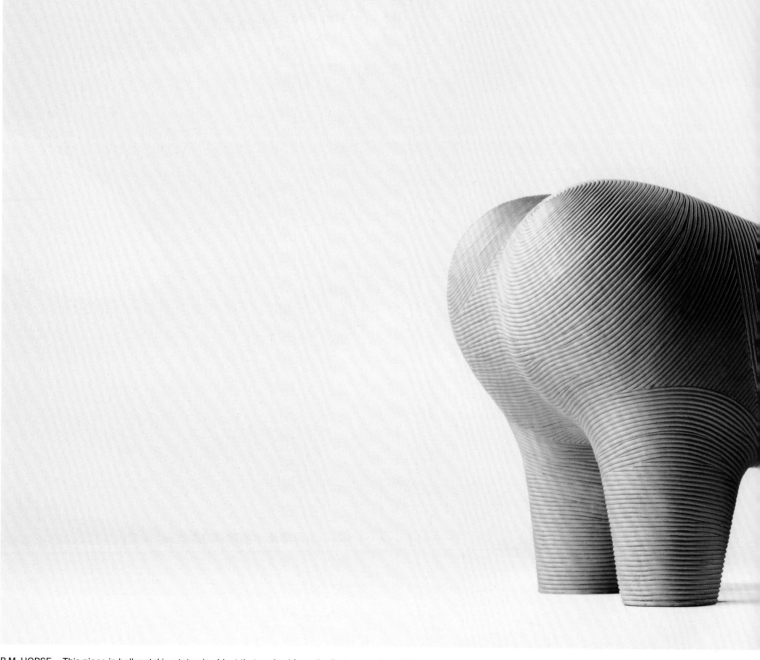

B.M. HORSE — This piece in bell metal is a totemic object that evolved from the first generation of B.M. Objects. Pakhalé wanted to create a larger, seamless piece using the lost-wax casting process. The size of the B.M. Horse made it impossible to cast it in one piece using the traditional process. Four self-financed attempts were made to cast the chair at a foundry in India between 2000 and 2005, but each one failed. To cast a thin-walled object this big in one piece is challenging, as there has to be enough space for the metal to flow, and the outcome is never known until the mould is broken apart. In 2005 Pakhalé moved the exercise to Europe and started to think of an alternative to natural wax. He devised a new method by replacing the wax with specially made, semi-flexible PVC cord and developing a silicone mould. He searched Europe for

a foundry to take on the challenge, and after several months located one near Milan, Italy, which was willing to give it a try. Meanwhile Pakhalé carried out a metallurgical test simulating mathematical models to study the flow of metal. Eventually the B.M. Horse was successfully cast in seamless bronze and first presented by ammann // gallery at Design Miami/Basel, Switzerland in 2007. It is the result of seven years of persistent research and development. The unique and innovative process combines old and new materials and technologies and makes the piece a limited edition in the true sense of the word. With its synthesis of design, technology, craftsmanship, engineering, material research and persistence, it holds a unique position in contemporary design.

LIMITED EDITION

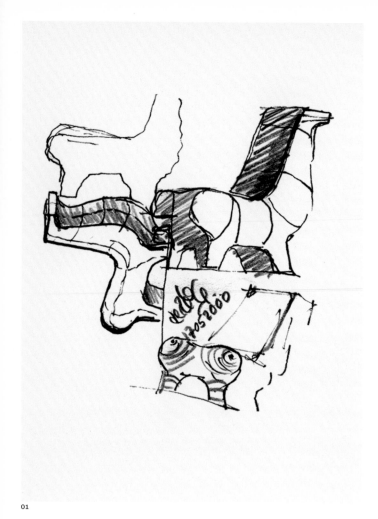

01

A

B

C

D

01 B.M. Horse sketch by Satyendra Pakhalé.
02 This totemic piece carries an energetic physical presence halfway between soft and hard, between flesh and object, between craft and industry.

E

F

G

H

02

A, B Pakhalé shaping a plaster scale model in his Amsterdam studio. Model in natural wax during one of the four self-financed attempts to cast the chair at a maker's studio, Nagpur, IN.

C-F A semi-flexible PVC cord being made near Varese, Italy. A foundry near Milan took on the challenge after carefully studying the scale model.

G, H Articulate master model made using the semi-flexible PVC cord. A silicone mould produced to create a wax model for each casting.

STAR HORSE — Giulio Cappellini ❶ had hoped to present B.M. Horse at the 2001 Super Studio Cappellini show, but it was far from ready so Pakhalé created the Star Horse in fibreglass. A special version finished in velvet flock, it had the zodiac sign of Virgo on the front, Sagittarius on the back and Libra on the bottom, represented as light blue circles on a deep blue flocked background.

CERAMIC HORSE — The work on the making of B.M. Horse was still going on during Pakhalé's residency at the European Ceramic Work Centre (EKWC) ❶, so using the fibre-glass mould of the B.M. Horse ❷ he made a one-off in special glazed ceramic with hand-painted Ananda Totems ❸. There were no guarantees that the ceramic piece would survive the drying and high-temperature firing at 1200°C, but fortuitously it did.

B.M. HORSE FAMILY — Scale 1:3 models of the B.M. Horse Family consisting of B.M. Horse, B.M. Horse Chaise Longue, B.M. Horse Stool, B.M. Horse Lo Table and B.M. Horse Hi Table all made in limited editions. The Satyendra Pakhalé Archives contains several 1:3 scale models of works in real materials.

◐36–39   ◐40–45   ➲282–287

01

02

01, 02   This piece is the largest one in the entire B.M. Horse Family so far. It is made with the same bell metal lost-wax casting process used for the B.M. Horse. The chaise longue is produced in limited editions with sandblasted and patinated surface finishing. Pakhalé studying the scale models made by the same process.
03   B.M. Horse Chaise Longue close-up illustrating highly articulate craftsmanship.

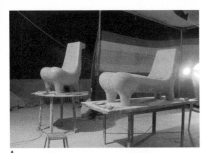

A

B

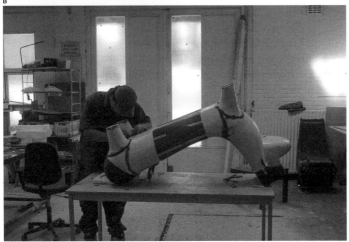

C

D

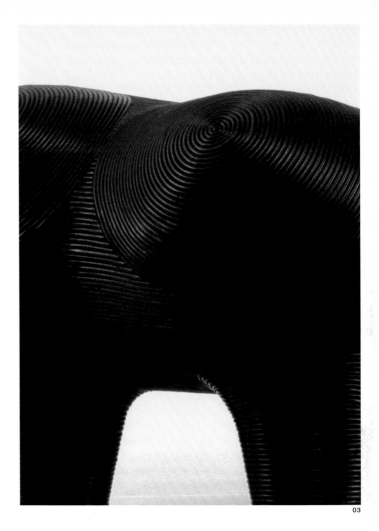

03

_{A, B} B.M. Horse Chaise Longue model being sculpted at a maker's studio in Nagpur, India. Semi-flexible PVC cord being modelled on a fibreglass base in preparation for the silicone mould.

_C The modelling of the B.M. Horse Chaise Longue, like the other B.M. Horse Family and B.M. Objects, required great craftsmanship to achieve the continuity of line and pattern on the three-dimensional surface.

_D B.M. Horse Chaise Longue with the B.M. Horse Stool and B.M. Horse, placed upside down ready to receive the limited edition piece labels at Pakhalé's studio.

Born and raised in the heart of India, trained in both his homeland and Switzerland, and currently a resident of Amsterdam, Satyendra Pakhalé is cosmopolitan in the truest sense of the word – a citizen of the world with a global, rather than a national or provincial scope. Pakhalé calls himself a 'cultural nomad', thus playing down the urban aspect often associated with cosmopolitan thinking and directing attention instead towards something more modest and universal. The designer's origins in India, as well as the traditional handicrafts still practised there in many places juxtaposed with innovative materials and state-of-the-art technology, play a decisive role in his ground-breaking and highly original designs.

The materials and surface structures of Pakhalé's design objects stand out because of their inherent sensuality and timelessness. He is acutely aware of the lack of sensorial quality in industrial design, which has become divorced from the senses and has thus lost its cultural and symbolic meaning, responding instead to short-lived fashion trends. By going back to the basics and working with traditional materials and techniques to create his contemporary design pieces, Pakhalé succeeds in reversing this process.

In keeping with his credo – 'originality comes from origins' – in 2000 Satyendra Pakhalé began working on what was to become his most iconic work yet: the B.M. Horse chair. This sculptural design piece, which is marked by a sense of timeless beauty, is the core of an entire family of bronze works, which – after a long journey and numerous production trials in India – was ultimately brought to life with the support of the Ammann Gallery in a foundry in Italy. These pieces also marked the beginning of a long-term and successful collaboration between Pakhalé and the gallery, which premiered the B.M. series together with Pakhalé's large ceramic Flower Offering Chair in his first solo exhibition, *OriginS*, in Cologne in November 2008. Eleven years on, these works have lost nothing of their original fascination, and the creative journey continues with a new series of B.M. Bronze Vases ❶.

— Gabrielle Ammann

A   The B.M. Horse Stool in a scale 1:3 model being studied prior to modelling with semi-flexible PVC cord at Pakhalé's studio.

B   The B.M. Horse Stool wax model is corrected before casting in bronze.

C, D   Patina being applied on the B.M. Horse Stool. The piece being weighed before shipping.

03

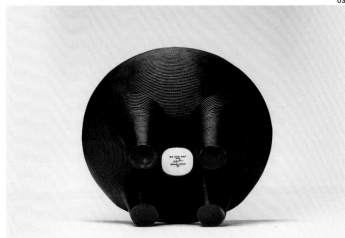

04

03   This limited edition piece is made using the same bell metal lost-wax casting process as that used for the B.M. Horse. The stool is produced with a sandblasted and patinated surface finish coated with natural wax.

04   Bottom view of the B.M. Horse Stool showing the limited edition piece label. All limited edition pieces created by Satyendra Pakhalé in various materials are labelled, numbered and signed.

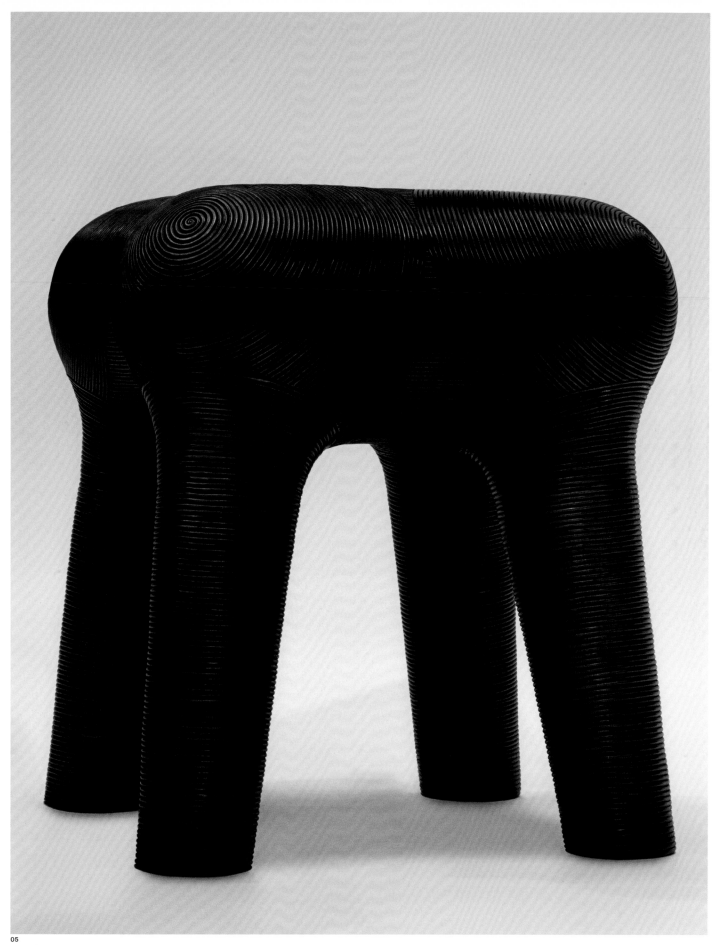

05

05   Part of the B.M. Horse Family, this piece is also made with the bell metal lost-wax casting process. It can be used as an active seat or a side table. The square shape of the top lends this object its unique sensorial feel.

06   Articulate sandblasted surface finish of B.M. Horse Lo Table in bronze.

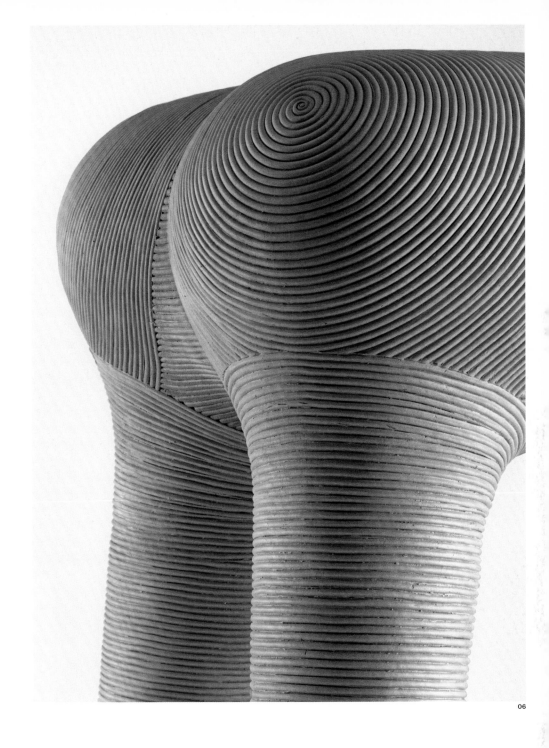

06

SATELLITE CHAIR — This occasional chair fulfilling our nomadic needs in a contemporary setting began life as a travel project ❶ created while Pakhalé was on an exploratory trip in a Brazilian National Park – the UNESCO World Heritage site of Chapada dos Veadeiros being one of the world's oldest and most diverse tropical ecosystems. He was inspired to create a piece when he discovered a wood craftsman making basic furniture in a small village. Pakhalé often develops projects while on the move, calling them 'travel projects'. 'These are spontaneous works based on a cultural particularity I discover,' he says. 'Sometimes, having quickly made prototypes with the local artisans they are further developed at the studio.'

A

B

C

D

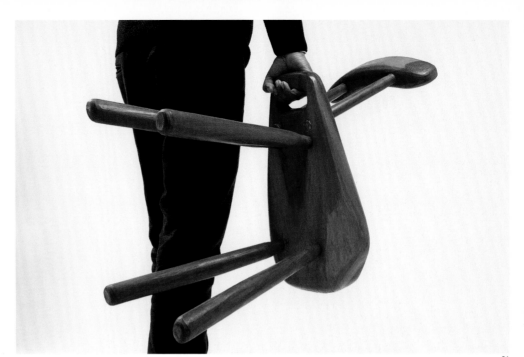

01

02

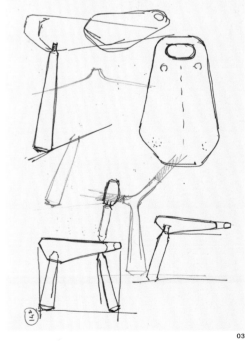

03

A–D	Young craftsman working near Chapada dos Veadeiros. Pakhalé selecting the material and communicating the project idea.

01, 02	Detail of the handle that allows the Satellite Chair to be lifted with one hand and taken outside or fetched as a seat for a surprise visitor.

03	Design sketch illustrating the idea of disassembly for flat packaging and shipping.

O-LED DESK LAMP — In 2006, Yamagiwa, Japan, invited Satyendra Pakhalé to create a desk lamp using one of the first commercially available OLEDs (organic light emitting diodes). This gave a large area spotlight that was cool, bright and white. The OLED generated significant heat and needed cooling. Pakhalé's innovative solution of mounting the OLED in a reverse direction creates, with the reflector, an indirect, soft, warm light, while the air circulation provides natural cooling. The essential design consists of just two moulded components.

01

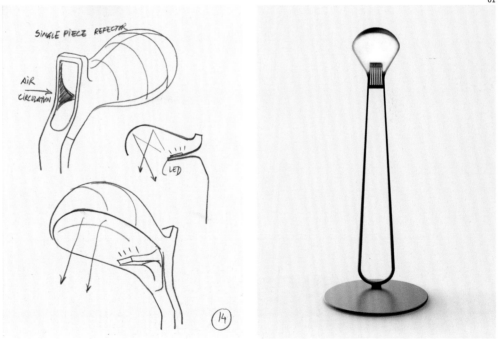

02

03

01 The first generation OLED is mounted on a central element. The lamp reflector and the central element let air circulate thus providing natural cooling as well as a soft, reflected light.
02 Design sketch illustrating the reflector, the central element and air circulation by Satyendra Pakhalé.
03 The reflector and central OLED element are mounted on a base with a tilted double arm that allows the desk lamp to be orientated in any direction.

07

DESIGN FOR SENSORIAL BEINGS

The world as presented to human beings is far from being a fixed and definable set of data,

but more likely an aggregate of sensations and perceptions

that forms the foundation of experience.

Tiziana Proietti

DESIGN FOR SENSORIAL BEINGS
Tiziana Proietti

The belief that we see through our eyes is inaccurate, as is the idea that our perception of surrounding reality mainly happens through the eyes.

We think that we see through our eyes but it is the brain that elaborates the rays of light perceived by the eye and translates them into an image we do indeed see – through our brain and mind. We often associate the idea of seeing with the idea of understanding or acquiring knowledge, unconsciously placing sight above the other senses. We say 'I see' when we understand the situation; or 'Do you see what I mean?' to check we are understood. The heritage of the Modern Era and its glorification of the sense of sight weighs enormously on our shoulders and even if numerous scientific studies state that perception is a complex process entailing the integration of all the senses in the cerebral cortex, we still rate seeing more highly than the other senses. Yet our eyes are mainly just a conduit for transmitting visual input to the brain. This input is just one of several other inputs – coming from all the other activated senses – that simultaneously reach the brain, ending up in what we call the process of perceiving. To quote Merleau Ponty: 'It would seem that we can fathom [the external world] simply by opening our eyes and getting on with our lives. Yet this is a delusion.'[1]

The world as presented to human beings is far from being a fixed and definable set of data, but more likely an aggregate of sensations and perceptions that forms the foundation of experience. According to the early Buddhist realizations, human beings are assemblages of five aggregates (*skandhas*), which include all bodily, perceptual and intellectual qualities and can be listed as follows: form (*rupa*), sensations or feelings (*vedana*), abstract ideas or perception (*sanna*), tendencies of mind or formation (*sankhara*), and mental powers or consciousness (*vinnana*).[2] Thus the complexity of human existence is carefully examined in all its various aspects. Buddhist 'realizations' can be said to have anticipated Edmund Husserl's phenomenology and studies in perception and cognitive science.

1   Maurice Merleau-Ponty, *The World of Perception* (1948), London: Routledge, 2004, UK, 2004, p. 39.
2   Davids Rhys, *Buddhism*, London: The London and Norwich Press, 1912, p. 90.

Mind as a Sense

In Buddhism, the Aristotelian five-fold division of the senses is extended to six: vision, hearing, olfaction, taste, touch, and 'mind'. Mind is thus another organ or faculty with which to perceive the external world — like the eyes or the ears. As Iain McGilchrist says, 'We are not sure, and could never be sure, if mind, or even body, is a thing at all. Mind has the characteristic of a process more than a thing; a becoming, a way of being, more than an entity. Every individual mind is a process of interaction with whatever it is that exists apart from ourselves according to its own private history.'[3]

Many centuries ago, by associating mind with the other five senses, Buddhist philosophy dealt with the perception of both the visible and invisible world, the last of which is constituted by thoughts and ideas. Bodily senses give rise to emotions, which in turn provide the basis for rational thought. When the five aggregates are united in one body, they bring into being a living existence. None of them can be disregarded when examining the human being in relation to the world. Perception, appreciation, comprehension and the experience of objects are all relevant parameters for its creation, allowing the construction of forms with content which can enrich human life. With this in mind, Satyendra Pakhalé sees the true nature of phenomena as based not on rules, dogmas or beliefs, but rather on direct experience and perception. He explores the connections between the early Buddhist realizations and contemporary studies on behavioural science, phenomenology and cognitive science.

Sense Spheres

This understanding of experience as an aggregate of reception, sensation, perception, mental formation and consciousness describes the human being as a sensorial being gifted with six main senses, or receptacles of experience (sight, hearing, touch, smell, taste, mind) alongside many others (sense of life, movement, balance, temperature, speech and so on). There are six *internal* sense bases (six sense organs: eye, ear, nose, tongue, body, mind) and six *external* sense bases (six sense objects: sight, sound, smell, taste, touch, mental objects). Thus, there are six internal-external (organ-object) pairs of sense bases. These constitute twelve 'sense bases' or 'sense spheres', called *āyatana*. These are instruments

---

3   Iain McGilchrist, *The Master and His Emissary: The Divided Brain and the Making of the Western World*, Yale University Press, New Haven, Conn. and London: Yale University Press, 2009, UK, 2009, p. 184.
4   Stanford Encyclopedia of Philosophy, *Mind in Indian Buddhist Philosophy, 3.2 Sensation and Perception*, 2009, reviewed in 2012.

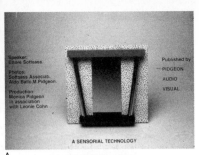

A, B　Ettore Sottsass Jr., *A Sensorial Technology*, Pidgeon Audio Visual, London, UK. Sottsass illustrates the idea that the environment can be read through the senses, emphasising the sensorial rather than the structural aspects of design, 1984. Courtesy: Hong Kong Polytechnic University, HK.

or mediums that join together the external spheres of sensory activity with the internal spheres of perception.[4]

This expanded idea of the senses and human experience represents the very core of Pakhalé's design work. Having grown up in India, a culture evolved from a strongly tactile, sensorial enthusiasm and rooted in the celebration of human experience as a complex multi-sensorial phenomenon, Pakhalé invests design with a positive, warmly sensorial feeling that humanizes the objects that we use every day. His projects are conceived to resonate with our senses. He is constantly in search of those forms, materials, colours and tactile textures that offer an experience that goes beyond the act of seeing, acknowledging the utility of the object or appreciating its general appearance.

Ancient Indian culture with its roots in early Buddhism, its negation of rituals and religious dogmas and its pondering of the human condition touched the imagination of many artists and creative minds around the world, such as Costantin Brancusi, Isamu Noguchi, Ettore Sottsass Jr., James Turrell, Bill Viola and many more. Nevertheless, the essence of the Buddhism that originated in India remains undiscovered, being frequently (deliberately) misinterpreted in later centuries in India and (more recently) in the world. Today, major misunderstandings of Buddhist insights have arisen due to mystification and deification, as well as the post-Buddhist decline of India and the social and political conditions resulting from it.

Sensorial Technology

Satyendra Pakhalé draws on India's cultural origins with a deep understanding of its realizations, shining a light on its distorted and ambiguous interpretations, and directing attention to the notion of 'secular humanism'. This has nothing to do with questions of either ritual or theology,[5] and is simply about promoting human welfare by rejecting any conventional notion of religion, animism or mysticism. Indeed, secular humanism encourages mental and emotional, as well as social, economic, and above all moral and ethical human development.

Early Buddhism probes human sensibilities and aptitudes in an effort to understand the truth about life and the universe. It is concerned with the human mind of the external order of things, seeing them as they are through focused sensitive experience.

5　T. W. Rhys Davids, *Buddhist India* (1903), Delhi: Motilal Banarsidass Publishers, IN, 1993, p. 292.

　DESIGN FOR SENSORIAL BEINGS　TIZIANA PROIETTI

An expanded idea of the senses and human experience

represents the very core of Pakhalé's design work.

Tiziana Proietti

C

E

Pakhalé believes very deeply, therefore, that every created object embodies an act of making – a refined process representative of humanity's ability to work with materials and tools in order to build its own environment – as well as all the senses activated at the stage of creation. A 'sensorial technology', as Ettore Sottsass Jr. would have named it, reaches objects, furniture and the whole environment not only through the brain and purely structural processes, but most of all through the senses. Being as free as possible – politically, professionally and linguistically – with the understanding that design is a cultural and not a technical event, as articulated by Ettore Sottsass Jr.,[6] finds a new expression in the work of Pakhalé.

Experience is the Core

Pakhalé's objects are charged with powerful sensorial energies. The form of the piece KUBU (2009)❶, to mention just one example, is so elegant and essential that it seems to have come about naturally without any effort at all. But that simplicity and essentiality comes from his tireless investigation of all the details, his control of form, his attention to the techniques used, both digital and artisanal, and the sensorial process of designing. In the end, the result is an object that is a compound of suggestions – visual, sensuous, tactile and kinetic – offering an experience that resonates with human perceptual aptitudes. It is then evident that when Pakhalé talks about 'sensorial design' he is not attaching any label to the act of making, which for him is the most universal and perhaps indefinable human act meant to manipulate and transform nature and make it accessible to human senses; rather, he is bringing our attention back to 'experience' (to paraphrase John Dewey), as the core of art.[7]

C   Kubu at the Designers' Lounge, Art Fair Cologne, DE, 2009. Curated by Gabrielle Ammann, ammann // gallery, Cologne, DE. Courtesy: Satyendra Pakhalé Archives, Amsterdam, NL.

D   Surface of Kubu with texture specified by Pakhalé being carved by an artisan living in the Italian Dolomites. Courtesy: Satyendra Pakhalé Archives, Amsterdam, NL.

E   John Dewey, *Art as Experience* (1934), rounds off his philosophy of experience with a notable and epoch-making statement on the place of art in the life of man: 'Since the actual work of art is what the product does with and in experience, the result is not favourable to understanding. In addition, the very perfection of some of these products, the prestige they possess because of a long history of unquestioned admiration, creates conventions that get in the way of fresh insight. When an art product once attains classic status, it somehow becomes isolated from the human conditions under which it was brought into being and from the human consequences it engenders in actual life experience'. Courtesy: Satyendra Pakhalé Archives, Amsterdam, NL.

6   Ettore Sottsass Jr., *A Sensorial Technology* (1983), recording produced by Monica Pidgeon in association with Leonie Cohn, London: Pidgeon Audio Visual, UK, 1984.
7   John Dewey, *Art as Experience* (1934), New York: TarcherPerigree, 2005.

When Pakhalé talks about 'sensorial design',

he is not attaching any label to the act of making,

but bringing our attention back to experience as the core of art.

Tiziana Proietti

CONTENT

ASSAYA CENTENARY ARMCHAIR — To mark the centenary of the design manufacturer Poltrona Frau, Italy, Satyendra Pakhalé was invited to design a centenary armchair by reinterpreting the classic Poltrona Frau armchair for the 21st century and beyond. The design concept of Assaya was inspired by life in the connected world. It is the result of three years of collaboration on design research and development between Pakhalé and Poltrona Frau. Assaya draws on the age-old tradition of saddle-making, coupled with a fresh interpretation of industrial leather craftsmanship. The objective was to create a long-lasting design that would be cherished and celebrated for decades to come by connecting with new generations. The way we are connected to the world nowadays is being transformed and will continue to evolve with more personalized, wearable and mobile

devices. Adjusting the legs on a table to sit more comfortably is no longer revolutionary; now, bringing more 'home' into the office and more 'office' into the home is a reality. Assaya addresses this by enabling relaxation and work in comfortable postures. 'I recall my first trip to the wonderful Italian factory in the Marche region, where industrial and handmade blend in a seamless manner, creating uniquely crafted, serially produced objects,' recalls Pakhalé. 'I was curious, keen to grasp, assess and evaluate in my own manner the legendary heritage of Poltrona Frau. The centenary armchair I designed as a new step forward is called Assaya. The name refers to the act of analysing, assessing and evaluating. Besides, in Marathi, my mother tongue, it also means to give comforting support, to create a comforting feeling.'

01

01 Assaya has simultaneously contradictory and complementary features – the high backrest with integrated armrest made of hard saddle leather is skilfully sculpted in a body-hugging form, recalling the memory of a sensuous waist. Assaya also features Kvadrat upholstery with saddle leather.
02 Design sketch illustrating several details of the Assaya Centenary Armchair.
03 A watercolour sketch captures the initial concept of the hard saddle leather backrest.

ASSAYA CENTENARY ARMCHAIR

A

B

C

D

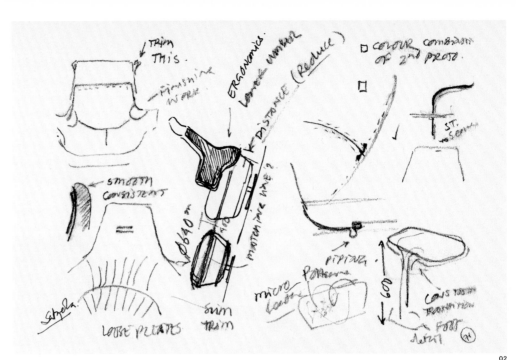

02

03

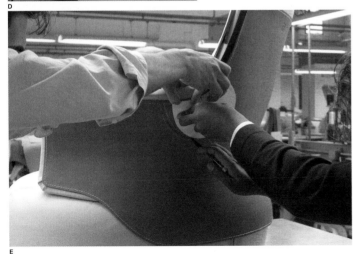

E

A, B Pakhalé defines the final leather details on the CNC machined model at the studio.

C, D The highly skilled staff of Poltrona Frau in the last stage of building the sixth and final prototype.

E Pakhalé drew the saddle leather detail at the junction of the backrest and armrest, from his memory of leather elbow patches on classic tweed sports jackets.

04

05

04, 05 The Assaya Centenary Armchair for the connected world is a concept that embodies a new way of working by providing a new typology – the Assaya Laptray for the flexible use of digital devices and the Assaya Side Table for a comfortable, personal, relaxing-working area.
06 Backrest details of the saddle leather made with an iconographic cut.

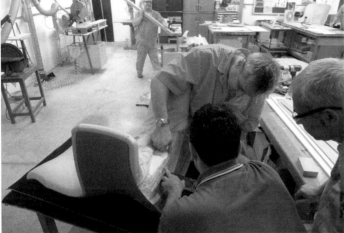

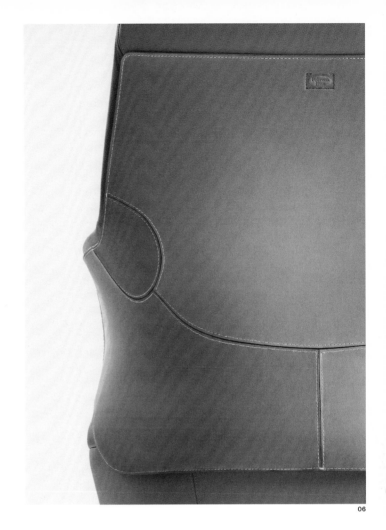

06

F   Pakhalé marking the refinements on the sixth and final prototype of Assaya.

G, H   Product development team at Poltrona Frau study backrest fixture detail and saddle leather cut of Assaya.

I, J   Pakhalé compares two prototype corner details before defining the saddle leather part of the integral armrest.

Tea

In 2014/2015, Satyendra Pakhalé was invited by Danish design companies Stelton and Eva Solo to explore new product typologies focusing on contemporary tea and coffee culture. Simultaneously invigorating and relaxing, tea is an ancient beverage and highly popular in contemporary life. It unites many health benefits with a deep significance as part of our daily rituals. Tea is one of the most widely consumed drinks in the world. From China to Russia, and from the Middle East to Japan, tea is served in a culture-specific manner that is frequently associated with a range of cultural themes from incorporeality to hospitality. Over time, tea ceremonies have evolved from being strictly religious to social and cultural activities. For some years now, there has been new awareness of tea in general and green tea in particular, the kind that is mostly drunk in Indonesia, Japan and China. This East Asian custom is now becoming a way of life in all the cosmopolitan cities of the world. In Europe, the demand for loose, whole-leaf tea and single-estate teas is rising. A growing number of Europeans purchase quality teas in specialty stores. Satyendra Pakhalé's Tea and Coffee Culture products reflect these evolving developments.

Coffee

Pakhalé was invited to create a series of contemporary coffee culture-related objects and Moka Syn was one of the results. The designs are based on Pakhalé's insights into coffee culture as a global phenomenon. Cultivated for centuries, coffee is enjoyed around the world in a wide range of culture-specific ways. Coffee is roasted, brewed and drunk in various manners. Coffee culture is social and comes with a series of associated social behaviours. Consumed in company, it acts as a social lubricant. The coffee culture currently prevalent around the world brings back to life a more hands-on, human aspect. Just like other artisanal food and drinks, coffee is perceived as an artisanal drink rather than a commodity, with a focus on authenticity as opposed to speed. Having spent significant time in cafés in Vienna and Paris, Pakhalé drew from his personal experience of the age-old, intangible cultural heritages of Viennese, Parisian and Indian coffee-house cultures with their unique social atmospheres. In urbanized metropolitan centres around the world espresso-drinking has become the dominant form.

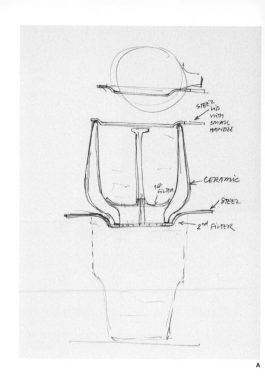

A

B

C

D

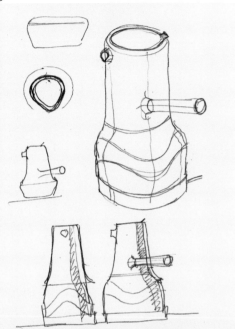

E

Responding to these developments, which are particularly evident in cosmopolitan cities, Pakhalé explored and created several object typologies to redefine current coffee culture and facilitate a contemporary series of design objects that facilitate a social atmosphere in a private and public setting.

Tea and Coffee Culture

Having tea and coffee are rituals of daily life. These stimulants and their effect on our bodily perceptions, sensations and imaginations provide a framework for the everyday social act of drinking tea or coffee together as a catalyst of social cohesion. These societal habits, customs, specialities and routines, the particularities of various cultures and the objects and places associated with them, retain undeniable significance all over the world. In his tea and coffee ranges, Pakhalé explores these diverse cultural roots and creates contemporary objects for tea and coffee culture around the world.

F

A–C Pakhalé creates a new single coffee maker in stainless steel, ceramic and glass based on his memory of Vietnamese coffee makers.

D Tea-coffee set consisting of thermos with integral grip, tea-coffee cups, sugar pot, creamer and wooden tray.

E, F Design sketch by Pakhalé illustrating the protruding shoulder-like form derived from the synthesis of two curves. Working out the details on the Moka Syn at Pakhalé's studio.

G

H

I

J

G   The Jingdezhen Tea Set is a contemporary interpretation of the traditional tea set of this region. It is designed keeping the long tea culture of Asia, especially China, in perspective.

H,I   The 3D-printed technical ceramic shell of the kettle with stainless steel handle and spout detail has a distinct identity.

J   Tea for Two is an all-in-one tea set designed for Scandinavia, where a cup of tea is enjoyed outside in good weather.

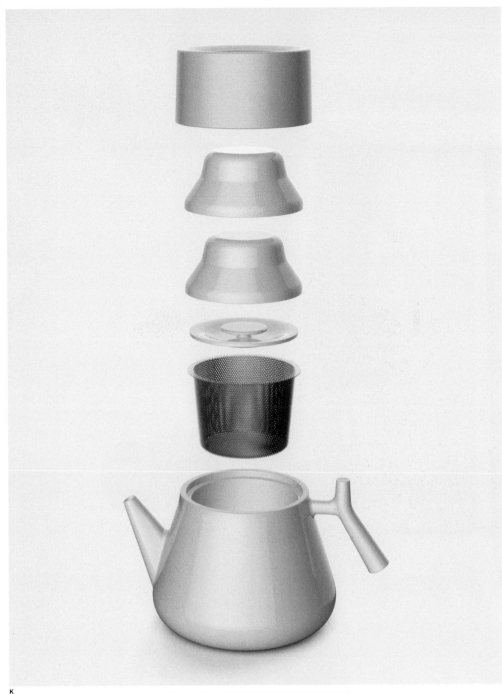

K

L

K   Tea for Two consists of a teapot and two cups stacked inside the lid. The portable set is made of porcelain with a steel infuser and sieve.

L   The two cups are formed in such manners that they are nice to hold and can be easily stacked.

MOKA SYN — A familiar yet distinctive object, Moka Syn is made from stainless steel with a wooden handle. The top coffee collection chamber has a tapering oval form at the top, transitioning into a circular form where it connects with the bottom chamber. The bottom chamber has a one-directional, protruding shoulder-like form derived from the synthesis of two curves. This facilitates the easy dismantling and refilling of the moka, hence the name Moka Syn.

01

02

01 The Moka Syn family consists of an electric moka maker in stainless steel; ceramic sugar pot, cream jug and espresso cup; and a compact wooden tray.
02 Top view of the electric Moka Syn in stainless steel.

STACKING TEAPOT — This teapot allows tea drinkers to dilute their tea to taste by adding water from the lower pot. This age-old technique of preparing tea to personal requirements is reinterpreted in a contemporary way. The Stacking Teapots fit firmly on top of each other thanks to their finely crafted square base and top. The teapots become one object when stacked on top of each other and also work perfectly well when they are used independently. The tea pot family is completed by a stacking sugar and creamer set, all made in porcelain.

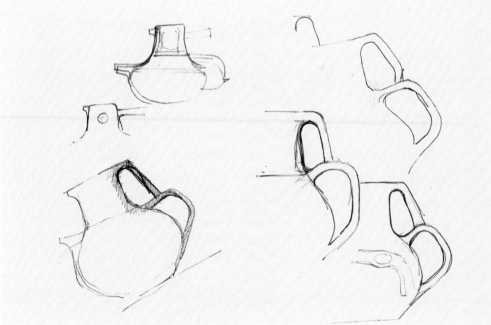

01   The two teapots can also be used independently.
02   Design sketch illustrating the concept behind the Stacking Teapots.

ALINATA SHELVING SYSTEM — This modular shelving system is made of three extruded aluminium parts and offers a variety of combinations. Invited to design a shelving system using aluminium extrusion technology, Pakhalé created an innovative joint with extruded aluminium parts. This allows endless combinations and hence a modular system of shelves. Pakhalé married the highly industrial manufacturing process of aluminium extrusion with materials such as bamboo and wooden panels, striking a balance between industry and craft and at the same time returning human warmth back to an industrial product. Alinata can also be used as a space divider in a domestic or office space. It is designed not only for efficient manufacture, but also for reduced shipping volumes, being easy to assemble and disassemble besides having a very sturdy

structure. Pakhalé: 'Extrusion is a technology that needs a lot of care and attention. There are very few technologies that, even in the planning phase, demand as much deliberation as the production of extruded aluminium profiles. I have always believed that when it comes to extrusion technology, the result ought to be a product that can be used in several ways and is both economical and intelligent. We achieved that combination in by producing not only the aluminium profile but also the joint of the Alinata Shelving System in extrusion technology.'

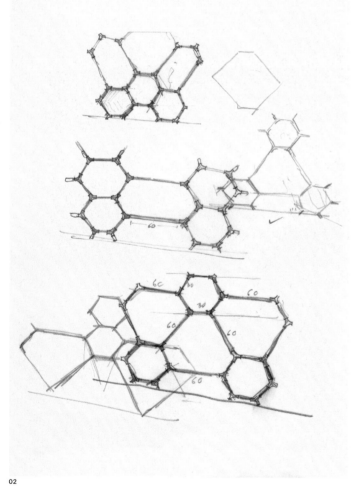

01

02

A

B

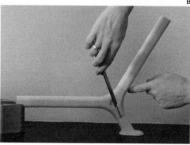

C

D

01   Natural plyboo panels made of bamboo are used in the Alinata Shelving System to create a complementary effect with the industrial extruded aluminium.
02   The Alinata Shelving System design sketch by Pakhalé illustrating the modularity concept.
03, 04 Various configurations of Alinata using three extruded parts.

E

F

G

H

03

04

A Alinata proportions being studied at Pakhalé's studio.

B–D Studying the joint with the sketch model and testing the first 3D-printed joint.

E–H Stored extruded profiles and product assembly line at the Erreti factory.

MEANDER TEXTILE — Satyendra Pakhalé was invited to research and design a new textile for Väveriet, the historic Swedish textile company, established in 1895, whose name translates as 'the weavery'. After studying its textile-making process, Pakhalé decided to create a pattern that would interpolate Swedish textile craft with state-of-the-art weaving technology, while referencing the beautiful meandering rivers of the Scandinavian landscape. The resulting meander pattern is consistent with the tapering loop iconography found in several of Pakhalé's objects. Pakhalé first created a sketch before using a 3D CAD drawing to work out the precise geometry of the pattern. Careful mathematical calculations were needed to arrive at the right combination of warp and weft. Wool is a living material, so several trials were required to ascertain the amount

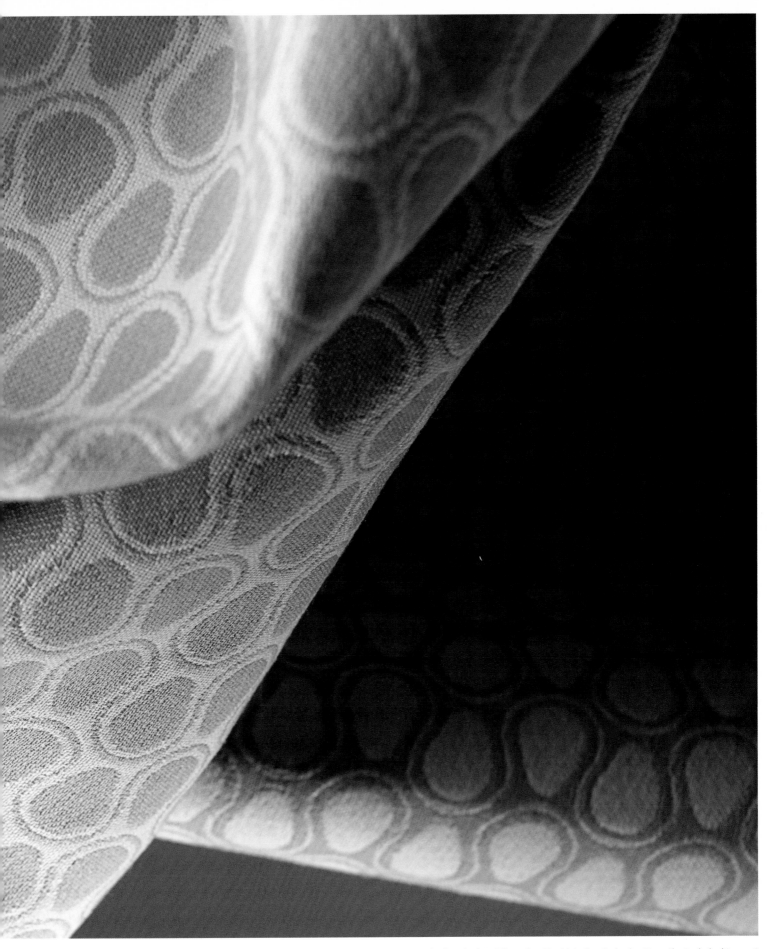

of shrinkage possible. Finally, the right information was fed into the loom, which automatically calculated the ratios. To obtain the desired pattern, the technical team at Väveriet and Pakhalé had to recalibrate the machines. The Meander Textile is a sturdy upholstery material suitable for public and domestic use.

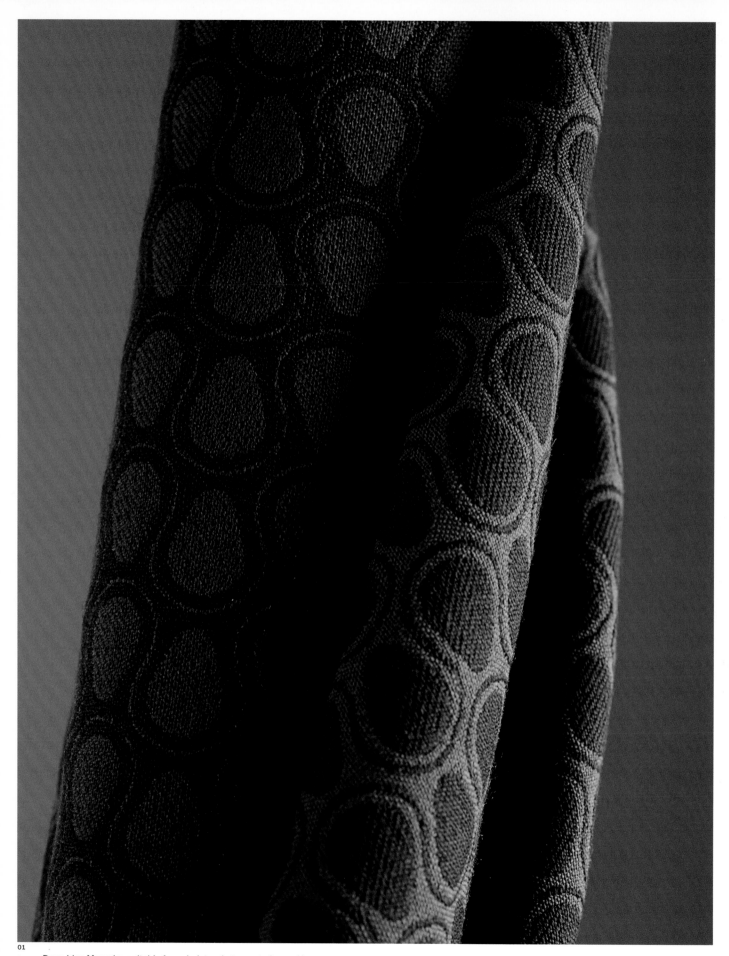

01

01 Deep blue Meander, suitable for upholstery in trams, trains and buses.
02 Seven colours from the range that went into production.
03 Design sketch by Pakhalé illustrating the meander pattern.

A

B

C

D

02

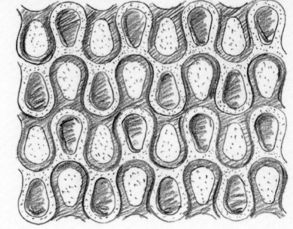

03

A   First prototype of Meander.

B, C   Meander in production at Väveriet, Sweden.

D   At the factory the loom and yarn colours are prepared with an automatic spindle machine.

08

BEYOND PANGÉA

We no longer really relate to products or develop any affection for them.

We never really make friends with them:

they remain casual acquaintances or incidental business contacts at the edge of our real existence.

Stefano Marzano

BEYOND PANGÉA
Stefano Marzano

All too often, the comforts of our technological society and the needs of the environment appear antagonistic to each other. People fear that sustainable design means giving up the handy inventions of the past century, taking a step backwards. But design can show us that such a pessimistic scenario is not inevitable. It should be possible to design ecologically minded, sustainable products that are attractive and charismatic enough for people to buy, while at the same time contributing to improving our quality of life. It is an ambitious goal, certainly; but it is one worth pursuing, on both ethical and economic grounds. If we accept the challenge, there are various paths to follow, potential strategies for realizing products compatible with sustainability and poetics.

One major factor burdening the environment is the relatively short life span of many products. We need to make products which last longer, and – more importantly – which people want to keep. To understand how to do that, we need to consider what it is about modern products that makes it easy for their owners to throw them away; and to recall what it was about objects in the past that made people keep them and pass them on to their children as treasures.

Relating to Products

Just as we are continually being bombarded by advertising and media messages so numerous that they cease to have any meaning, so the products we use often overwhelm us with their excessive number of features. The unused and irrelevant possibilities they offer us litter our minds like mental garbage. As a result, we no longer really relate to products or develop any affection for them. We never really make friends with them: they remain just casual acquaintances or incidental business contacts at the edge of our existence. And, because we do not feel bad about throwing away products we are not attached to, they end up polluting the environment.

While we have been creating this quantity-mad world, an essential human need has been neglected. Consider the sort of relationship our ancestors had with their objects – trusty tools, family heirlooms, totems or magical objects. Such objects not only served a practical function but they were also carriers of memories, of personal or family history; they were magical or ritual objects that gave protection or expressed belonging. They remained in society. We have lost this affectionate relationship with most of our contemporary objects. We no longer form an emotional bond with them.

Envision the Future

These concerns and views are found in the works of Satyendra Pakhalé. In the mid-1990s, Pakhalé was part of the New Business Creation Team at Philips Design, working on various projects. Under my design leadership, we initiated several collaborative projects with other corporations, joining forces to envision the future. These included Philips and Alessi, Philips and Levi's, Philips and Leolux, Philips and Lucent Technologies, and – last but not least – Philips and Renault.

During this period, we undertook several projects to investigate and create future scenarios in the hope of creating products and services that could potentially last and that people could bond with emotionally. In a multidisciplinary, collaborative spirit, designers worked in close cooperation with cultural anthropologists, social scientists and technologists. Together, we engaged with the design of lasting, sustainable possibilities for the future.

The Car as Companion

The Pangéa was one of the projects to look ahead and explore the world of objects and tools as life companions. Pangéa – Connected Wheels – was a visionary concept car project, created in collaboration with Renault, with Philips Design envisioning digital technology well ahead of its time. It is important to remember that the Pangéa was conceived long before Google was founded, well before GPS technology became accessible, and in advance of the all-pervasiveness of flat-panel displays, tele-media cameras, voice-activated input technology, digital graphic tablets and the internet.

In 1995, we asked: What if we take two companies working in ostensibly quite different fields but sharing the common goal of creating a better quality of life and then say the magic words – what if? – and just follow through. What if they joined forces in pursuit of that goal? In 1995, this was the starting point of a remarkable

A   Stefano Marzano and Patrick Le Quément during the Pangéa concept car development, Turin, IT, 1996. Courtesy: Renault Design, FR.

B   Pangéa concept car during a photo shoot in the south of France, simulating remote area exploration, 1997. Courtesy: Renault Design, FR.

C   Full-scale study model of the Pangéa interior, envisioning the nomadic way of working with technologies, a decade ahead of its time, 1996. Courtesy: Philips Design, NL.

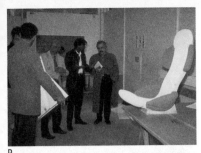

collaboration. Inspired by their respective design directors, Patrick Le Quément and myself, designers from Renault and Philips took up the challenge of working together on this joint, exploratory project.

Sustainable Society

As a part of the environmentalist call for a global view of the world, governments, organizations and individuals are becoming increasingly aware of the need to monitor the environment, not only for present generations, but also for future ones. The accelerating deterioration that has been observed in recent years has made it abundantly clear that our world is highly vulnerable. If it is to survive in a recognizable and agreeable form, we need to develop a sustainable society – sooner rather than later. Although improvements are already visible in some areas, it seems likely that this pursuit of sustainability will need to involve scientific research, advanced fieldwork, laboratory analysis and careful monitoring of the environment on a permanent basis.

The design departments of Philips and Renault decided to explore the possibility of developing a totally new kind of vehicle in concept form, one which would reflect this new situation. Making use of the latest environmentally friendly technologies, it would be a 'mobile laboratory': a multi-purpose professional vehicle which could contribute significantly to improving the quality of life.

Products that Last

After working on the Pangéa project, Pakhalé went on to orientate his independent practice towards researching the fulfilment of various human needs. By cultivating a sense of design aimed at rethinking our contemporary throw-away culture, Pakhalé acknowledges the improvements introduced by the modern lifestyle, while at the same time remaining deeply critical. Above all, modernity has opened the door to the age of discoveries, urbanization, the acceptance of technology, mass information and production, ending up, after two world wars, with the foundation of democratic values, which positively affected human, social and individual lives. A quick look at the contemporary world confirms that it is dominated by modernity in all its forms. With this in mind, Pakhalé recognizes and welcomes modernity's great innovations, while simultaneously rejecting its conformism and dry approach to life based on a limited awareness of the world and a lack of cultural sensibility.

D   Satyendra Pakhalé in discussion with Patrick Le Quément during the making of the Pangéa concept car, Turin, IT 1996. Courtesy: Philips Design, NL.

E   Pangéa concept car before its unveiling at the Geneva Motor Show, Paris, FR, 1997. Courtesy: Renault Design, FR.

Pakhalé works diligently to cultivate a design sensibility,

a language that could last and create products that will hopefully become part of a collective human culture.

In so doing, he proposes new design typologies,

ingenious combinations of materials, forms and techniques.

Stefano Marzano

F

G

H

In a fast-moving world with an unpredictable future and with social contacts being increasingly remote, people feel a need to establish a balance between living in the 'now' and being part of a tradition with an unchanging geographical base. Roots, traditions and rituals should be restored and cherished in order to give our lives depth. The throw-away society would – not solely for ecological and sustainable reasons – give way to a society which recycles short-term products and values others for a history that can be passed on to our children to continue the chain of the generations. Pakhalé has focused on creating objects and products that will hopefully last, eventually being handed over to the next generation.

Technology as a Tool

Technology never becomes something to be displayed to embrace the laws of the market or commercial consumerism in Pakhalé's projects. Technology is a tool he keeps on cultivating, just as he did when I first met him, to allow his objects to speak to people and shape their lives, and hopefully the lives of the next generation. Every day in his studio he engages with this challenge, opting for the universal appreciation of human making, the richness of its values, and an all-embracing understanding of the significant role assumed by objects in human life.

With this intention, he continuously explores the functional, sensorial and technological qualities of his design projects in order to bring to light a universally graspable meeting point between various human needs and objects, which in turn mediate the encounter between humans and the surrounding environment. He works diligently to cultivate a design sensibility, a language that could last and create products that will hopefully become part of a collective human culture. In so doing, he proposes new design typologies, ingenious combinations of materials, forms and techniques. For instance, the Add-On Radiator ❶, the Alinata Shelving System ❷ and the Kalpa vase and bowl ❸, can all be truly said to introduce new functional typologies. The Kalpa can be used as a vase or a bowl by simply turning it upside down. It can hold fruits or flowers. Similarly, the Alinata Shelving System can be used as a wall, dividing spaces, and at the same time hold objects, but if a glass slab is placed on top of one of its modules it can also become a table.

What if?
The future is not something that is created by the efforts of only a few individuals, companies or governments. It is the result of many contributions, of moments initiated in various places, of decisions whose impact may not be immediately apparent, but which ultimately can become highly significant. It all starts with asking: What if? What if we could do something, create unexpected collaborations, envision innovative future scenarios?

Therefore, at the risk of being charged with hubris, we, as producers of goods and services, and as designers, can – indeed, must – make our contribution in whatever way we can. Creating a new household appliance or domestic object may seem a minor venture in the grand scheme of the future, but that does not mean it will be without effect. Everyone must take a position and act with a clear goal in mind in those areas in which they have expertise and influence, joining with others who share the vision of a sustainable society to try to guide things in the right direction. This is, in essence, the ethic of our time. Pakhalé embodies this ethic through his diligent design practice.

CONTENT

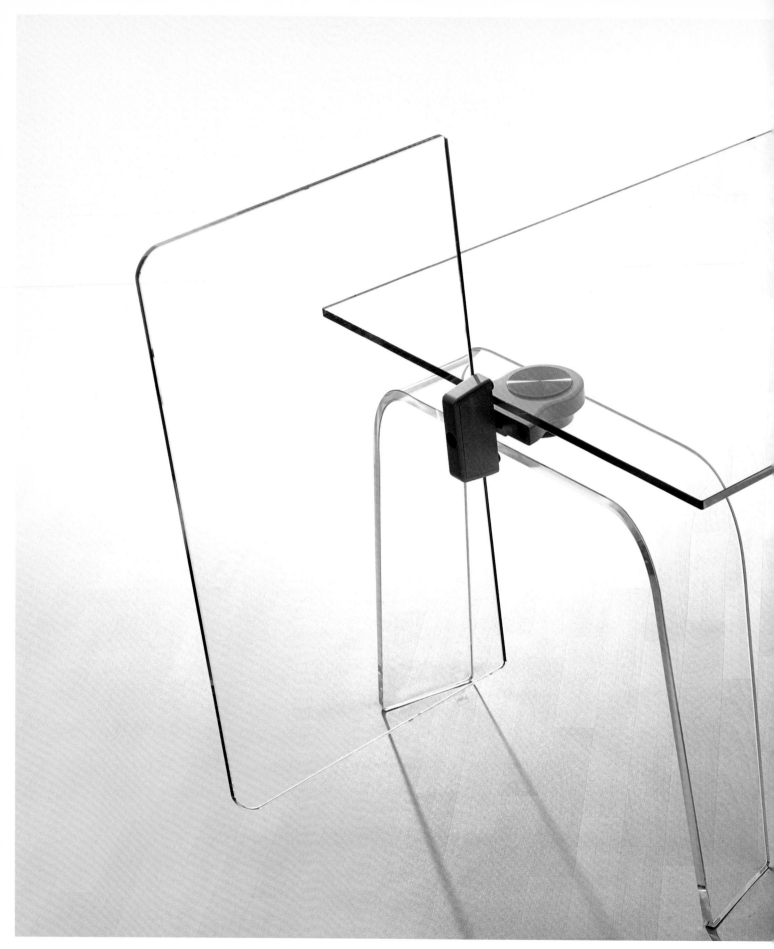

KAYO EXTENSIBLE TABLE — The way things are produced has not changed much over the years. Objects have been made using similar processes and materials for hundreds of years. But once in a while there is a breakthrough and an object is made in a manner never realized before. When Satyendra Pakhalé was invited to visit the FIAM pioneering manufacturing plant near Pesaro, Italy, 'It felt like being in the aerospace industry, where passionate people in thermal protective aprons with great skills and techniques were forming, engineering and making objects out of industrial glass using high-temperature furnaces.' Glass is a magical material with futuristic associations and characteristics such as transparency, hardness and structural strength. These allowed Pakhalé to create a table with only two supporting pivots, without compromising

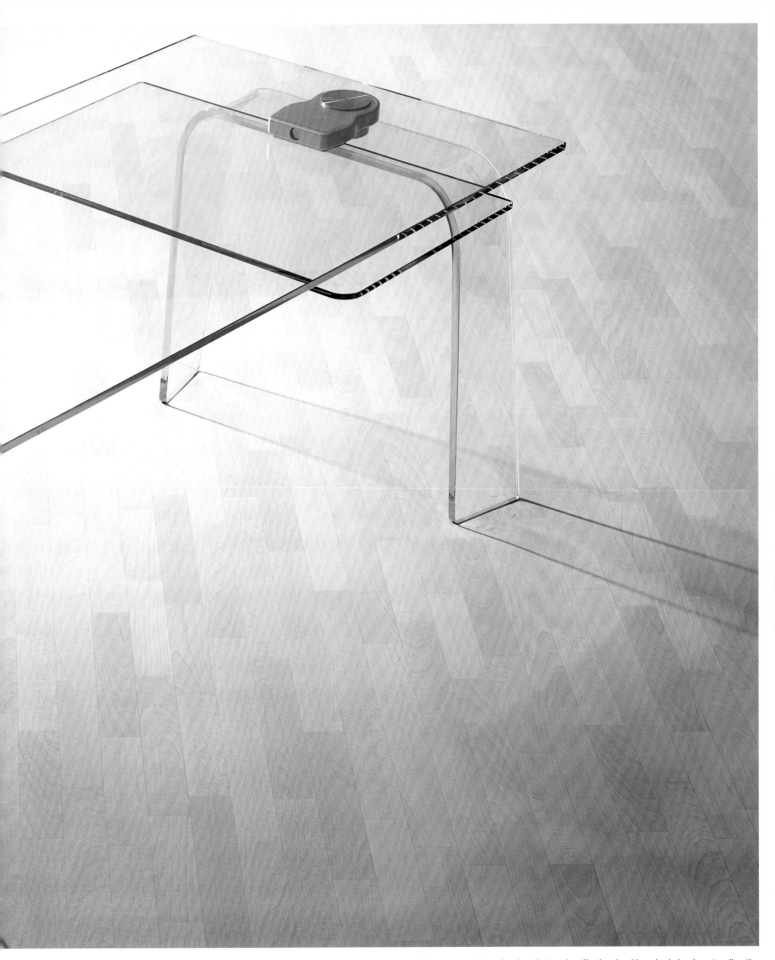

its stability. Kayo's main plane on bent glass legs and its extensible parts are connected by a compact mechanism that works effortlessly with a single knob, extending the table from a two- to an impressive three-metre span. Pakhalé: 'It was a real challenge to create a new compact mechanism and the seemingly obvious bent glass legs. They required three years of rigourous design and product development work [...] I recalled Hannah Arendt mentioning a table in *The Human Condition* (1958), in which she wrote "The table brings everything and everybody together in a spirit of gratitude. It creates possibilities and inspires whilst remaining itself, as it were, invisible (...)." An invisible table that is elegant and magical – literally unseen – is what I wanted to create. It could be achieved with FIAM's pioneering bent glass technology.'

INDUSTRIAL DESIGN

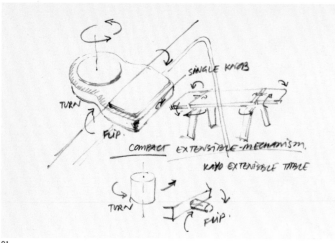

01

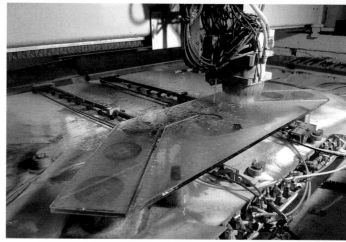

A

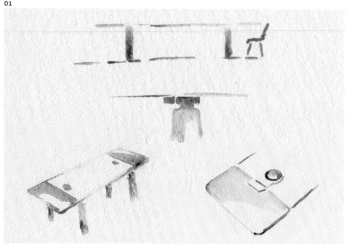

02

C

D

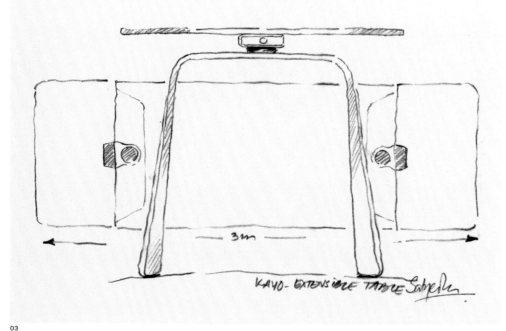

03

E

01 Sketch showing Kayo's compact mechanism that works with a single knob.
02 A watercolour sketch visualizes a table three metres long with just two supporting pivots.
03 Sketch illustrating the 3-m-long span on two pivot points held by the compact mechanism.
04 The table leaves can also be used in a lower position, making them ideal for children and other uses.
05 The seemingly obvious bent glass solution for the table legs required a long period of design and product development work.

KAYO EXTENSIBLE TABLE

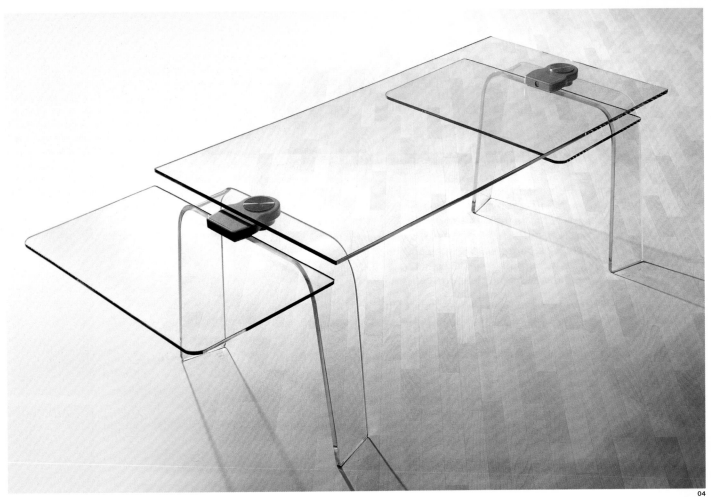

A, B The glass profile is first cut with a water jet; the cut glass is then bent in the furnace.

C, D Study sketches during the product development process. Pakhalé checking the fifth prototype.

E The top management and technical team at Fiam's technical office during one of many product development meetings with Pakhalé.

Satyendra Pakhalé is known for pushing boundaries and exploring the unknown. He is always open to new discoveries and innovations. I remember our first visit to his studio with our management team some years ago, well before starting our collaboration on Kayo. We were so impressed by his studio's research – we saw so many raw materials, lots of experiments and curiosities, and a library full of books on everything from anthropology to astrophysics, not just design and architecture.

It was obvious that he is a very meticulous kind of person, a perfectionist by nature – so we naturally trusted him. For Kayo, the research took a long time, with him constantly wanting to improve every detail. Regardless of the amount of time it took, he just wanted a product that worked beautifully – which it does.

Satyendra can be quite stubborn creatively. For Kayo, we had lengthy discussions about a particular detail, and it was difficult to make him change his mind without a very good reason. In this we recognize ourselves a bit, in the sense that we are also quite tenacious. It took time, but in the end, we found a solution that worked well for both of us. Satyendra puts his heart into a project; he is ideas-driven and something new emerges from that passionate involvement.

Now, after closely collaborating with him, I can say that he is a research designer, and he wants to understand the material and go beyond the material in such a way as to bring to bring it to its maximum value. This makes him the perfect designer for FIAM, a company which uses glass as it was never used before.

Satyendra is the kind of designer who is not limited to the sign. He is one of the few designers who knows how to use their hands in the sense that in each of his experiences with other companies, where he has entered into the technology and technique and has gone beyond the form, there has always been an industrial thought behind every action.

He loves to create expressions of modernity yet also rediscovers the aesthetic canons of the past, giving them a new shape and meaning, making them modern again.

— Vittorio Livi and Daniele Livi

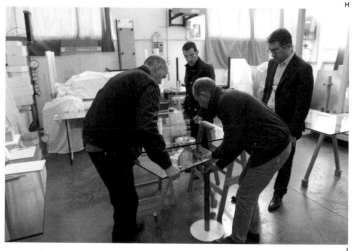

F   Pakhalé draws while explaining his ideas and thoughts during one of many product development meetings at Fiam's R&D department.

G–J   Studying the V-arm mechanism; and exploring the metal leg during the development phases. Examining a specific detail of an extensible mechanism.

K,L   Pakhalé holding the Kayo bent glass study model in sheet metal. He draws the definitive proportions of the compact mechanism on the sixth working prototype.

KAYO EXTENSIBLE TABLE

J

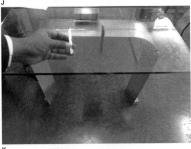

K

L

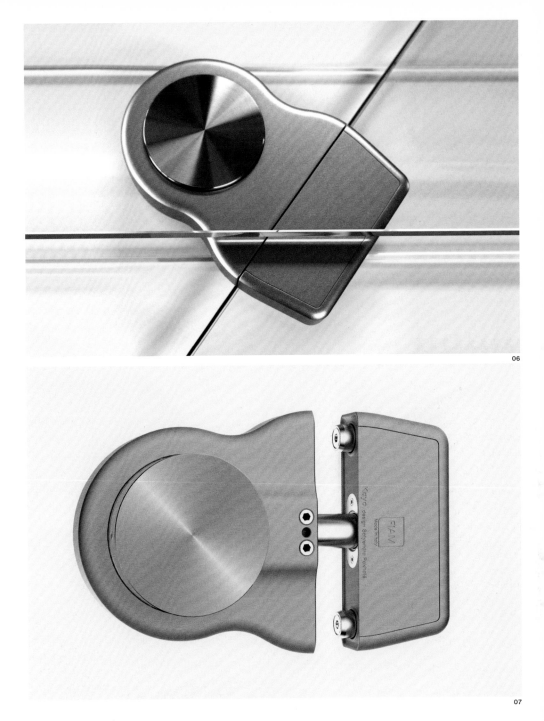

06

07

06   Compact extensible mechanism in the closed position, viewed from above.
07   Rear view of the Compact extensible mechanism with all the design details specified by Pakhalé, viewed from below.

LOOP O2 – In 2003, Pakhalé was invited to design a mobile phone by O2, then a subsidiary of British Telecom's Mobile Division. Pakhalé created the Loop O2 mobile, which with its circular LCD display easily fit into the palm of the hand as a compact personal object. Loop O2 is made of two stainless-steel shells designed for disassembly and for easier materials recycling at the end of the product life cycle. The phone is designed simply for making calls and sending voice messages, with basic features such as an analogue clock and a calendar as homage to Enzo Mari's Formosa Perpetual Wall Calendar. It has a wedge-like form that provides a comfortable view for the user when the phone is resting on a table-top.

01

02

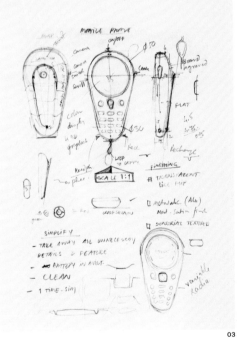

03

01,02   The Loop O2 mobile has a concave back. This creates a space for the on-off button to nestle in and a rim that acts as a base for placing the phone on a flat surface. The wedge-like form, developed from the configuration of the internal components, provides a comfortable view of the LCD display for the user, showing the time and a calendar as homage to Enzo Mari's Formosa Perpetual Wall Calendar. It is a compact 85 × 50 mm phone.

03   Design sketch of Loop O2 mobile by Satyendra Pakhalé.

MOONWĀKĀ — This hiking gauge assists eye-hand coordination in microgravity and evokes a sense of security in first-time Moon travellers. A playful object, it allows users to intuit the changing microgravity line of sight and distances on the lunar terrain. The Moonwākā has a stick-like form with a mass-volume distribution that ensures it always stays upright in microgravity. The top part has an anti-slip handle that enhances grip force control while manoeuvring, walking and hiking on the Moon. Moonwākā was presented at the Moon Life Concept Store, the first shop on Earth with items for future life in space. After its debut in Shanghai, it travelled worldwide as part of the Moon Life Foundation, which raises questions that are relevant today and for the future.

260–263 264–267 268–271

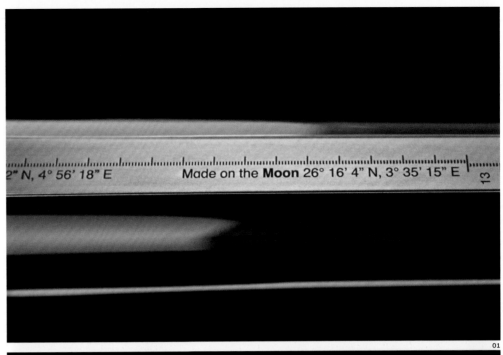

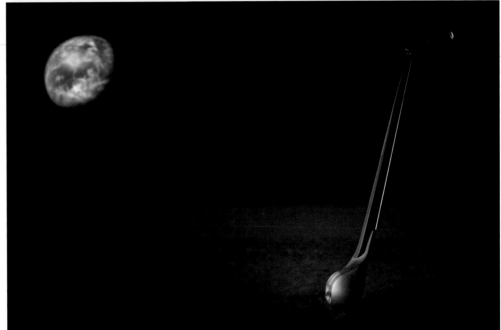

01

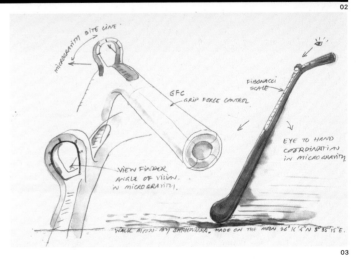

03

01   Moonwākā was to be made on the Moon, using the material resources available on the Earth's only known natural satellite.

02   To appreciate and value our mothership Earth, Pakhalé argues, 'Everybody should go to the Moon, once in their lives.'

03   In the Moon's microgravity environment, the angle of vision changes considerably, while Grip Force Control (GFC) is a primal human need. For hiking on the Moon to be enjoyable, it is crucial that space travellers have a utilitarian object which facilitates eye-hand coordination and references the Earth.

01

02

PANGÉA CONCEPT CAR — This concept car for research in extreme environments was developed by Philips and Renault. Pangéa was designed for use by the scientific community, development and relief organizations, and other groups which need to undertake field research. The vehicle is particularly suited for work in remote or inhospitable areas, or work which requires a high degree of mobility as well as interaction with a base station or other units. Pangéa was designed in 1996 and presented at the Geneva Motor Show, Switzerland in 1997. The design envisioned a nomadic way of working and the application of technologies which would become real only a decade later. The flat-panel LCD display and telemedia cameras, voice-activated input technology, digital graphic tablets and the internet – all the things we take for granted today

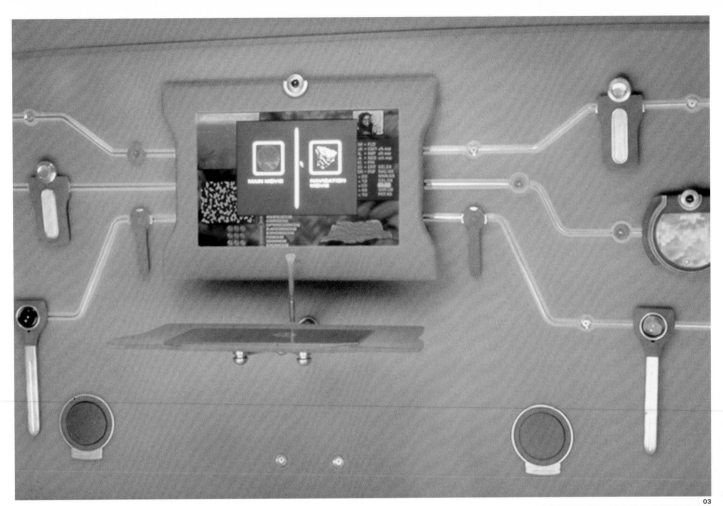

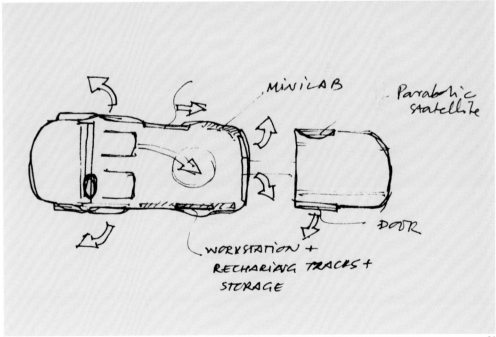

MINILAB

Parabolic
satellite

DOOR

WORKSTATION +
RECHARGING TRACKS +
STORAGE

were then in an early developmental stage. GPS technology was still not available for civilian use. Smart phones and other handheld mobile devices were created more than a decade later. The objective was to explore the possibility of developing a totally new kind of vehicle, one that would reflect a new, nomadic human condition. Making use of the latest environmentally friendly technologies, it would be a 'mobile laboratory', a multi-purpose professional vehicle which could contribute significantly to improving the quality of life.

05

06

01–04 The interior of Pangéa with its mobile working space, where tools such as the flat-panel computer display, telemedia camera, and graphic tablet can be stored away. The passenger seat can be moved on rails and transformed into a task chair with an upright ergonomic posture.
05–08 The Pangéa concept car features a satellite antenna for worldwide communications, an onboard analytical lab and communications centre, a 360° panoramic camera in a roof-mounted turret for all-round vision, and external temperature, relative humidity, air-quality sensors and toolkit for repairs.

A

B

C

D

E

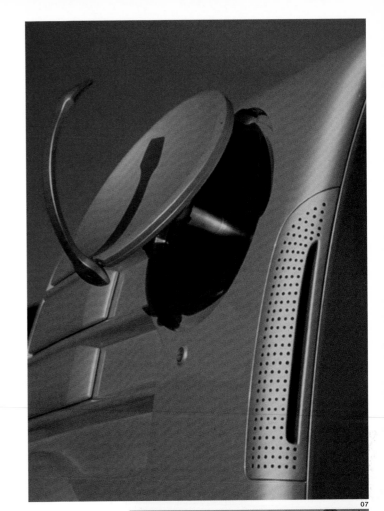

07

08

A, B   A clay model of the Pangéa. Pakhalé presenting the design for the mobile workspace to Le Quément – envisioning the nomadic way of working with technologies a decade ahead of its time.

c, D   Full-scale model of the Pangéa concept car in plaster. Illustration presenting the technological features and package.

E   Stefano Marzano and Patrick Le Quément review the Pangéa concept car before shipping to the Geneva Motor Show.

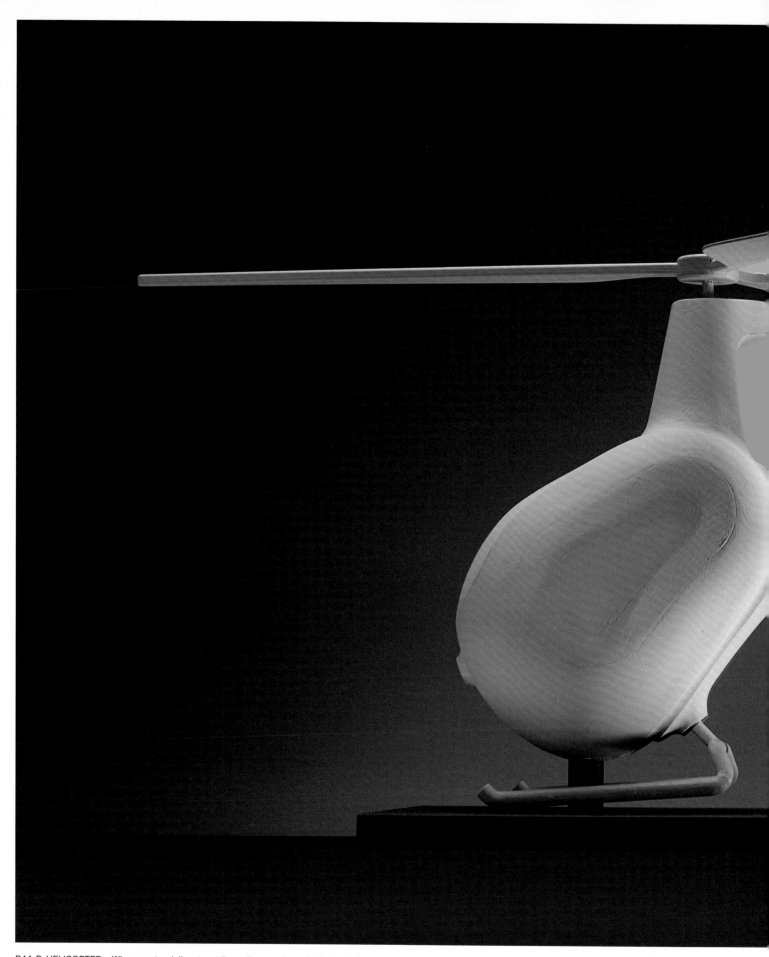

R44-D-HELICOPTER — When a natural disaster strikes, all we can hope for is that help comes fast. Inspired by his own experience of a tsunami in 2006, Satyendra Pakhalé created a humanitarian helicopter for civilian use in 2007. The hybrid-powered rotor system is integrated to increase the helicopter's safety and greatly reduce external noise, allowing it to be used both day and night in urban and rural scenarios. Helicopter R44-D has a unique central connection for its landing skids, which can also be used as a step-ladder easing access to the cabin. Pakhalé focused on what he calls a 'secular-humanistic and culturally engaging design approach' to develop this idio-syncratic work.

258–259   260–263   268–271

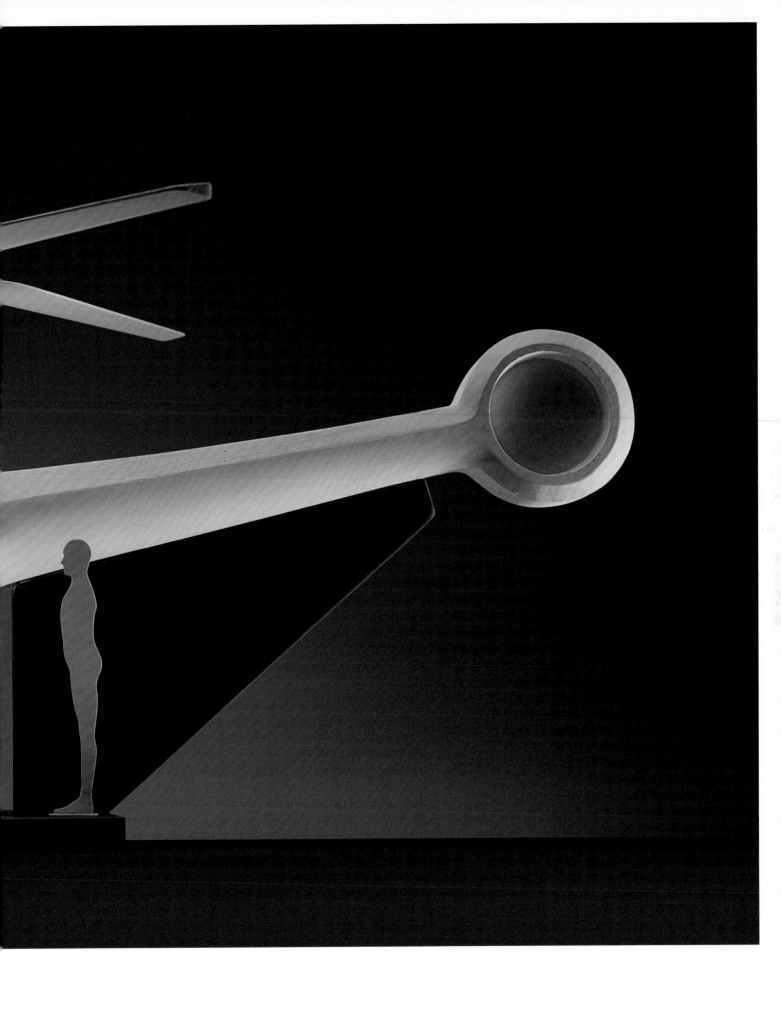

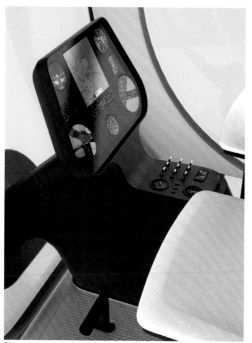

01

A

B

C

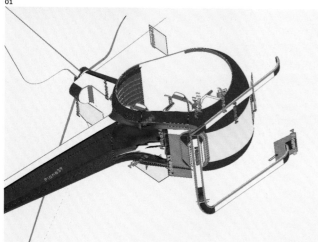

02

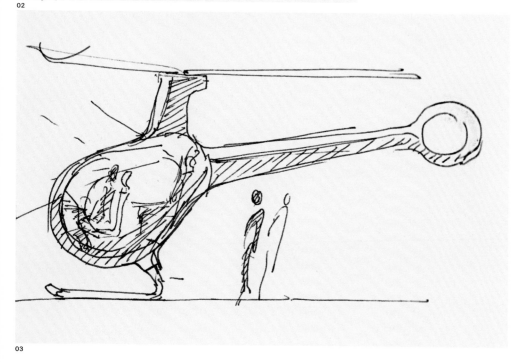

03

A–C Working on a series of models in the studio.

R44-D HELICOPTER

04

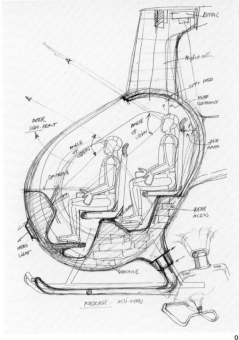

05

01   The helicopter flying system controlled from the digital-analogue console.
02   3D CAD simulations for the component analysis.
03, 05 Working drawing illustrating passenger visibility and overall configuration study and a design sketch by Pakhalé.
04   The hybrid-powered rotor system is integrated to increase safety and greatly reduce external noise, allowing the helicopter to be used both day and night in urban and rural scenarios. The large windows allow for greater visibility, and contribute to the helicopter's lightweight appearance.

TRANSPORTATION DESIGN

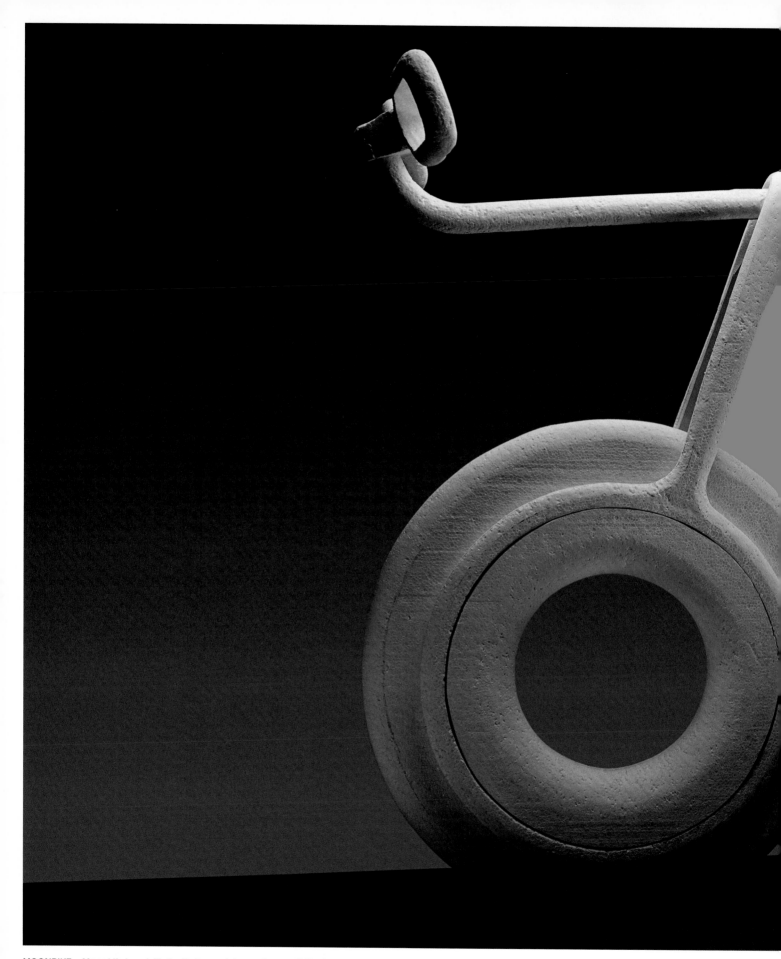

MOONBIKE — Moon Life is an initiative that speculates on the possibility that humans will live in space in the near future. Its objective is to take a creative approach and an artistic, design-led and architectural perspective, rather than a governmental or military standpoint. With this in mind, the project is a stimulus for designers, artists and architects to create futuristic, realistic and radical yet human concepts for habitat design in an extreme lunar environment. Satyendra Pakhalé was invited by Alicia Framis, the multi-disciplinary artist and founder of the Moon Life Foundation, Amsterdam, to contribute a project. Pakhalé created Moonbike and Moonwākā ❶ for life on the Moon. The Moonbike project examines the potential and challenges of life on the Moon from a design perspective. In a microgravity lunar environment, it is important for humans

to perform physical exercises. Pakhalé created a Moonbike with a direct cranking mechanism that requires more effort than a normal bicycle on the Earth. The aim was to compensate the comparative lack of gravity. Though the image of the Moonbike looks distinctive, the riding posture is similar to the standard trekking bike. The torso tilts towards the ground and the distance between the handlebar and the saddle is relatively large, making it particularly well suited to longer rides.

01

01   Moonbike's distinctive bike riding posture can be adapted to the rider's needs by adjusting the wheelbase. The wheels are made of a woven, semi-flexible, metal-alloy wire mesh. This material can support dynamic loads on the lunar terrain.

02   Moonbike's synchronized steering system and centre-of-gravity, self-balancing system integrated in the rear wheel.

03   Integral saddle and frame for a microgravity environment with a technical ceramic coating that can resist extreme temperatures.

04   Moonbike in the microgravity lunar environment.

A

B

C

02

03

04

A   The ergonomics, overall Moonbike pro-portions and riding posture studies.

B, C   Study models on various scales at Pak-halé's studio.

09

DESIGN BY DREAMING

The magical encounter between the world of dreams and the real world

has inspired the very origin of human making, communication, behaviour and thinking.

Tiziana Proietti

DESIGN BY DREAMING
Tiziana Proietti

'It is important to keep in mind that the necessity for dream is stronger than any utilitarian need... Man's first expression, like his first dream, was an aesthetic one,' writes Barnett Newman in his essay, *The First Man Was an Artist* (1947).[1] Barnett describes the very origin of human action, thinking and behaviour as a genuine and instinctive act of dreaming: that is, the act of opening the doors for the aesthetic experience born in the creative mind. Dreaming comes before any necessity-driven action and is at the very root of all human expression. It is in itself an artistic act: that is to say, as Barnett states: 'The artistic act is man's personal birthright.' However, when thinking about those people who give birth to the objects that become part of our life, it is customary to think of them as 'form givers' in a traditional sense. With the focus often on form and function, attention is rarely given to the powerful act of imagination, the immersive act of 'dreaming', that is vital for the full expression of human making.

Watching Satyendra Pakhalé approach a design project, you see a man dreaming like a child, searching and patiently waiting for that powerful moment when the aesthetic experience comes to answer the simplest question of addressing a human need. But that aesthetic experience, as Pakhalé knows very well, is completed only when the dream is brought back to reality and starts to take its shape, to patiently mould itself from the inside. That magical encounter between the world of dreams and the real world has inspired the very origin of human making, communication, behaviour and thinking. Design, meant as the action of shaping the human microcosm, was born of dreams that too often are left behind.

Continuation of Ideas

At the beginning and during the development of every project, whether a limited-edition piece or an industrial design product, Pakhalé keeps on dreaming. The challenge is equally valid, and industrial production should never be perceived as an obstacle to dreaming. Pakhalé is one of those few designers who has successfully created industrial design works for leading design companies like Cappellini❶, Fiam❷, Poltrona Frau❸, and Tubes❹ to name a few,

1   Barnett Newman, *The First Man Was an Artist*, Tiger's Eye Magazine, USA, October 1947.

as well as some germinal pieces – which he calls 'studio pieces' – resulting from several years of exploration and experimentation, such as the B.M. Horse, Black-White Swan and others. As Henri Focillon reminds us, the formation of forms 'does not occur on the spur of the moment, but results from a long series of experiments. To speak of the life of forms is inevitably to invoke the idea of *succession*.'[2] Succession comes in Pakhalé's work from the daily back-and-forth between dreaming and reality, which in the end is an expression of the dreaming itself, and equally the reality.

Pakhalé's dreams are nurtured by an instinctive curiosity that he feeds with constant research. Pakhalé is a designer driven by his research into the deep culture of making things. In each of his pieces, he is committed to exploring design typologies, examining rituals and cultural gestures, understanding the human sensorial response and pondering the way the object expands beyond its physical limits to create atmospheres. To make this happen, he looks at materials, technology, and design tools with a fresh mind, constantly imagining how to enhance and even challenge the possibilities that each tool offers, while collaborating with industries, artisans and craftsmen from various parts of the world.

Cultivation of Mind

At the core of his design thinking, or 'cultivation of mind' as he calls it, is a dynamic approach to history and to the notion of what is past and what is future. Pakhalé neither approaches tradition with nostalgia nor glorifies contemporary technologies. Neither a traditionalist nor a futurist, he gives no credit to dualities and seeming opposites. In his design, he seeks the 'present' by embodying a blended spirit of 'past' and 'future'. He believes that any object is meant to express the encounter between the object and the subject, a timeless encounter beyond any style, mannerism or tradition. The materials and surface structures of Pakhalé's design objects stand out because of their inherent sensuality and timelessness.

'Every decision and action taken from the inception of an object to the final form is a result of the 'cultivated mind' of the person or team creating it,' says Pakhalé. 'Design that comes from a sensitive mind, through the personal experience of the creator as an author – that is what I am after.' In Pakhalé's view, the privilege of designing is twofold: it entails both shaping the built

2   Henri Focillon, *The Life of forms in art* (1942), New York: George Wittenborne, Inc., USA, 1948, p. 53.

A

B

C

environment, which means shaping the way people live in it, as well as the society they will develop in, and revealing a personal way of looking at the world. This is something that must be handled carefully, in order to enable that magical encounter between human sensorial qualities and unlimited nature that transcends time and space and produces authentic totems that can live with us as companions.

As Pakhalé says, 'Design is a process that transcends itself. In the end the object outlasts the creator. Designing means cultivating one's own mind and expressiveness to create things that make life easier for people, while nurturing their senses. One has to create a point of view capable of shaping a specific design in that context – that is what I see as authorship. Design is really getting in touch with the broadest necessities and nurturing all of them.'

Futuristic yet Archaic

Pakhalé's pieces have an energetic physical presence halfway between soft and hard, between flesh and object, between craft and industry. The B.M. Horse series❺ is a perfect example of this blended character. It not only shows unique technicality or ingenuity in terms of the way the material is handled or pushed to its limit to achieve the desired results, but is also refreshing in its sensuality, re-eroticizing the world, as it were. After a long journey and numerous trials in India, the various pieces – B.M. Horse Chaise, B.M. Hi, B.M. Lo, B.M. Table and B.M. Stool❻ – were ultimately brought to life in a foundry in Italy. It took a continuous exploration lasting more than seven years to translate the idea that Pakhalé had in mind to create a seamless, single-piece casting in bronze. Pakhalé immersed himself in the traditions of the Muria community and its bell metal craft technique, searching for the essence of those gestures and techniques that bring Muria objects into being and reinterpreting them as though exploring them for the first time. This is how Pakhalé was able to embody the B.M. Horse series with a sense of lasting presence.

The B.M. Horse family pieces are archaic and futuristic at the same time. They look at the past and the future in a single stroke. They do not simply occupy space, they complement it by creating powerful atmospheres or auras with their sensorial, analogical and totemic presence. This makes them very much 'present' in space

A   B.M. Horse was first presented by ammann//gallery, Cologne, DE after the seven-year-long development period at Design Miami/Basel, CH, 2007. Courtesy: Satyendra Pakhalé Archives, Amsterdam, NL.

B   B.M. Horse Chaise Longue at *Satyendra Pakhalé: OriginS*, solo exhibition, Curated by Gabrielle Ammann at ammann//gallery, Cologne, DE, 2008. Courtesy: Satyendra Pakhalé Archives, Amsterdam, NL.

C   B.M. Horse Family at group show at ammann//gallery, Cologne, DE, 2008. Courtesy: Satyendra Pakhalé Archives, Amsterdam, NL.

Watching Pakhalé approach
a design project,

you see a man
dreaming like a child,

searching and patiently
waiting for that powerful
moment when the aesthetic
experience comes

to answer the simplest
question of addressing
a human need.

Tiziana Proietti

– almost like an object that has always been there, that has come from the distant future and the past at the same time.

Dreaming Hand

The same thing happens with industrial design pieces designed by Pakhalé. This is indeed the peculiar twofold character of his design. Pakhalé is acutely aware of the lack of sensorial quality in industrial design, which often risks being divorced from the senses by losing its cultural and symbolic meaning and responding instead to short-lived fashion trends. Over the years he has explored and investigated the meaning of the senses and how objects can nurture them, and he welcomes the challenge to instill industrial design with sensorial thinking, as in his Fish Chair (2005)❼, made by rotational moulding with a special insert making it a bi-colour object, produced in seven different colours but always with the white inside.

As Focillon says, 'The hand finds every instrument useful for writing down its signs [...] The hand means action: it grasps, it creates, at times it would seem even to think,'[3] or to expand it further, even to dream. It is through the laborious work of the hand, with all the possible tools that human evolution has brought, that the artist acts, immersed in the process of creating. Pakhalé is constantly in search of those meaningful and thoughtful working hands in order to instill into his objects a joyful sense of being and of the fullness of life with a great economy of means – so that the object belongs not to any specific time, but to collective human culture in its broadest social and sensorial nature.

D   Fish Chairs at *Satyendra Pakhalé: Meeting of Minds*, solo show at Hästens flagship store, Stockholm, SE, 2010. Courtesy: Satyendra Pakhalé Archives, Amsterdam, NL.

3   *Ivi*, p. 65 and 74.

He believes that any object
is meant to express the
encounter between the object
and the subject,

a timeless encounter
beyond style,
mannerism or tradition.

Tiziana Proietti

CONTENT

B.M. OBJECTS THIRD GENERATION — This bell metal object belongs to the most recent third-generation series of B.M. Objects. These were developed in a similar manner to the second generation using a silicone mould, but with greater formal complexity since they have an off-centre starting point. This results in two types, one that keeps the form symmetrical on both axes, and another with an asymmetrical form on at least one axis. This process leads to a unique opening at the top and front of the object which has a distinctive form, creating an effect that makes us think about how this object was made. The new language of the third generation B.M. Objects with their controlled geometric forms and strong totemic presence is evident in B.M. Kanheri, B.M. Kondane, B.M. Kuda and B.M. Karad. In spite of the advanced level application of current

state-of-the-art parametric software, such geometry could not have been resulting into a distinct opening form, could not have been achieved without the continuous evolution of the making process of the B.M. Objects over an extended period of time. Pakhalé: 'We could not achieve the desired outcome by modelling these objects with 3D CAD. They are the result of the high level of craftsmanship that we evolved over the years.' He therefore calls these pieces 'post-3D CAD objects'.

02

A　In the process of making the B.M. Objects elaborate craft skills were cultivated at Pakhalé's studio to achieve the desired results.

B　With the studio's focus on making things, new ways are devised to build objects. An ingenious hands-on turning fixture was created using a bike-crank mechanism to generate larger turned forms.

C-E　After the modelling, a silicone mould is made and an impression in wax is taken and prepared for the lost-wax casting process.

01 With an off-centre opening, B.M. Kuda provides various possibilities for displaying flowers.
02, 03 Balancing on a rounded base, B.M. Kanheri has an asymmetrical departure point giving rise to a uniquely shaped opening.

04

04 Controlled geometry, rhythmic patterning and an asymmetrical departure point result in the elegant B.M. Kondane.
05 B.M. Kuda, view of the base. Notice its asymmetrical departure point.

B.M. OBJECTS THIRD GENERATION

F

G

H

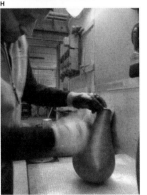

I

J

05

F   Molten bronze ready in the furnace for lost-wax casting.

G, H   After chiselling, the bronze pieces are ready to be patinated or sandblasted.

I, J   The pieces are treated with natural wax to retain the lustrous finish of sandblasting.

SPOUT OBJECTS

Satyendra Pakhalé is fascinated by everyday utilitarian objects. He cherishes them and remembers all the curious, interesting objects found on his travels around the world. He is particularly interested in how such objects of utility evolve over time and in different cultures. All these found objects in his studio are from Brazil, Syria, Japan, India, Finland and many other countries.

Pakhalé has a long-standing fascination with objects with spouts, and he particularly admires the utility of the innovative soy sauce dispenser of Kikkoman Corporation, designed by Kenji Ekuan. 'I don't recall when I first used this object, but I am so fascinated by the way it just works,' he says. 'It is one of my favourite industrial design objects. It somehow seems deeply Asian, and rooted in Japanese culture, yet it has become a universal object that you can find in any supermarket around the world. Technically, a common problem with objects with spouts is that they drip and spill, so I have always been fascinated by the cultural condition that created such an object with its sensitive gestural innovation – the way you control the amount of soy sauce pouring out by simply controlling the airflow with your index finger. It's a beautiful application of physics in the most culture-specific way, yet it has been produced on an industrial level for more than half a century, and looks likely to be around for far longer still. This is rare, and it makes the Kikkoman bottle very special.'

Taking a specific utilitarian feature rooted in a specific culture and making it genuinely universal – you could say that this is one of the aspirations of Pakhalé's own design practice. Indeed, he set out to playfully explore the theme, creating a diverse set of objects with spouts. His travel sketchbooks feature a long series of spouted object sketches. Eventually, these sketches were swiftly translated into clay models, which were fired in a ceramic kiln and then photographed. These 'sketch objects', as Pakhalé calls them, became a reference for further development; they were evolved into detailed three-dimensional mathematical models using 3D CAD, and so refined further. Later, these objects were made into various scale models at the studio.

At Pakhalé's studio, free exploration like this allows the evolution of pieces with a distinct character and utility, producing new typologies of objects.

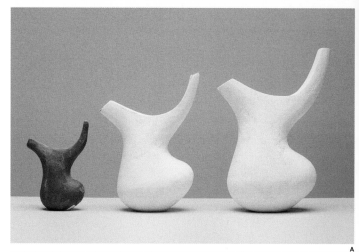

A

B

C

D

A, B   The first sketch models made in clay on various scales in order to refine the proportions and surface continuity.

C   The above reference models are further developed to produce detailed 3D mathematical models ready to be made in various materials.

D   Test piece in electro-deposit copper.

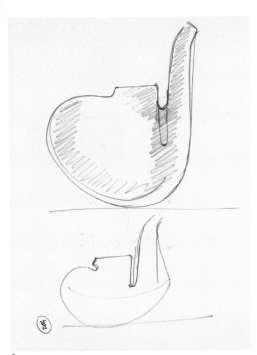

E

F

G

E   The travel sketchbooks in the Satyendra Pakhalé Archives are full of sketches carried out seemingly without any specific intention in mind. Such sketches often emerge as part of a continuous process of intuitive exploration.

F   Often two identical models are made to allow subtle refinements of all the features to be studied.

G   Sometimes these themes also appear in the watercolour sketches that Pakhalé produces almost daily.

SPOUT OBJECTS

H

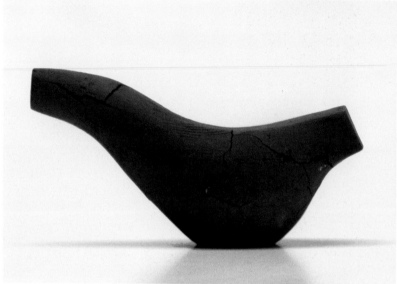

I

J

K

H, I   Based on the chosen sketches, spout object clay models are made and then fired in the ceramic kiln for further development.

J, K   Pakhalé creates new typologies with distinctive proportions from these sketch models.

L

M

N

L   Sketch model in clay of open dish with spouts on either side.

M   The clay model is further developed into spout object with lid for serving oil.

N   Sketch model – in clay – capturing the essence of Pakhalé's sketch and ready to be developed.

SPOUT OBJECT FAMILY — Creating objects with spouts has been a fertile period of design exploration at Pakhalé's studio. Fascinated by objects with spouts, the designer pondered why they so often spill over on pouring. Internal research led to a new take on some age-old objects with spouts, along with some new typologies made in different materials such as copper, electro-deposit silver and porcelain. The way each object pours was worked out individually, depending on its proportions, size and form.

 302–303

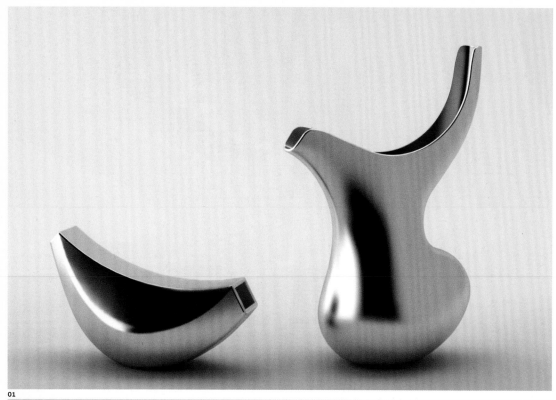

01   Asymmetrical small object and a taller object that can be used as oil dispensers.
02   Open dish and a pitcher with spouts on either side.
03   A larger object with symmetrical spouts that can also be used as a pitcher or vase.

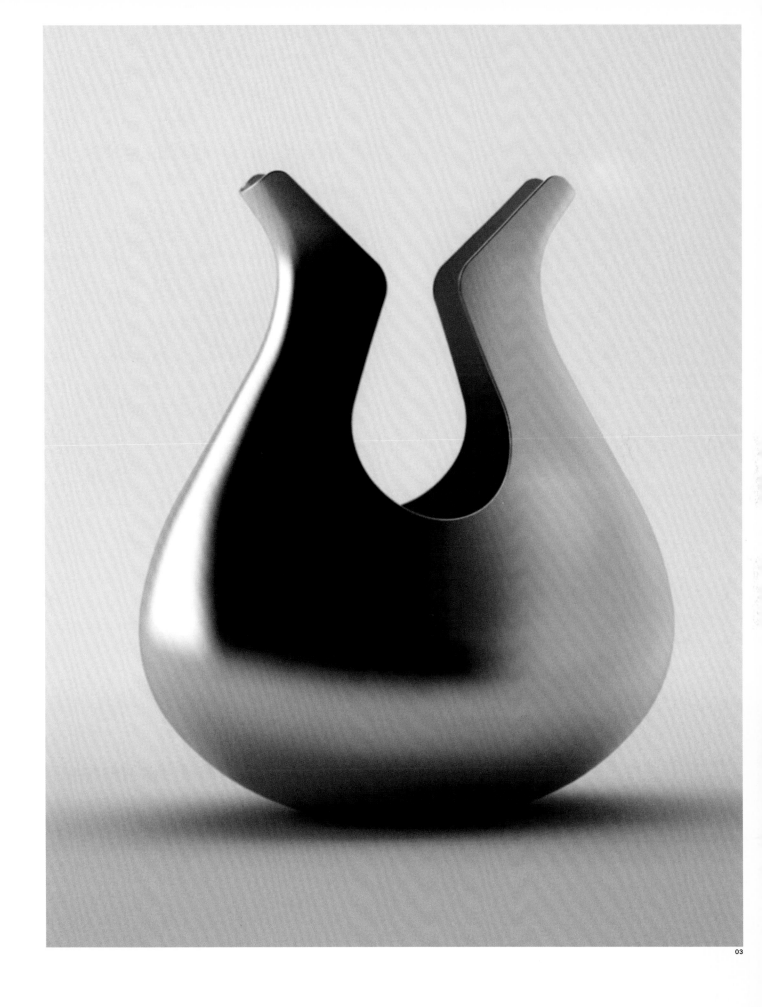

03

PUZZLE CARPET — A modular play surface, Puzzle Carpet is made of expanded PU. It helps children aged 2 to 6 to enhance their motor skills while encouraging fantasy play - grass, sand and water patterns are digitally printed onto the Puzzle Carpet surface. 'The idea was born in my solo exhibition, *Design by Heart*, at Gallery Otto, in Bologna, Italy,' explains the designer. 'There we had each area of the gallery floor digitally printed with images of sand, grass and sky to evoke different feelings. When Eugenio Perazza, founder of Magis, came to visit the exhibition, the idea evolved of creating a modular carpet for children that eventually became part of the Me Too collection.' Puzzle Carpet also helps children to tidy up their space after playing, encouraging them to put together and take apart the modules playfully.

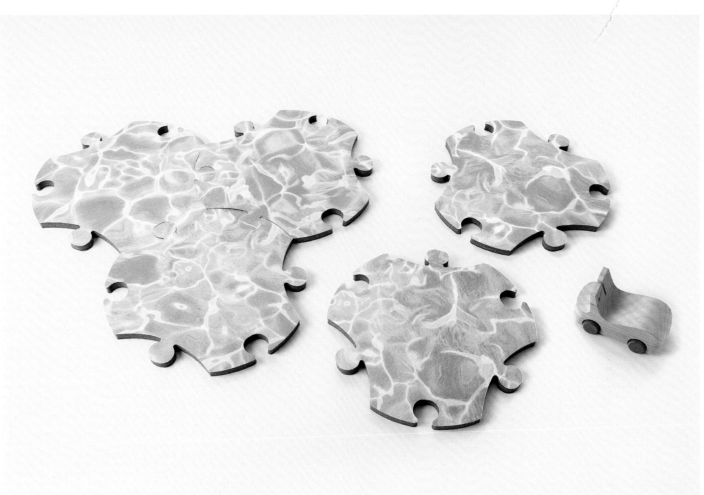

01, 02 Sand and water patterns are digitally printed onto the Puzzle Carpet surface, simulating the idea of memory playing on a fantasy island.

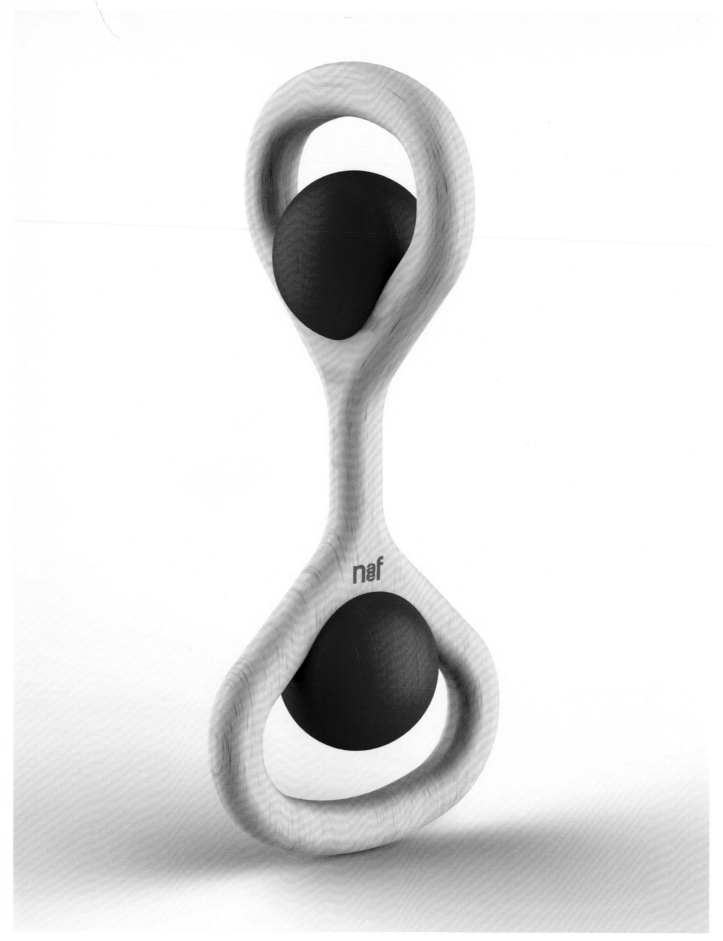

SINGULARITY TOYS — Learning from the sensory experience and development of babies, Pakhalé designed Singularity Toys for little ones up to 3 years old. In natural wood and brightly coloured non-toxic paint, these help cultivate babies' haptic perception, the process of recognizing objects through touch. Babies enter the world equipped with senses for discovering how to engage with the world to meet their needs. They pay more focused and intense attention to new stimuli, especially those coming from the human world. As babies watch and listen to what goes on around them and become more aware of what they see, hear, touch, taste and smell, so they differentiate between shapes and sounds and formulate whole images by synthesizing sensory information. These objects are designed to help babies cultivate their sensory skills playfully.

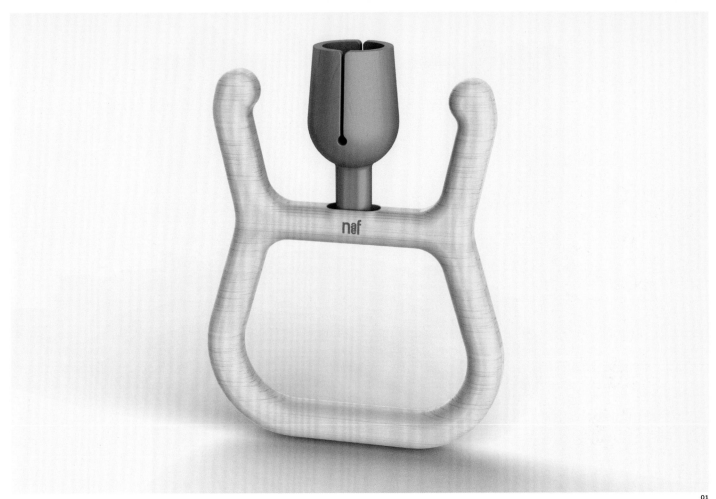

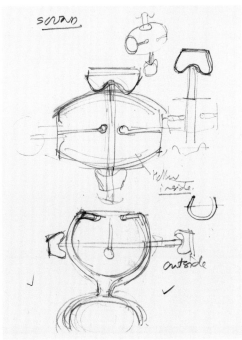

01 Sound Object is a basic toy that helps babies of 3+ months to develop sensory experiences focusing on the sense of touch and the sound an object when it moves, thanks to the acoustic qualities of wood. Sound Object helps babies develop basic motor skills and learn how to get feedback via sound.
02 Design sketch of Sound Object by Pakhalé.
03 Sound Object consists of a handle form in natural wood and a hollow wooden element that generates sound.

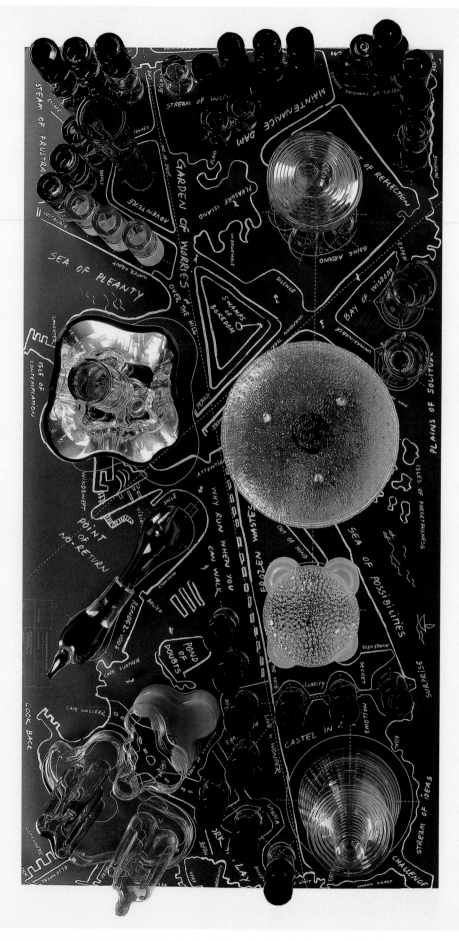

URBAN COMPATIBILITY — Pakhalé was invited to create an installation of using littala products for Designboost 2008 in Sweden. He chose the theme 'Sustainable City'. The resulting installation, called Urban Compatibility, is a poetic and optimistic take on the current urban crisis in major metropolitan cities around the world, and particularly megacities in India. It evokes positive notions of how a city might be modelled based on human emotions, so there is an Avenue of Happiness, a Swamp of Boredom and a Sea of Possibilities, all represented by classic littala products by the famous Finnish glassware manufacturer. Currently, more than half of the global population lives in urban areas. In the Indian context the situation is more critical – there has been and still is serious neglect regarding comprehensive development, both urban and rural.

The resulting explosion of the urban population presents challenges but also wonderful design opportunities to create innovative solutions that have a positive impact. 'I feel we ought to take an inventive look at the urban setting,' says the designer. 'How can we return to the idea of humanizing our cities without segregating "work" from "play" and "entertainment" from "life"? I thought of giving a playful answer to this serious question at Designboost 2008. I felt it was appropriate to try to visualize an urban setting, illustrating a secular humanistic point of view, so I chose to use mainly the classic Iittala products created by the great humanists Alvar Aalto and Aino Aalto. I aspire to create a truly emotional human city by seamlessly blending "work" and "play" and "entertainment" and "life".'

DESIGNERS VS CHANEL NO. 5 — Al-Sabah Art and Design, Kuwait, invited Satyendra Pakahlé to create a personal product concept for the I Love Souk Gallery Store using the classic Chanel No. 5 perfume bottle. 'Considering the historic significance of the Chanel No. 5 perfume bottle, the idea was to celebrate it by creating a pedestal or "altar" for it. And to make it with state-of-the-art DMLS (direct metal laser sintering) technology, popularly known as the rapid prototyping process for metal.' Pakhalé used bronze alloy to make the DMLS pieces – an earthy, heavy material designed to enhance the daily ritual of using the iconic Chanel No. 5 perfume.

01

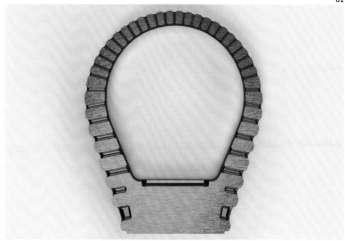

02

01   Celebrating the iconic Chanel No. 5 bottle: the DMLS limited-edition pedestal with LED lights.
02   Cross-section of the piece made in bronze alloy, illustrating how it was agglomerated using the DMLS process.

10

THE ATMOSPHERE OF AN OBJECT

As we enter a space,
the space enters us,

and the experience is
essentially an exchange

and a fusion of the object
and the subject.

Juhani Pallasmaa

A

B

THE ATMOSPHERE OF AN OBJECT
Juhani Pallasmaa

Modern architecture and design have been dominated by vision, and especially focused vision, following the Gestalt principles of psychology. However, focused vision makes us outside observers in relation to what we are seeing. Le Corbusier's famous credo of 1923 exemplifies this retinal position: 'Architecture is the masterly, correct and magnificent play of masses brought together in light.'[1] The master's own works create dramatic and moving sensations of presence, emotion and unifying ambience, but modernity at large has been obsessed with pure form and visuality. We like to visit vernacular and historical settings, often of lesser formal qualities, due to their embracing and caressing sense of materiality, texture, scale and atmosphere. Atmosphere, feeling and empathy were theorized as early as the late 19th century in German research and literature, but modern architecture and design have been oriented towards 'pure' form so obsessively that immaterial, formless and measureless overall ambiences and atmospheres have been neglected. We must recognize, however, that artistic and empathic sensibilities have usually produced captivating atmospheres, although they have not been conscious goals in the designer's thinking or working process.

Multi-Sensory Fusion
The character of a space, place or object is not merely a visual perceptual quality. The judgment of environmental character is a complex multi-sensory fusion of countless factors, which are immediately and synthetically grasped as an overall atmosphere, feeling, mood or ambience. 'I enter a building, see a room, and – in the fraction of a second – have this feeling about it,' Peter Zumthor confesses.[2] This experience is multi-sensory in its essence, but it also involves judgments beyond the five senses. Indeed, our immediate judgment of the character of a space calls for our entire embodied and existential sense, and this character is perceived in a diffuse and peripheral manner, rather than through precise and conscious observation. Moreover, this complex assessment engages a temporal process as perception, memory and imagination are fused. As we enter a space, the space enters us, and the experience is essentially an exchange and a fusion of the object

A   Proto-object by Constantin Brâncuși, *Atelier Brâncuși*, Paris, FR. Courtesy: Satyendra Pakhalé Archives, Amsterdam, NL.

B   Stoup by Le Corbusier, *Chapelle Notre-Dame-du-Haut de Ronchamp*, Ronchamp, FR. Courtesy: Satyendra Pakhalé Archives, Amsterdam, NL.

1   Le Corbusier, *Towards A New Architecture* (1923), London: The Architectural Press, UK, 1959, p. 31.
2   Peter Zumthor, *Atmospheres: Architectural Environments. Surrounding Objects*, Basel: Birkhäuser, CH, 2006, p. 13.

Our immediate judgment of
the character of a space calls
for our entire embodied and
existential sense,

and this character
is perceived in a diffuse
and peripheral manner,

rather than through
precise and conscious
observation.

Juhani Pallasmaa

and the subject. Each space and situation is an invitation and suggestion to distinct acts. It provides the unifying coherence and character of an object, a room, a space and a landscape, or a human encounter. Atmosphere is the common denominator of the colouring, tuning and feel of the experiential situation. It is a 'quasi-thing'[3] suspended between the perceived object and the sensing subject.

Atmosphere in the Arts

Atmosphere seems to be more conscious in literary, cinematic and theatrical thinking than in architecture and design. Even the imagery of a painting is integrated by an overall atmosphere or feeling; the most important unifying factor in paintings is usually their specific feel of illumination and colour, more than their conceptual or narrative content. In fact, there is an entire painterly approach, as exemplified by J.M.W. Turner and Claude Monet, which can be called 'atmospheric painting', in both senses of the word, atmosphere being both the subject matter and these paintings' mode of expression. 'Atmosphere is my style,' Turner confessed to John Ruskin, as Zumthor reminds us. The formal and structural ingredients in the works of these artists are deliberately suppressed for the benefit of an all-embracing and shapeless atmosphere, suggestive of temperature, moisture and subtle movements of the air. Colour field painters likewise suppress form and boundaries and utilize large areas of the canvas to create an intense interaction and presence of colour.

Great films, such as the films by Jean Vigo, Jean Renoir, Michelangelo Antonioni and Andrei Tarkosvsky, are also steeped in a characteristic atmospheric continuum. Theatre, too, relies heavily on atmosphere which supports the integrity and continuity of the story regardless of the often abstracted and vaguely hinted features of place or space. An ambience can be so suggestive and dominating that very few cues are needed, as in Lars von Trier's film *Dogville* (2003), in which houses and rooms are often indicated by no more than chalk lines on the dark floor. Yet the drama still grips the spectator's imagination and emotions.

Somewhat paradoxically, we can also speak of 'atmospheric sculpture', such as the sketch-like modellings of Medardo Rosso, Auguste Rodin and Alberto Giacometti. Often it is the atmosphere of the works, as in the abstracted sculptures of Constantin Brâncusi, that create the unique sense of a singular artistic world.

C   Passive ventilation system at Agra Fort, UNESCO World Heritage site, built in red sandstone by Emperor Akbar, Agra, IN, 1565-1571. Courtesy: Satyendra Pakhalé Archives, Amsterdam, NL.

D   The Pantheon is one of the best preserved Roman buildings in the world. The open dome of the Pantheon has a diameter of 8.7 metres and provides the special light and atmosphere. The total dome has a diameter of 44.4 meters and is the largest dome in the world made of unreinforced concrete. The Pantheon was built between 118 and 125 by Emperor Hadrian, Rome, IT. Courtesy: Satyendra Pakhalé Archives, Amsterdam, NL.

E   Sacromonte, Granada, is famous for its cave dwellings. It is located in the hills of Valparaiso, north-east of the historic Arab quarter of El Albaicin, founded in the 17th century. Inspired by the *Gitanos* native to the area, the poet Garcia Lorca gave a lecture on their *Canto jondo*, in which he described it as 'Siguiriya the prototype of deep song [...] the only genre on our continent that preserves in all its purity, as much structurally as stylistically, the primary qualities of the primitive songs of the oriental peoples'. Courtesy: Satyendra Pakhalé Archives, Amsterdam, NL.

3   Tonino Griffero, *Quasi-Things: The Paradigm of Atmospheres*, New York: State University of New York Press, USA, 2017.

THE ATMOSPHERE OF AN OBJECT   JUHANI PALLASMAA

All great works of art in painting, sculpture, theatre, film and music project

atmospheres and specific attunements.

Juhani Pallasmaa

F

G

H

Artists seem to be more aware of the seminal role of ambience than architects, who tend to think more in terms of the 'pure' qualities of space, form and geometry. Among architects, atmosphere seems to be judged as something romantic and shallowly entertaining. Besides, the serious Western architectural tradition is entirely based on regarding architecture as a material and geometric object experienced through focused vision. Standard architectural images seek clarity rather than ephemerality and obscurity.

Of all the various art forms, music is particularly atmospheric and has a forceful impact on our emotions and moods regardless of how little or how much we intellectually understand musical structures. That seems to be the very reason why music is commonly used to create the desired atmospheric moods in public spaces, shopping malls and even elevators. Music creates atmospheric interior spaces, ephemeral and dynamic experiential fields, rather than distant shapes, structures or objects. Atmosphere emphasizes a sustained being in a situation rather than a singular moment of perception. The fact that music can move us to tears is convincing proof of the emotive power of art as well as of our innate capacity to simulate and internalize abstract experiential structures. Or more precisely, to project our emotions on abstractly symbolic structures.

A Specific Air

The notion of atmosphere is usually related to weather, environments, places and spaces, but even singular objects project a specific mood or tuning, and they evoke distinct associations and feelings. All great works of art in painting, sculpture, theatre, film and music project atmospheres and specific attunements. Modern architecture at large has been obsessed with clear and pure form, and atmospheric qualities have been neglected and bypassed. Yet even Modern environments have their atmospheres, and what is frequently called 'style', either periodic or personal, is based on atmospheric characteristics as much as on formal criteria.

The objects designed by Satyendra Pakhalé embody poetic analogies, which project strong and embracing atmospheres. They have a specific air around them, which has a direct effect on our perception, behaviour and feelings. Pakhalé's design works exude a benevolent, friendly and inviting atmosphere, like the comforting presence of life companions.

Pakhalé's design works
exude a benevolent,

friendly and inviting
atmosphere,

like the comforting presence
of life companions.

Juhani Pallasmaa

CONTENT

ADD-ON RADIATOR — In 2002 Satyendra Pakhalé was invited by Tubes Radiatori to create a product. The brief was simply to design a new radiator. In the literal sense, Pakhalé created Add-On Radiator with a beginner's mind, as if the radiator was being made for the very first time. This defiance to rely on conventional notions of the generic radiator led to a design that implied something not merely novel, but actually new. He started from the premise of what a radiator ought to do, which is to effectively warm the air around it. Proceeding to sculpt the piece with a high degree of abstraction as an assembly of modular elements creating rhythmic volumes and densities, Pakhalé created a unique modular heating system based on an element which can be integrated into any architectural setting. Add-On Radiator can be placed on a wall, recessed or used as a space

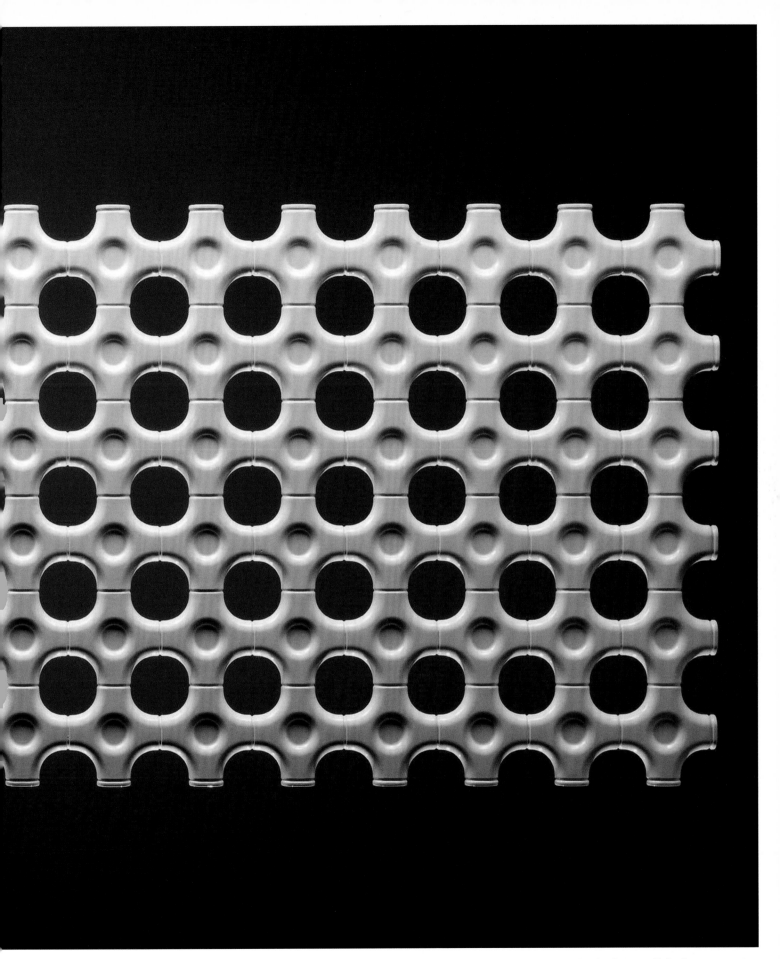

divider connected to floor and ceiling. It is not only a typological innovation, but also fulfils more utilitarian needs than conventional radiators – offering faster temperature regulation with less power – and conforms to international safety requirements. Pakhalé: 'In architecture, radiators are technical-looking components and rather neglected products, even though they are one of the most utilitarian products in an architectural setting. So the first thought that came to my mind was to create a radiator that has an effectively larger surface area. I wanted to design a radiator which also has the personality of an object – a presence in an interior with its own modest dignity.'

01

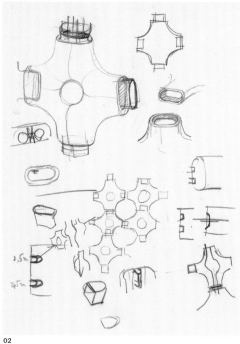

02

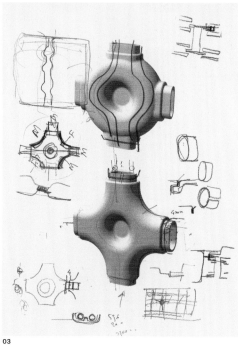

03

01   Installed in the wall, Add-On Radiator becomes an integral part of an architecture, effectively warming spaces on both sides as the air passes through it.
02, 03 Design sketches exploring modularity, solution for the joint between the modules and how air might pass through a radiator.
04   Installed between ceiling and floor, the radiator becomes a space divider.

A

B

C

D

E

04

A, B   The Tubes technical team and Pakhalé discussing the connection between the module and the frame of the radiator; prototype illustrating the connection.

C   The radiator is tested for hydraulic pressure using an automated process at the Tubes manufacturing facility.

D, E   Product development meeting between the management and technical team of Tubes and Satyendra Pakhalé to define the core for aluminium die-casting and subsequent work at the studio.

Satyendra Pakhalé brought something new to Tubes. With Add-On Radiator, he pushed us to create things together with him, to achieve new goals that were not only impossible, but perhaps unthinkable before.

With Add-On, his first proposal was in ceramic, a material absolutely unknown in the world of radiators. It is extremely refractory, delicate and therefore not particularly suitable from our point of view, yet he wanted to use ceramic, and eventually technical ceramics, so much so that the first prototype we presented at the Salone del Mobile in Milan in 2004 was a ceramic prototype. Satyendra has the power to make you develop things that were unthinkable at the beginning.

Finally, we developed the radiator in aluminium, a material much closer to the world of radiators and industrial production, as technical ceramic was economically not feasible. What is noteworthy about Satyendra is his precision, his meticulousness and his passion to think through every single detail. In every project collaboration, one feels his deep desire to manage everything – not only the product, design and manufacturing, but also the packaging and communication. This deep involvement, taking care of every single detail, resulted in a product that is long lasting and has become a part of the permanent collection of the Centre Pompidou, Paris, and the Montreal Museum of Modern Art, besides being a successful product in the market. That is a source of great pride for us.

Satyendra is a unique character; it is not easy to find such a designer. Working with him on the product development process is a wonderful experience. He hooks you, slowly, slowly, and takes you wherever he wants to go.

He is an extremely innovative designer, always looking for something new, something more. He gives you so much; he is a persistent visionary who loves what he does. He works with passion, putting so much effort into each creation. But all that hard work, from the initial idea through to the rigorous product development, is immensely satisfying because then you realize what you have done is something wonderful and unthinkable.

— Cristiano Crosetta

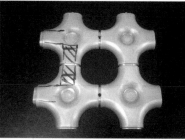

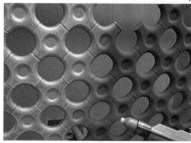

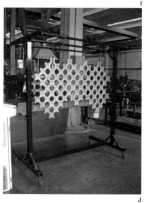

F, G   The first working prototype is CNC machined.

H   The radiator is assembled at the production facilities of Tubes, IT.

I, J   The radiator is produced in die-cast aluminium with a powder-coated surface.

ADD-ON RADIATOR

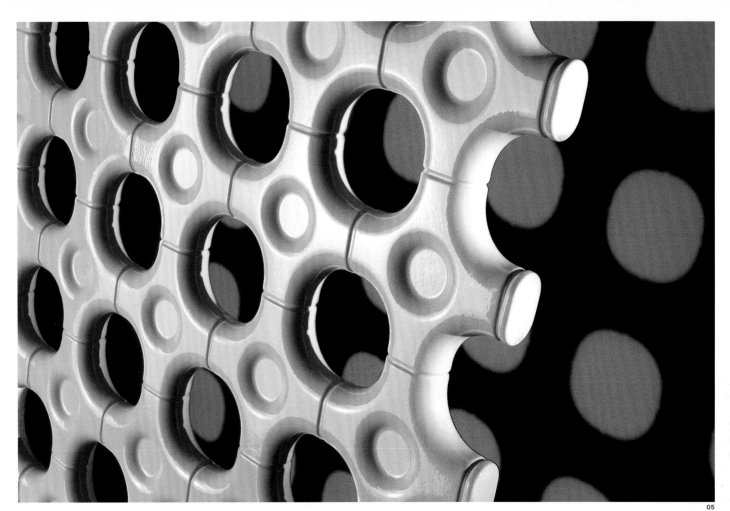

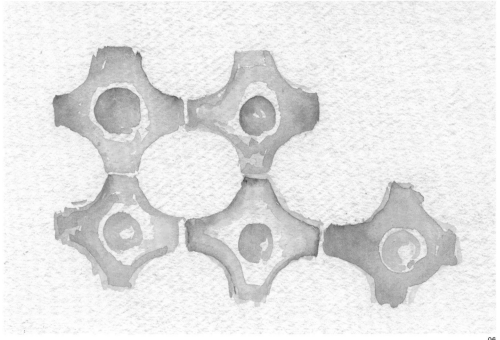

05   The freeform version of the Add-On Radiator is closed with cap details.
06   Watercolour sketch conceiving the form of the Add-On module by Pakhalé.

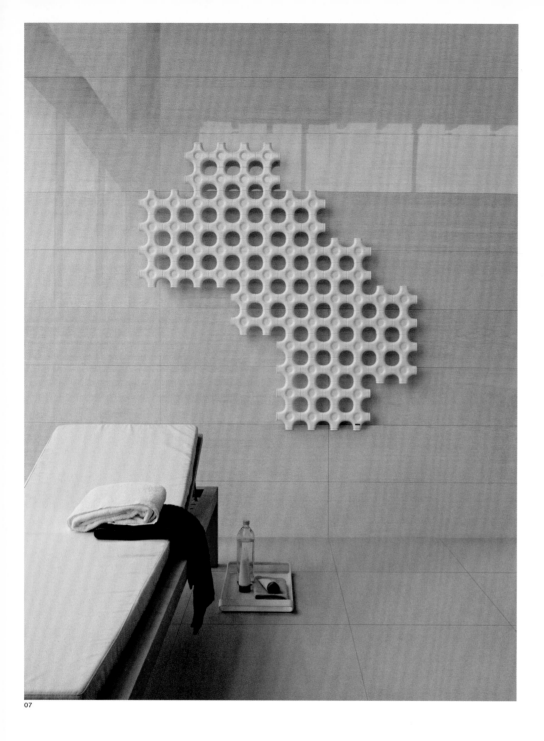

07

ADD-ON RADIATOR

07   Freeform version of the Add-On Radiator mounted on the wall. The modular heating system can be customized for any architectural setting.
08   The Add-On Radiator available in hydraulic and electric versions can be mounted between the ceiling and the floor in any architectural setting.

LDC LEATHER DINING CHAIR — Few objects have the status of a cult object, but Les Arcs Chair is certainly among them. It is often associated with Charlotte Perriand, perhaps because she specified it for the French ski resort of Les Arcs in 1970. When Satyendra Pakhalé was invited to create a contemporary version of this cult piece, made in saddle leather with a tubular metal structure, he took on the challenge to create a contemporary re-interpretation of this object. The Les Arcs Chair was manufactured by Dal Vera in Italy, around 1919: the chair's 18 mm-diameter tubular structure, with a unidirectional bend of constant radius, reflected the technology of the time. The seat and backrest were made of two pieces of 4-mm-thick saddle leather, stitched together at the centre and slung from the tubular frame of the chair rivets, creating a modernist look. 'I like the

directness and clarity of the Les Arcs Chair,' says Pakhalé. 'However, I felt the necessity to rethink it for the new millennium. It was important to work on the comfort of the chair.' Due to the nature of the material, sitting becomes slightly uncomfortable as one feels the tubular structure through the leather. Responding to this, Pakhalé came up with the idea of a 'leaf-spring', a compression spring made of flat, laser-cut steel plate that is attached to the tubular structure. This innovative feature not only helps to improve the ergonomics of the chair, but it also creates a refreshing contemporary image. The leaf spring supports the outer edge of the saddle leather seat and also guides the cross stitching on the chair, lending the two-dimensional saddle leather a three dimensional sculptural quality.

01, 02 LDC (Leather Dining Chair) is designed as a homage to the classic Les Arcs Chair. Full-scale 3D-printed laser sintered nylon prototype.
03 The design sketch illustrates the innovative leaf spring that enhances the ergonomic comfort and the aesthetic quality of the chair and the mounting of the leather on the profile.
04 The design innovation of the leaf spring is further developed to provide the necessary support for the outer edge of the saddle leather.

A

B

C

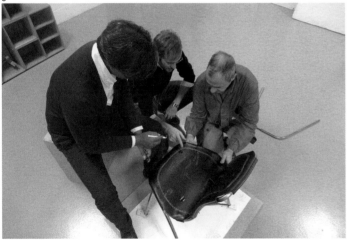

D

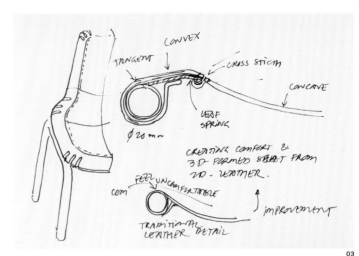

03

04

A   Studying the Les Arcs Chair at Pakhalé's studio.

B   Pakhalé discusses the leaf spring idea idea with the product development team.

C, D   Discussing the leather stitching detail with the model maker and checking the first working prototype.

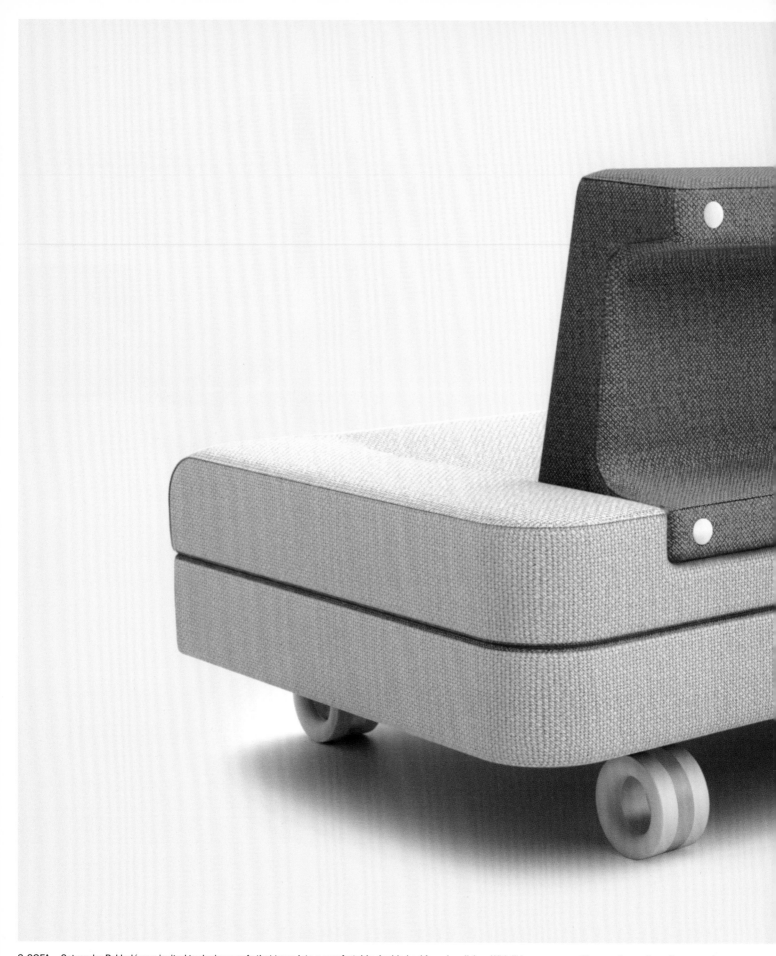

S-SOFA — Satyendra Pakhalé was invited to design a sofa that turns into a comfortable double bed for urban living. With living spaces getting smaller and smaller around the world, especially in major cities, objects for urban living condition should ideally have more than one purpose. This is a theme we see repeatedly in Pakhalé's work. The Kalpa vase ❶, for example, can also be used as a fruit bowl, Add-On Radiator ❷ also serves as a space divider and Frida Pitcher ❸ can be used as a vase. With the same concern for creating better urban living conditions, Pakhalé created the S-Sofa that elegantly transforms into a bed. The uniqueness of this concept is that there are no visible technological fixtures or mechanisms. All the articulated hinges are smartly concealed. The backrest simply folds in on the cavity of the seat and the entire top part

of the sofa can be flipped open to become a bed. The sofa-bed has anti-skid wheels and so can be easily moved around. In its closed form it is a compact sofa; when unfolded it becomes a comfortable double bed.

01

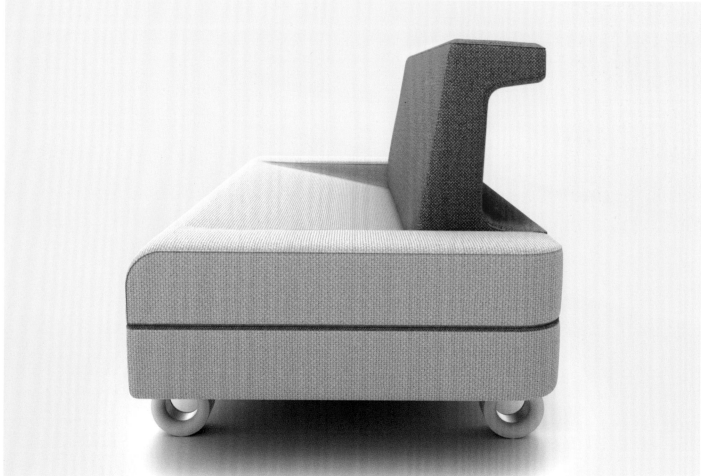

02

01, 02 Three-seater sofa that transforms into a comfortable double bed with anti-skid wheels.
03   S-Sofa, the single-seater sofa that transforms into a comfortable single bed.
04   Design sketch illustrating the concept of the S-Sofa by Pakhalé.

A

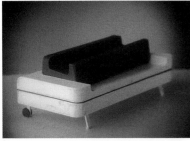

B

C

D

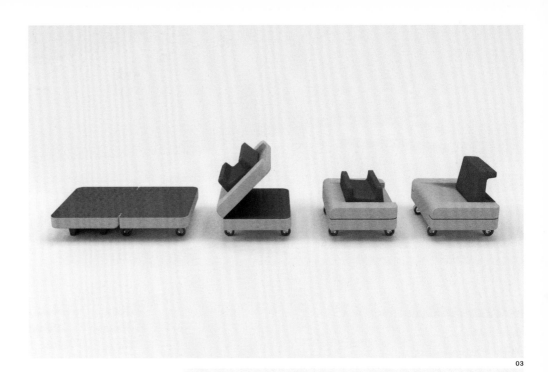

03

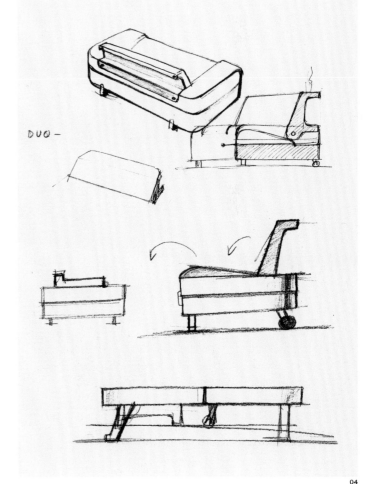

DUO —

04

A–D   Scale 1:5 sketch model in cardboard made during the design process at Pakhalé's studio, illustrating how the S-Sofa becomes a double bed.

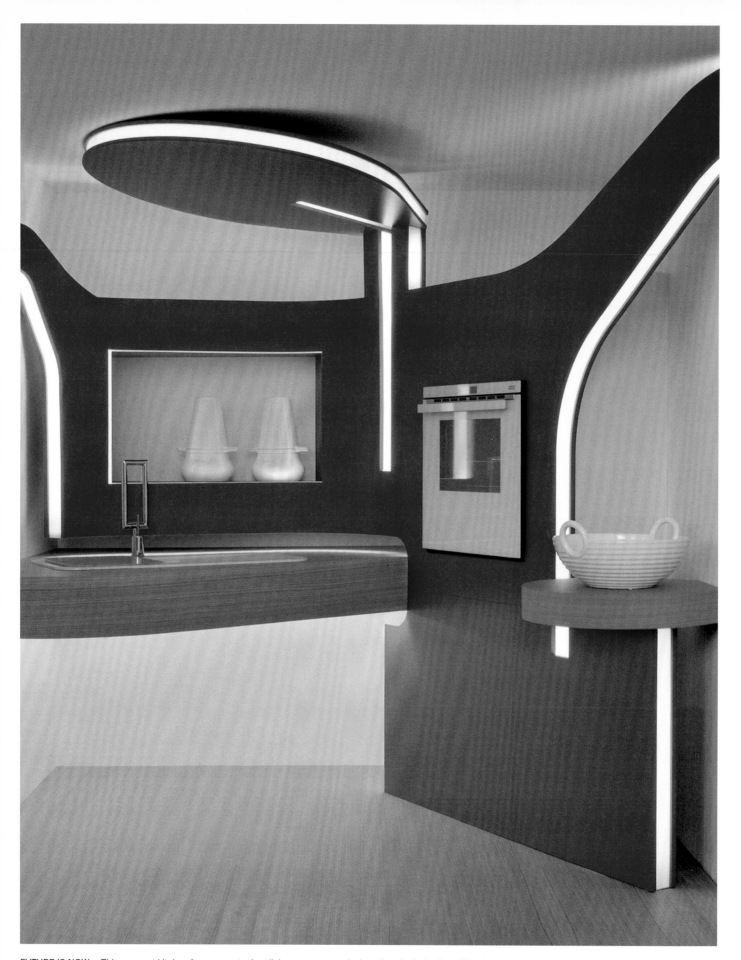

FUTURE IS NOW — This concept kitchen for compact urban living spaces was designed on the invitation of Franke to celebrate its centenary year at Milan Design Week 2012. Responding to increasing urbanization and the shrinking of city homes, Pakhalé decided to create a compact solution in just 2.5 cubic metres. It nevertheless incorporates the usual kitchen requirements such as an oven, hob, refrigerator, storage space and sink. The design, with its continuous wrapping form, creates an intimate feeling – a contemporary vision of the kitchen as the heart of home.

01

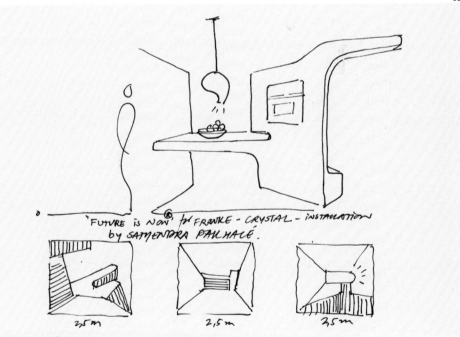

'FUTURE IS NOW' for FRANKE - CRYSTAL - INSTALLATION
by SATYENDRA PAKHALÉ.

2,5 m   2,5 m   2,5 m

02

01   Watercolour concept sketch capturing the essence of the centenary concept kitchen for compact urban living.
02   Design sketch illustrating the concept for a compact kitchen in 2.5 cubic metres of space.

ALU-ROCKING — With its sensuous form for active sitting, the Alu-Rocking invites you to touch and feel the beauty of its contours. Alu-Rocking has rhythmic punctuation, convexity and flowing continuous lines rooted in the world of experience and perception. It evokes a symbolic meaning stimulated through its materiality by creating an upright sitting posture that also rocks. This allows rocks – allowing users to be relaxed and still move somewhat, encouraging free and creative thinking. Pakhalé: 'Every office should have rocking chairs for the managers to rock!'

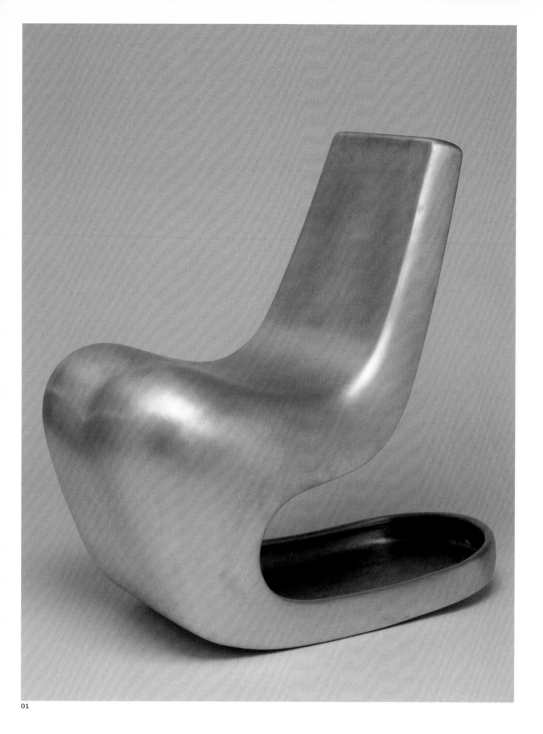

01

A

B

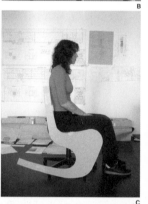

C

D

E

01   The Alu-Rocking in sand-cast aluminium with a natural brushed finish.
02   The chair in deep red-purple. With its voluminous forms, this piece invites you to touch and feel the sensoriality of its contours.
03   Design sketch illustrating the idea of a sculptural shell that later became the Alu-Rocking.

F

G

H

02

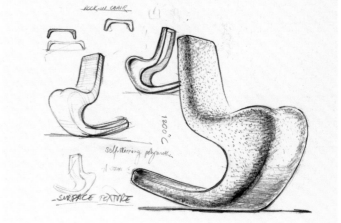

03

A, B The first prototypes being built in India in plaster and fibreglass.

C, D Sitting posture and ergonomics are being studied and the fibreglass model being refined at the studio.

E-H Pakhalé discussing the possibility of using aluminium sand-casting with a master artisan in Italy.

11

AXIOMATIC DESIGN

Pakhalé cultivates ideas and critical thinking about what he calls 'social modernity'.

These are rooted not only in his knowledge of history,

but also in his own life experiences.

Jacques Barsac

AXIOMATIC DESIGN
Jacques Barsac

The avant-garde movements of the 1920s and 1930s shared a concern with social and even political issues. The creators' struggle for modernity – and it was very much a struggle – aimed at bringing progress and wellbeing to everyone. Most joined the communists, hoping to contribute to the creation of a 'paradise on earth'. Consumer society did not yet exist, nor did design as we understand it today, and its creations were not yet known as products.

European avant-garde architects gathered under the name Congrès Internationaux d'Architecture Moderne (CIAM). Founded in 1928, CIAM sought to develop a new doctrine of urban planning to meet the housing needs of a rural population that had been pouring into urban areas since the industrial age. In 19th-century Europe, millions of farm labourers joined the ranks of the working class in increasingly unsanitary cities where tuberculosis was rampant and slums proliferated (a massive migratory movement that cannot fail to remind us of the recent situation in emerging countries). The aim, therefore, was to invent 'the modern city' by using every kind of innovation in the field of urban planning and architecture, and also home equipment – including furniture, storage, household appliances and so on, all the while taking account of the economy and mass production for the greatest number as a prerequisite for meeting social needs.

Craft and Pragmatism
In the 1930s, however, the economic crisis, the failure to mass produce furniture and housing, and the economic reality of production methods prompted Charlotte Perriand to take a different approach. "We will no longer engage in formalism or constructivism," she wrote 1935. "We will no longer favour curved or straight lines, stone or cement, blue or red, wood or metal, but instead, we will use each of them where it is most practical – technologically and physiologically."[1] Her pragmatic approach led her to reconsider traditional crafts as production methods equivalent to industrial manufacture – complementary, and not in conflict with each other.

The advantage of crafts, which are found all over the world, is that they benefit from the proximity between the production site

A   Congrès Internationaux d'Architecture Moderne (CIAM) at the Chateau de la Sarraz, CH, 1928. Courtesy: Archives Charlotte Perriand, Paris, FR.

B   Charlotte Perriand with Le Corbusier and Pierre Jeanneret, CIAM, Athens, GR, 1933. Courtesy: Archives Charlotte Perriand, Paris, FR.

1   Charlotte Perriand, 'L'habitation familiale: son développement économique et social', in *L'Architecture d'aujourd'hui*, Boulogne-sur-Seine, FR, January 1935, p. 25.

and place of use. They also favour a fruitful dialogue between designer and craft practitioner, allowing them to benefit from each other's knowledge and creativity. Crafts offer the opportunity for a fair relationship on a human scale in a local economy. They provide knowhow and express different regional and national sensibilities, helping to preserve cultural diversity and not reducing creation to a unique, universal functionalist formula. Crafts broaden the creative palette by offering a wide diversity of locally produced materials and unusual techniques that industry cannot provide.

Formula-Free Design

In the mid-1930s, Charlotte Perriand reacted to the International Style then spreading, as evidenced by the laudatory Philip Johnson exhibition at MoMA in 1932. 'There is no formula,' she argued. 'We should take the production site, practices, cultures and programmes into account.' A similar understanding of the artisanal combined with industry and animated by socio-cultural concern belongs to Satyendra Pakhalé.

Pakhalé cultivates ideas and critical thinking about what he calls 'social modernity'. These are rooted not only in his knowledge of history, but also in his own life experiences. His ideas about the human being as a social animal come directly from his birth country, his continued curiosity about the human condition, and the socio-cultural awareness of his family upbringing and education. Pakhalé highlights a new perspective on social modernity in contemporary societies around the world. Keeping in mind the idealistic views of the early modernist movement, and at the same time with a keen awareness of the problematic side effects of those early modernists on society at large, Pakhalé takes the view that: 'The project of modernity is still a work in progress in most societies seen from the point of view of social cohesion. Design has to help to bring the disintegrating elements together and unite them in a given society. It ought to rebuild society on the foundations of "social modernity".'

Human Skills

Stepping away from any glorification of the industrial process and technological innovations alone, Pakhalé pursues the appreciation of very different, apparently opposite, production techniques, by returning attention to human skills – both of the hand and the

intellect. The artisanal element represents a world in itself and offers the advantage of proximity between workshops and users, but also a fruitful dialogue between designers and craftsmen. For each, it gives access to mutual knowledge and creativity. It offers the possibility of a fair relationship on a human scale. It also spreads knowledge and expresses different sensibilities from one region to another, and from one country to another, and therefore maintains an international cultural diversity rather than reduce creativity to a universal, unique and functional formula. The consideration of craftsmanship enlarges the creative field and offers a great diversity of locally produced materials and special techniques that industry cannot offer.

Pakhalé understood all this intuitively even at the beginning of his practice. It is evident in his approach design, which entails engaging with a wide range of projects with industry as well as artisans across the world. By actively seeking collaborations with craftsmen as well as industry, he acknowledges complementary opportunities which require the creator to be flexible and accommodating in his approach and design possibilities.

New Craftsmanship
Glancing at history, the gap between industrialization and manual work has never been as unbridgeable at that described by historians who refer to the ideological conception of modernity as the enemy of crafts. From Pakhalé's perspective, this is a bizarre point of view. He is interested in 'new craftsmanship', which allies modernity with tradition and daily folklore with advanced technology in the eclecticism of its methods, by establishing itself as the catalyst of universal communication. Creation is indeed part of tradition. This is the refreshing view that stands out against the conventional notion of modernity, and with this approach he articulates a view of modernity that his ideas, notions about social modernity that at its core is social cohesion rather than social charity for the third millennium.

Looking at European societies with their migrant populations, a new vision of social modernity is very much needed in our times, as Europe learns to put its Eurocentric perspective aside to accommodate the newcomers with a renewed energy. At the same time, fast-developing economies like China, India and Brazil cultivate their own approach to social modernity in their own manner.

c–e *International Style* exhibition by Philip Johnson at the Museum of Modern Art New York, USA, 1932. Courtesy: © 2019. Digital image The Museum of Modern Art, New York, USA, Scala, Florence, IT.

The project of modernity
is still a work in progress in
most societies,

seen from the point of
view of social cohesion.

Design has to help to bring the
disintegrating elements
together and unite them in a
given society.

It ought to rebuild society
on the foundations of 'social
modernity'.

Satyendra Pakhalé

F

G

It will be fascinating to see how designers contribute to this journey of social reconstruction in the third millennium.

Cultural Innovation

Pakhalé's keen interest in material and technological innovations is evident in several projects. 'When we speak about innovation,' he says, 'most of the time we just refer to technological innovation which is important and often challenging to achieve. However, the ideas, especially design ideas, that make an impact on social change could be termed 'social innovation'. Furthermore, if society accepts those innovations and they then become part of the culture, they could eventually be called 'cultural innovation'. I like the idea that design could lead to cultural innovation.'

Pakhalé is enthusiastic about one of Charlotte Perriand's innovations, that of bringing the kitchen into the living room. He considers it a germinal example in the history of design, a praiseworthy innovation that has had an emancipating impact on societies around the world, freeing women from the traditional kitchen that used to be located at the end of the corridor of the apartment or house. Thanks to Perriand's vision, the kitchen became part of the living environment and the woman became part of the family once more, sharing the cooking and at the same time being together in the living space adjacent to the kitchen. She is in the midst of the living environment and engaged with family and friends and no longer cut off.

Pakhalé thinks such cultural innovations are of great importance for our current human condition as we learn to live together as a global human family and learn to achieve social cohesion.

Global Contexts

Although Charlotte Perriand was one of the greatest modern designers and a pioneer of contemporary design, for her the creation – the design – of furniture or objects extended far beyond the object itself and was situated within a global context.

The positions held by Charlotte Perriand in the 1930s and thereafter are shared by Satyendra Pakhalé. They are an echo of the contemporary world and the world of tomorrow in that they strive to satisfy the needs of the many with a social aspect. They demonstrate cultural diversity in their human scale, in their use of artisanal capacities to complement industrial ones and in their singular products. They produce honest and fully useful objects in

F, G Charlotte Perriand, prototype of the kitchen-bar for the cell of the *Unité d'habitation* in Marseille by Le Corbusier, fabrication CEPAC, 1949. Courtesy: Archives Charlotte Perriand, Paris, FR.

consonance with the present and not dominated by it, and never lose sight of the object's socio-cultural, socio-political dimensions and aesthetics.

The human being is a social animal and at the root of human life is hope. Designers have a commitment to empower social messages. Social modernity, and with it social justice, is more important in a vertical society than economic or political justice. Almost all societies to a lesser or a greater extent are vertical societies – especially India, even today. As Pakhalé points out, 'What we see as modernity in India is a visual modernity, there is still no comprehensive modernity in all walks of life. Unless there is social modernity no society or country can be called modern.'

Design Shapes Society

Design is not the result of society but in fact the very opposite. Design is the shaper of society, the foundation that allows people to know more about how to live in the world. It is a source of knowledge in itself, yet it is hidden. People can discover it by experiencing and allowing the design piece to disclose all the potentialities of the atmosphere it creates, showing the many sensorial, intellectual, social, modernist aptitudes a human being has. Design is a way of knowing more about ourselves as humans and social beings. It is the foundation of a way of life – if created with a deep understanding of its meaning.

With its secular-humanist insight and inquiry into the human condition, design is a primary aspect of cultivating social modernity to rebuild society; and social modernity has to be further cultivated in order to reconstruct society as the basis of secular humanity. With this sensibility, it will be fascinating to see what sort of axiomatic design for social modernity Pakhalé will evolve in the years to come.

CONTENT

DR. AMBEDKAR NATIONAL CENTRE FOR SOCIAL JUSTICE — The architectural programme of the centre consists of four components: a public library with research centre; a media-cum-introspection centre; a convention hall; and an administrative wing. Taking the given programme as a starting point, Pakhalé treated the four components as separate elements that are held together, for as Ambedkar ❶ himself said: 'The strength of a society depends upon the presence of points of contact, possibilities of inter-action between different groups that exist in it. These are what Carlyle calls "organic filaments", i.e. the elastic threads which help bring the disintegrating elements together and reunite them.' This quote accompanied Pakhalé in the design process, providing him with a powerful metaphor for uniting the separate elements of his design. The

emblematic 'elastic threads' thus became elastic bands and a core concept. The bands on this building are designed to shield against the sun's glare, while encouraging air to pass through. The significance of the bands goes much further than their symbolic meaning. The idea facilitates the age-old practice of harvesting rainwater, for evaporative, passive cooling. The water is first collected and stored on the roof. Gradually, it circulates in channels integrated in the bands, cooling the air as it passes through the fins, and collecting in the water basin at the base of the building. The Social Justice Centre's design is open and accessible, expressing optimism with equanimity and representing the potentially non-stratified society that Ambedkar envisioned.

01

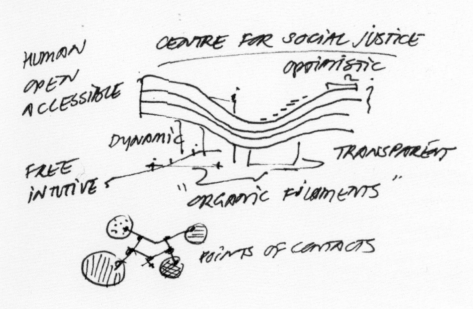

02

01   Rainwater harvesting and passive cooling are combined in the bands designed to be a shield against the sun's glare, while encouraging air to flow through. Shallow bodies of water are created on the ground using harvested rainwater to further facilitate evaporative cooling on the south-east and south-west sides of the Centre.

02-04 Architectural concept sketch. Pakhalé treats the four components of the programme as separate elements that are held together and united by an organic filament or band, as illustrated in the sketches. Design sketch illustrating evaporative cooling and rainwater harvesting.

A

B

C

D

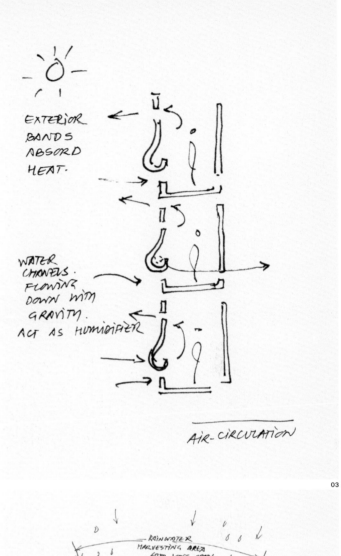

EXTERIOR
BANDS
ABSORD
HEAT.

WATER
CHANNELS.
FLOWING
DOWN WITH
GRAVITY.
ACT AS HUMIDIFIER

AIR-CIRCULATION

03

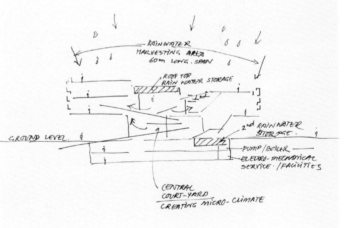

RAINWATER
HARVESTING AREA
60m LONG. SPAN

ROOF TOP
RAIN WATER STORAGE

2nd RAINWATER
STORAGE.

GROUND LEVEL.

PUMP/BOILER
ELECTRO-MECHANICAL
SERVICE /FACILITIES

CENTRAL
COURT-YARD
CREATING MICRO-CLIMATE

04

A The architectural programme and site model at Pakhalé's studio.

B Sketch model of the core idea of rain-water harvesting and passive cooling by means of the water channels integrated in the bands.

C, D Models of the architectural volume studies.

ARCHITECTURE

349

05   The centre disseminates the ideas and philosophy of social justice, inclusivity, diversity and social development by organizing symposia, workshops and exhibitions on related issues. Often public buildings are intimidating and not at all accessible and inviting as their as their presence exerts authority. To reflect Dr. Ambedkar's vision of a plural, non-stratified society, Pakhalé created an architectural space that is accessible and non-hierarchical. He did this by removing the conventional staircases and instead creating site-specific continuous ramps flowing through the entire architectural space. These form the central spiral rotunda that allows users of the building to seamlessly navigate the entire space in and around (and on top of) the centre in an intuitive manner.

ENDLESS ALCANTARA — Invited by Domitilla Dardi, Design Curator at MAXXI Architettura, and Giulio Cappellini, Artistic Director at Alcantara, and Patrizia Beltrami, Alcantara to interpret the material Alcantara, intrigued by the making process Pakhalé created the site-specific piece 'Endless Alcantara' for the 'Can you imagine?' Alcantara project, presented at MAXXI in Rome. 'The process of making this material is magical,' says Pakhalé. 'I wanted to create an endless stream of Alcantara, a kind of waterfall that keeps flowing endlessly, just like the process of making Alcantara.'

A

B

C

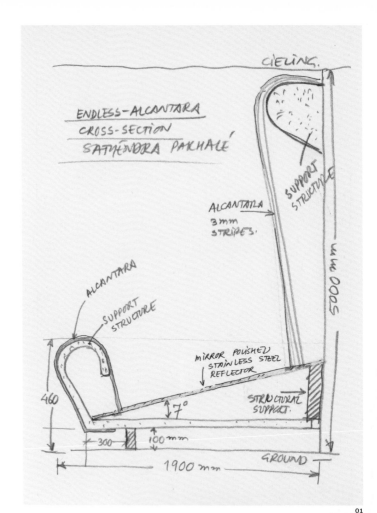

ENDLESS-ALCANTARA
CROSS-SECTION
SATYENDRA PAKHALÉ

CIELING.

ALCANTARA
3mm
STRIPES.

SUPPORT
STRUCTURE

ALCANTARA

SUPPORT
STRUCTURE

2100 mm

MIRROR POLISHED
STAINLESS STEEL
REFLECTOR

STRUCTURAL
SUPPORT.

460

7°

300   100 mm

1900 mm

GROUND

01

02

A–C   Pakhalé at his studio experimenting, testing and deciding the appropriate angle of reflection.

01   Design sketch illustrating the concept. The mirror-polished aluminium plate is mounted at a 7° angle in an oval, pond-like structure. It has laser-cut holes through which the Alcantara is woven, creating an illusion of endlessness.

02   The pond-like structure is made of wood and is covered with Alcantara, laser-cut into 3 mm wide strips in various selected colours. These strips are woven through the holes on the aluminium plate, creating a reflective, endless effect and making the audience curious about their own reflection.

CARVING THE SENSES — For Design at the Venice Architecture Biennale 2016 and at the invitation of the Global Art Affairs Foundation, Satyendra Pakhalé created a 3-metre-high piece that combines sculpture, design, architecture and nature. By integrating his innovative Add-On Radiator ❶ into a tectonic space, he produced a work called Carving the Senses. This archi-sculpture invites the viewer to experience its atmosphere through form, texture, colour and light, evoking all the senses at once. 'Architecture is not merely buildings, but the expression of the human ability to inhabit space,' says Pakhalé, 'The moment one puts an object in space it becomes architecture.' As a consequence, engagement with architecture has been a natural progression for Pakhalé. Architectural design has become an integral part of his studio practice though

industrial design remains the core. For the Venice Architecture Biennale, Pakhalé teamed up with Tubes, Matteo Brioni and Artemide to create an atmosphere to nurture the senses. Primal yet with a sense of nowness, the created space is a monolithic form whose tectonics lend the material a powerful presence. The idea was to convey the sensation of inhabiting a warm living space and to create imagery imbued with poetic analogies by allowing the user to step into the realm beyond all form. Carving the Senses is a statement on the nature of creating forms to dwell in the world with concern for humans as social beings.

01

01   Sculpture, design, architecture and nature combine in the Carving the Senses piece created for the Design at Venice Architecture Biennale exhibition at Palazzo Michiel, Venice, IT.
02   A watercolour drawing of Carving the Senses that sets out to capture atmosphere through form, texture, colour and light, evoking all the senses at once.
03   Design sketch illustrating the concept, proportions and orientation of Carving the Senses.
04   Design concept sketch by Satyendra Pakhalé.

02

03

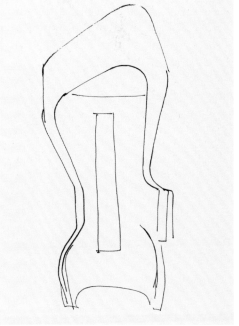

04

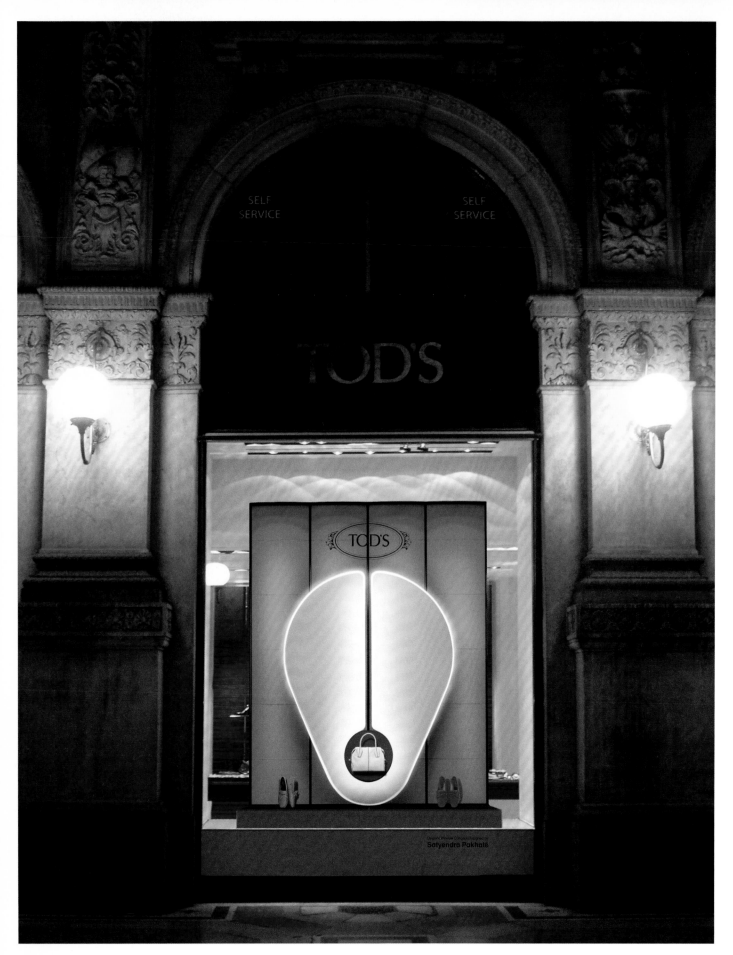

LOOKING AT TOD'S — Satyendra Pakhalé was invited by Tod's to create a window display design for the brand's Madison Avenue flagship store in New York, USA. Pakhalé created one basic, strong central display: a shell-like element fixed to a base. It makes a passing reference to a seashell, suggesting Tod's highly crafted products are as precious as a pearl. The overall form of the central, prototypical element helps to emphasize the quality and refinement of Tod's products. It creates a unique display area for showcasing a single Tod's product. It also allows light to fall beautifully onto the well-crafted works. The management of Tod's liked the project so much that they presented Pakhalé's window architecture in all the brand's flagship stores worldwide in the winter season 2008.

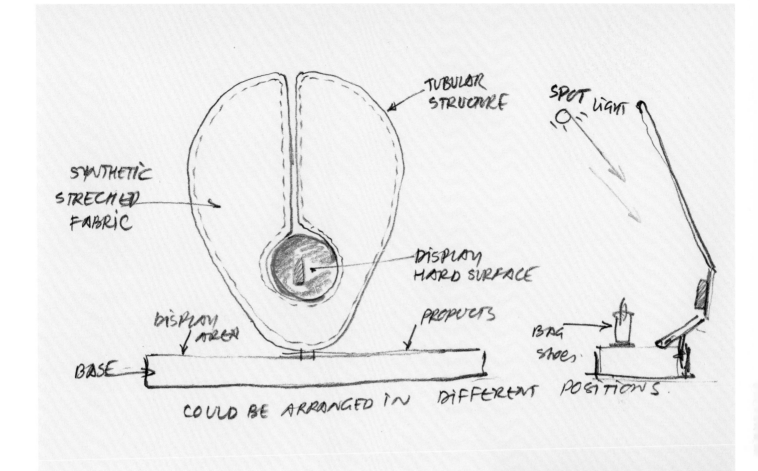

SYNTHETIC STRECHED FABRIC

TUBULAR STRUCTURE

SPOT LIGHT

DISPLAY HARD SURFACE

DISPLAY AREA

PRODUCTS

BASE

BAG shoes

COULD BE ARRANGED IN DIFFERENT POSITIONS.

01

02

01   Design sketch illustrating the concept of a large seashell, with a Tod's product displayed at the core like a pearl.
02   Looking at Tod's by Satyendra Pakhalé at Tod's flagship store at Galleria Vittorio Emanuele, Milan, IT.

DR. AMBEDKAR NATIONAL MEMORIAL — The memorial is a space for people to learn about the life and mission of Dr. B. R. Ambedkar. The memorial environment allows visitors to experience a contemplative mindset, internalizing Dr. Ambedkar's profound contribution to humanity ❶. Satyendra Pakhalé won the competition to design the Dr. Ambedkar National Memorial, one of the most prestigious projects of national importance. The memorial site programme at 26 Alipur Road, New Delhi, India (the last residence of Dr. Ambedkar) houses the memorial as a 21st-century interpretation of the classic stupa typology. It consists of exhibition galleries, a viewing ramp, amphitheatre, collection storage and administrative spaces. The adjacent dome-like structure – lowered below ground level – houses a public library and community space. The outdoor space has a prominent memorial plaque with

selected quotes by Dr. Ambedkar along with outdoor seating areas. Located at the entrance there is a café, a bookstore and utility facilities. Pakhalé's approach to the memorial was to establish a meaningful relationship to the unique site as well as a strong, lasting experiential resonance with Dr. Ambedkar's lifelong work and its significance for people. On the invitation of India's Ministry of Social Justice and Empowerment, Pakhalé created a serene architecture with plenty of open areas. A dense plantation of lush green trees surrounds the site, blocking noise and visual pollution. Except for the prototypical Stupa Gallery and the Stupa Dome of the public space and library, the programme is below ground. One essential feature of the architectural design is that one can walk straight from the street and enter the memorial without any barriers, making it easily accessible to all people.

01

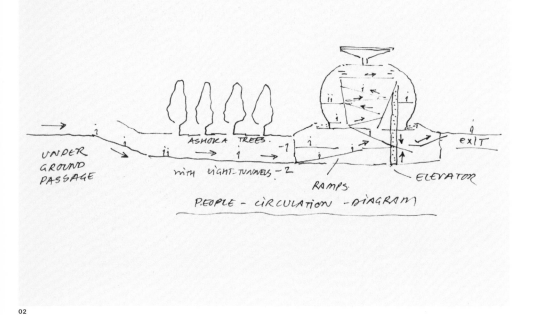

02

01 Visitors are greeted by a peaceful space with a single clear entrance within the green surroundings. Ashoka and flame of the forest trees block exterior noises and distractions, and provide shade from the sun. The wind passes through the trees and over the large bodies of water that are present on the site, reducing the heat and cooling the spaces. The walk-in entrance is set into the ground. Walking down the gentle slope suggests a change of gear and allows visitors to reflect and relax before entering the main architectural space of Stupa Gallery.
02 The entrance to the memorial and circulation diagram. Thorough consideration was given to safe and fluid pedestrian traffic flows through the entire site.

362   DR. AMBEDKAR NATIONAL MEMORIAL

A

B

C

D

E

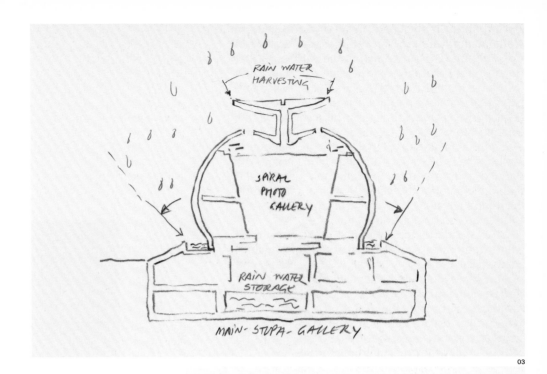

03

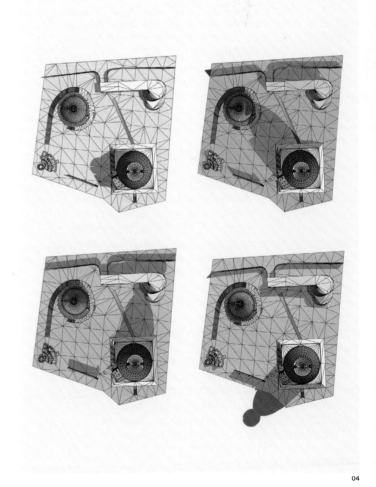

04

03   Design sketch illustrating rainwater harvesting and a concept for a spiral photo gallery inspired by the rock-cut architecture of Kanheri.

04   The Delhi climate is extreme, ranging from 45°C during the summer (April–July) to 5°C during the winter (December–January). Sun tracking studies for the site were carried out during the early design phase to implement 'passive solar design'.

Having spent many years living and travelling in Maharashtra, I am familiar with the many statues of the great Dr. B. R. Ambedkar in the villages of that region. I am constantly made aware of the people's reverence for their beloved leader, since in village after village one finds his statue set up in the centre of the town. He is always dressed in his formal blue suit, wearing his scholarly glasses, and holding (what else?) the constitution of India. Fittingly, a statue of the Buddha is often set up beside him, for both the Buddha and Ambedkar, through their insights and their actions, offer the same teaching, recognizing the world's adversity, but holding out the promise that something can be done about it.

It is wonderful to realize that these many local points of promise, scattered across the Indian landscape in Dr. Ambedkar's honour, will now – finally and most appropriately – find their ultimate expression in New Delhi, in the heart of India, the capital of the world in which he was so actively involved. It is heartwarming to realize, too, that the new Ambedkar Memorial will rise on the plot of land – wisely preserved by the Government of India – where the great man lived and worked.

What is particularly moving, to those who so greatly respect this saintly and hard-working man, is that the new Ambedkar Memorial planned by Satyendra Pakhalé so sensitively reflects both Ambedkar's effective involvement with the present, and his reverence for the past. I am glad that this splendid, innovative project, with its compelling references to India's long heritage which it brings so admirably into the 21st century, has been approved and selected by the committee appointed by the Prime Minster's office.

The planners, remarkably, have created an architecture that is both public and private, taking account of the needs and the demands of the hundreds of visitors expected every day and guiding them past the visitors' entrance, cloakroom, cafeteria, restrooms and other areas which realistically have to be planned for such a public monument. The visitor then moves into an increasingly meditative space and experience, sensitively developed in accord with the architect's enriching knowledge of his own India and Indian roots. The plan developed by Satyendra Pakhalé guides visitors into more and more private spaces, enhanced by a rich variety of trees, bordered by green grasses and peaceful water. Those who travel through the various reaches of the monument must inevitably feel the resonances of India's deep past, both in the familiar stupa shapes of the areas to which they are drawn, whether for learning or contemplation and relaxation, and in the quiet simplicity of the enclosing dome of the meditation centre.

The memorial is planned as a quiet, simple, and resonant space. In the midst of the turbulence of the surrounding city, such a place of contemplation and learning will be a most fitting tribute to Dr. B. R. Ambedkar. How wonderful to honour the great Ambedkar with something so appropriately modest and, at the same time, so appropriately impressive!

— Walter M. Spink

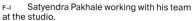
A–E Architectural model being assembled at Pakhalé's studio for presentation to the jury at the ministry in New Delhi, IN.

F–I Satyendra Pakhalé working with his team at the studio.

J–N Various scale models being developed during the design process. Model being fixed at the hotel by an enthusiastic staff member before the presentation in New Delhi, IN.

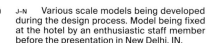

DR. AMBEDKAR NATIONAL MEMORIAL

K

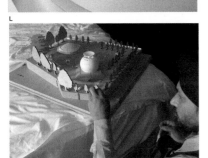

L

M

05

N

06

05   The photo gallery in the main stupa has an inviting, open and approachable feeling to it. The entrance to the main gallery is recessed underground, creating a unique architectural experience. The ramp represents the continuity of tradition and progress that is above all non-hierarchical.

06   As the visitors walk out of the photo gallery, a continuous ramp spirals down offering views of the memorial site. There are even lower viewing windows for children. An elevator is provided so that elderly and physically impaired people can access all the floors.

07   The architectural design of the Dr. Ambedkar Memorial refers to the long tradition of Buddhist architecture on the Indian subcontinent. These ancient sites were rather progressive, with sanitation areas and sophisticated ventilation systems. Continuing the tradition, the National Memorial is conceived with state-of-the-art technologies such as rainwater harvesting, water management and integrated solar power. The umbrella-canopy on the top of the Stupa Gallery is both a powerfully iconic form (evoking ancient canopy forms) and a roof for the amphitheatre. Amphitheatres are well rooted in ancient Buddhist architecture. One surviving example is at the Buddhist archaeological site of Nagarjunakonda, Andra Pradesh, which inspired the one in this design.

12

BEING AT
THE STUDIO

At Pakhalé's studio, the focus is never on the past as something to long for,

or on the future as something to reach.

In fact, there is no need to talk about past, present or future, since we can never really separate them.

What matters is the process, the action in the specific moment.

Wera Selenowa

BEING AT THE STUDIO
Wera Selenowa

Behind every daily action, behind what we do and how we do it, lies not only what we *are* in that specific moment, but also what we will *become*. Nothing is ever static, but in flux; and everyday actions lead to the making of the future. The idea of creating the future is incorporated in the actions of the present. Being is a state of unceasingly becoming. Paraphrasing John Dewey, experience is cumulative and it acquires expression thanks to this cumulative continuity. It is about living in the present with awareness as a process of being and becoming, with no reason to glorify the past or chase the future.

Experiencing daily life at Pakhalé's studio, it is clear that the focus is never on the past as something to long for, or the future as something to reach. In fact, there is no need to talk about past, present or future, since we can never really separate them. What matters is the process, the action in the specific moment, or better yet the journey of those actions inside which the notion of being and becoming refines itself.

A Way of Living

If you ask Pakhalé what design is, he will simply say it is 'a way of living' or 'just like breathing'. In his everyday design practice, Pakhalé looks at the world with curiosity and humility, thinking critically, and trusting only in direct knowledge grounded in experiential reality. He is informed by the Kālāma Sutta, which recommends avoiding 'blind faith and belief spawned from specious reasoning and its encouragement of free inquiry; the spirit of the sutta signifies a teaching that is exempt from fanaticism, bigotry, dogmatism, and intolerance'[1].

> *Do not believe in anything (simply) because you have heard it.*
> *Do not believe in traditions blindly because they have been handed down for many generations.*
> *Do not believe in anything because it is spoken and rumoured by many.*
> *Do not believe in anything (simply) because it is found written in your religious books.*
> *Do not believe in anything merely on the authority of your teachers and elders.*

---

[1] Tathāgata, *Kālāma Sutta, Anguttara Nikaya, Vol 1,188-193 PTS Ed.* The Buddha's Charter of Free Inquiry, translated from the Pali by Soma Thera, 1994.

But after observation and analysis, when you find anything that agrees with reason and is conducive to the good and benefit of one and all then accept it and live up to it.

Tathāgata (Anguttara Nikaya, Vol 1)
These five annotations are a summary of the ten expositions of the Kessaputtiya Sutta, popularly known as Kālāma Sutta.
— Kālāma Sutta

With this in mind, Pakhalé approaches the age-old field of creation and the story of human making in a fresh way. He looks at object creation in depth and with a non-conformist mindset. These are his only maxims when bringing his design projects into being.

Culture of Creation

One cannot fail to notice that Pakhalé seems to be intuitively aware of how design influences the human condition. His studio's everyday activities, gestures, critical thinking and cultivation of curiosity are all important components that nurture each other and animate life there. They are the constituents of a highly sensorial process, the foundation of a 'studio culture' or, as Pakhalé calls it, a 'culture of creation'. His approach to creation is deliberately artisan-like, even though he has mastered technology and is adept at using everything from state-of-the-art 3D CAD, to CNC, to 3D printing. In each project, he thinks deeply about every aspect of learning, researching and observing and then starts sketching, making 3D CAD drawings, sketch modelling along the way and then model-making and prototyping to reality before going back to thinking, drawing and sketching again, until he arrives at a satisfactory result. The process of experimentation, design, testing and execution is a sort of circular, cyclical process of thinking, sketching, making and back again.

This 'choreography of creating' is supported by meetings, presentations, documentation and sharing ideas over a meal with the team and collaborators. Experiencing materials is one of the active driving forces in the process of building the studio's culture of creation. Since the foundation of his studio in 1998, Pakhalé has cultivated this culture, refined it and made it part of each day's studio practice.

A

B

C

Why Design?

The synthesis between being and becoming is embodied in objects that belong not to this or that time, but to general human existence, while celebrating every day the dignity that design is meant to give human life. The culture of creation is the place of making, thinking, discussing, acting, contemplating, pondering, questioning and more. These are nurtured by continuous, tireless research at the roots of the meaning of creation. Why design? Why create? Pakhalé would say. That cumulative continuity, which brings expressiveness, manifests itself in the culture of creation: in the scheme of topics and subjects of investigation brought into the discussion as the direct consequence of everyday actions and gestures. Concepts involving atmosphere, poetic analogy, sensoriality, social modernity, technology and the culture of making are at the core of this thinking. All these themes are closely connected and are vital for the continuous development of the studio's culture of creation. Woven together through thinking and making, these topics are part of being, while becoming is still patiently shaping itself from within.

Observing and acquiring more knowledge and experience is one of the ongoing actions at the studio, leading to many discussions and an overarching, deeper insight into the human condition through all the topics brought into the conversation. Apparently contradictory ideas and paradoxes are nourished in the studio - discussed, thought through and cultivated further.

Something Magical

This cultivation of mind and critical thinking is supported by Pakhalé's drawings and watercolour sketches – which make room for something magical to happen – as well as models which go from physical modelling to three-dimensional digital drawings and vice versa. Indeed, being aware of the possibilities and limitations of 3D CAD modelling software, Pakhalé has cultivated a studio culture with constant attention to perception as the source of an experiential reality, alternating continuously between visual thinking, physical modelling and experience.

He accompanies every phase of a project, never forgetting that the goal is a final product that is able to speak to all the senses of the end-user. He himself therefore experiences the new reality created through his design and the sensorial effect of his output

A First-floor open studio space with shoji-inspired sliding doors at Pakhalé's studio, Amsterdam, NL. Courtesy: Satyendra Pakhalé Archives, Amsterdam, NL.

B Pakhalé's personal space filled with objects and curiosities collected from around the world. Courtesy: Satyendra Pakhalé Archives, Amsterdam, NL.

C First floor studio space. A long shelving system filled with numerous study models at Pakhalé's studio, Amsterdam, NL. Courtesy: Satyendra Pakhalé Archives, Amsterdam, NL.

No limitation should be given to the birth of an idea.

Wera Selenowa

in the studio. With the support of his team, collaborators and industries, he constantly questions the possibilities of improvement. In doing so, he does not merely look at the object, but he also seeks to generate atmospheres through objects. In this way, every single aspect of a given project is precisely controlled, ensuring an appropriately proportioned and meaningful result. The object becomes a presence that fills the space with both physical and immaterial boundaries. In addition, even if technology in a broad sense plays a leading role in Pakhalé's design projects, it is never dominant in the perception of the final result. Rather, technology is an essential assistant, which cannot be shown merely for its own sake.

The core of every project for Pakhalé is how to arrive at a deep insight into the project requirements and the inter-being of projects within the studio context as well as via the external collaborative partner – whether an industrial manufacturer, artisan, or cultural or educational institution. The intent is to create a refreshing approach to innovation, diligence, and aesthetic consistency with contemporary expression. Every project carried out in the studio is endowed with the commitment and determination to innovate and push boundaries.

Inside the Space

Pakhalé's studio is organized and designed as a creative environment reflecting all these positive energies. The industrial space that used to be a fur-making factory, and later a woodworking shop and office, is an unassuming place. Passing by on the Zeeburgerpad, you would not notice it. The front door opens onto the staircase that takes you to the first floor. On entering the upstairs, the gloominess of the staircase is left behind with the welcoming feeling of an open space that is well lit with daylight from the ceiling and a glass frontage overlooking an Amsterdam canal, filling the interior with bright northern light. A long shelving system is filled with numerous study models of various scales and materials. The single open space allows the team and collaborators to enjoy and experience the creative activities happening there. The daily studio work becomes the dynamic scenography of every event and meeting. On one side of the space a set of computer desks runs perpendicular to the windows, with a short partition system designed and made at the studio making them visually disappear.

D   The open space at Pakhalé's studio first floor is filled with ever changing study models. Courtesy: Satyendra Pakhalé Archives, Amsterdam, NL.

E   Ground floor studio work space filled with hand tools and study models. Courtesy: Satyendra Pakhalé Archives, Amsterdam, NL.

F   Satyendra Pakhalé Archives, Amsterdam, NL on the ground floor of the studio space. Courtesy: Satyendra Pakhalé Archives, Amsterdam, NL.

Shelves filled with everchanging study models of current as well as older projects create the backdrop to the daily studio activities.

The elegant *shoji*-inspired sliding doors, designed by Pakhalé, conceal his personal space and lend a touch of mystery. With their wooden frames, translucent off-white textile and articulate handle details in saddle leather, the doors are typical of Pakhale's way of making bespoke objects for his personal use. Situated behind the large oval table of the studio director, they gently introduce visitors and collaborators to a wonderland – a space within a space – filled with objects and curiosities collected from Pakhalé's travels around the world. An entire wall from floor to ceiling gives space to the extended library with rare books acquired over the years. A bespoke desk, equipped with a watercolour kit and handmade paper, neatly occupies a corner space for the daily morning practice of watercolour sketching, providing the silence needed to focus on the thinking and contemplation.

The Journey as Reward

The studio is a serene space, a silent space filled with fresh light, enthusiasm and lots of energy. As you walk down the stairs to the ground floor, there is another kind of atmosphere. Here, it is possible to breathe the studio's projects in their process of evolution and continuous refinement. The entire space is full of prototypes, archives and models, some packed in wooden crates ready to be shipped to industrial partners or exhibitions. No machines populate the space; most of the tools are hand tools. As Pakhalé says, 'We do not want to limit our thinking with any one type of technology or given machines facilities. We want to be free and allow the hand to connect to the mind and senses and be immersed in the process of creation'. No limitation should be given to the birth of an idea.

The studio's culture of creation is animated by enthusiasm and idealism that creates the conditions for closely working together and cultivating the mind in order to further collective development. Every activity is carried out with passion and an awareness of the impact of our actions and the responsibilities they bring. There is a subtle seriousness here, yet also the joy of creation and of sharing the challenges and results with collaborators and the rest of the world. After two decades, the studio practice is still evolving. The journey is the reward.

CONTENT

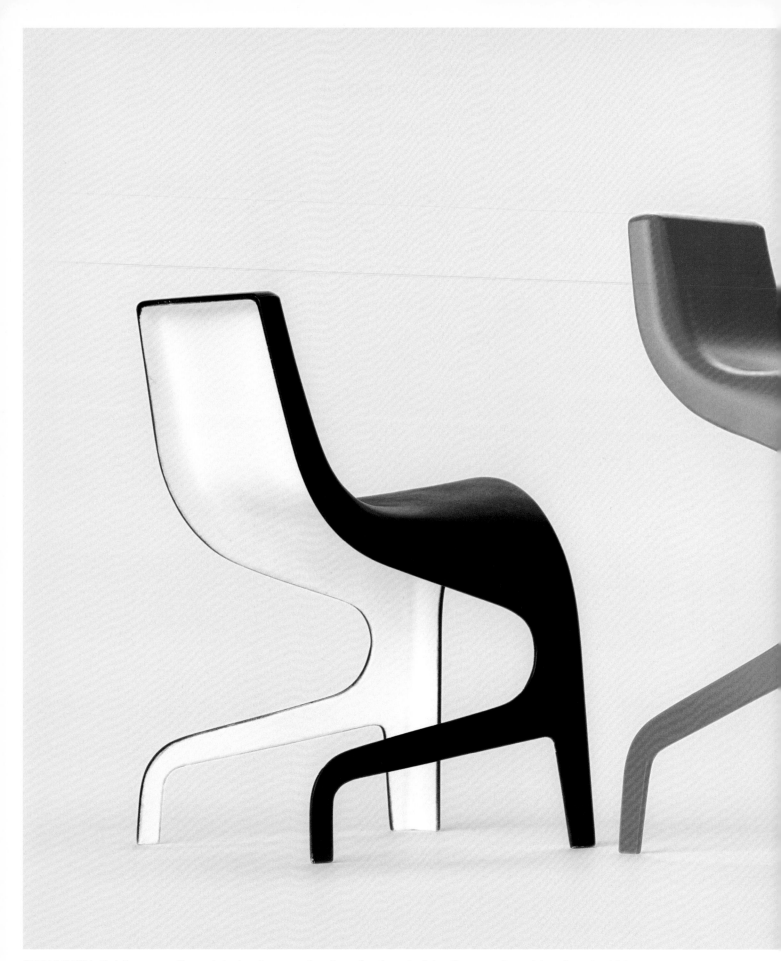

INSELLA FAMILY — Body language and human behaviour change over time. Currently active and collaborative spaces demand dynamic seating. While working on an architecture project, Pakhalé designed the InSella Chair for such a space to encourage interactive behaviour among users. The InSella Chair has a saddle-like seat for a casual body posture for informal sitting. It is a chair for lounges, university cafeterias and dynamic co-working spaces. The InSella Chair sparked a family of three active sitting typologies with seating heights of 45 cm (regular seating), 60 cm (active seating), and 80 cm (bar stool seating). The InSella Family is designed for contract projects which often require stackable chairs. It encourages a dynamic sitting posture, as if in a riding saddle – hence the name InSella.

01

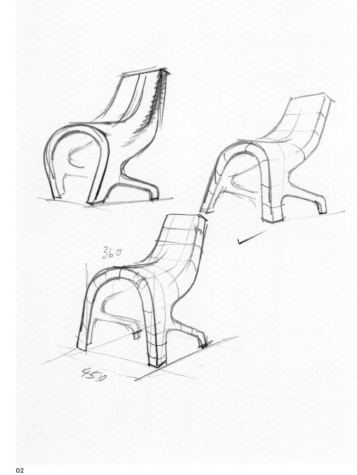

02

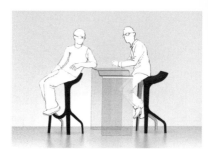

A

B

C

D

E

A   Study of human behaviour, postures and body language affected by the built environment. Pakhalé has carried out elaborate research on this topic.

B-D   InSella Family study models being made at Pakhalé's studio.

E   Double injection moulding being considered for the InSella Family.

INSELLA FAMILY

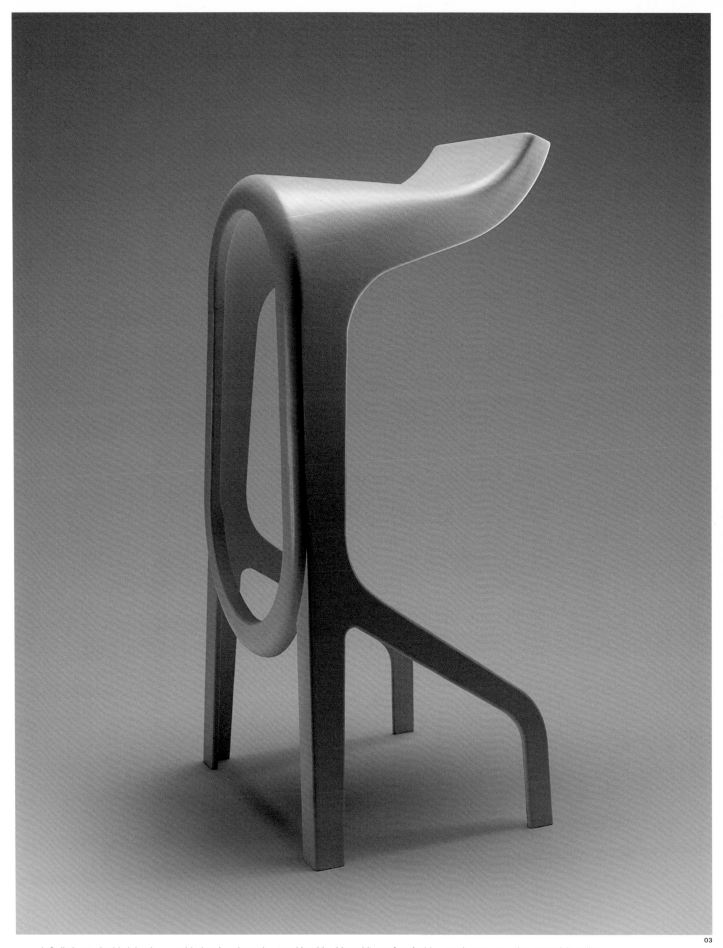

03

01 InSella has a double injection-moulded, soft-coloured outer skin with with a white surface inside, creating an evocative sensorial quality.
02 Design sketch for the InSella Chair by Pakhalé.
03 The footrest is integrated into the body of the InSella Bar Stool, creating a unique identity.

VIRCHOW 16 — A former chemical production plant is being transformed into the state-of-the-art R&D and management campus and HQ of healthcare company Novartis, Basel, Switzerland. Based on a master plan created by Vittorio Magnago Lampugnani, the campus has unique architecture by some of the world's most prominent architects, including Alvaro Siza, Frank Gehry, Fumihiko Maki, SANAA and Diener & Diener. Satyendra Pakhalé was invited by Rahul Merhotra to conceptualize the meeting, waiting and in-between spaces to enhance cross-disciplinary collaboration and so facilitate innovation in the advanced research centre: Virchow 16. With a dual structure, it has five floors of lab zones set alongside six floors of offices, meeting zones and technical services. Pakhalé researched the challenges of facilitating collaborative working conditions and

conceived various architectural spaces by addressing the needs of the centre within the multifunctional laboratory building with its focus on molecular biochemistry research. Pakhalé designed accessible collaborative spaces on various floors. These included the East Meeting Room on the ground floor, the waiting spaces on the first floor, quiet spaces, meeting spaces, in-between spaces, cafeteria and coffee areas, lounge areas, private rooms, the library and signage. Pakhalé's interior architectural design reflects the contemporary and future interpretation of the lab and ways of collaborating among teams and professionals from various disciplines. Through the inclusion of in-between spaces to facilitate the collision of ideas, a healthy, human and accessible atmosphere is created and a distinctive research space evolves.

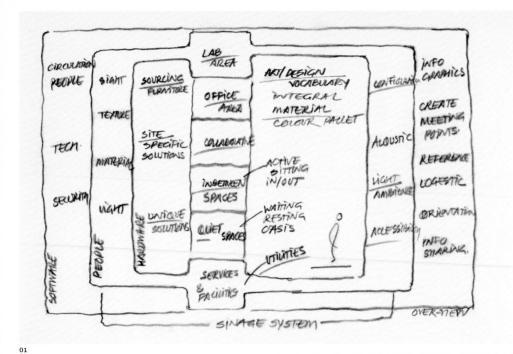

01

A

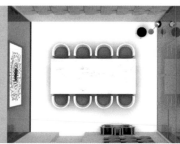

B

C

D

E

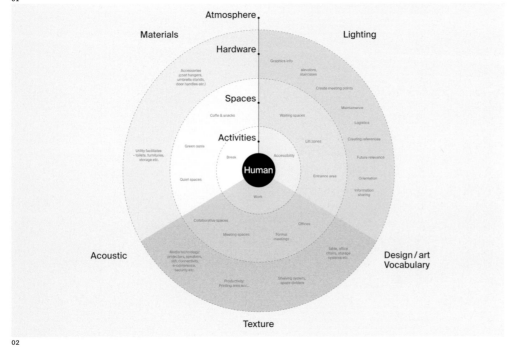

02

01   Design analysis sketch by Satyendra Pakhalé illustrating the complexity and multiplicity of the collaborative working conditions analysed from the point of view of people, software, hardware and activities. This led to the conception of various architectural spaces that address the needs and near-future development of the research centre within the building with its focus on research into molecular biochemistry.

02   Design analysis diagram by Pakhalé of the workings of the multi-faceted research laboratory. The open space in the architecture allowed for flexible layouts of furniture and objects, encouraging creative encounters among users.

03

04

A–K Study layouts of the East Meeting Room, waiting spaces, meeting spaces and in-between spaces carried out during the design process.

03 The Conference Room on the fifth floor hosts 20 people with extra seating options for board members, partners and collaborators.
04 The video conference room on the ground floor is designed for frequent use.

05

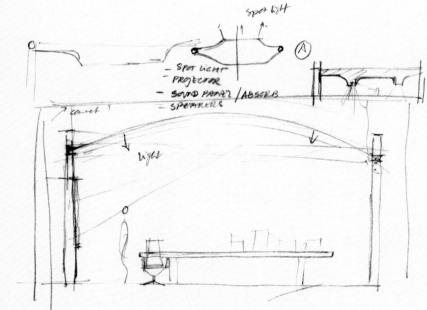

06

05   The East Meeting Room on the ground floor is a fully equipped conference room for formal business meetings with a state-of-the-art, three-dimensional display and ceiling roof with integral dynamic lighting and video conferencing. Ancient sculptures selected from the Novartis art collection are on display.

06   Design sketch by Satyendra Pakhalé illustrating the main conference room lighting integrated in the ceiling and storage column and the large board meeting table in wood with marble base with an in-built, high resolution display.

F

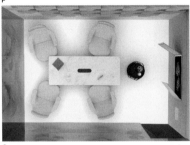

G

H

I

J

K

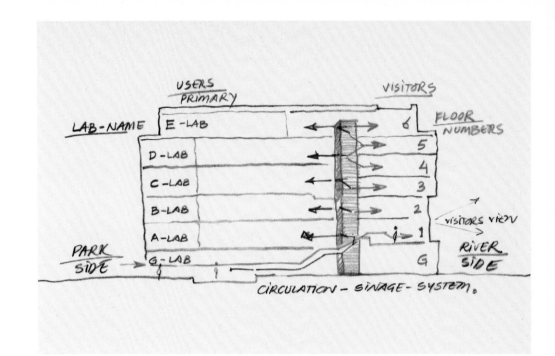

07

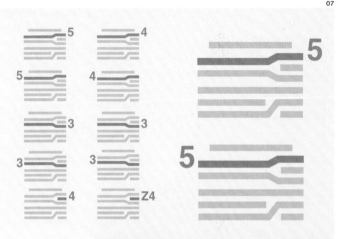

08

09

07 Design sketch of the signage system for orientation and circulation throughout the architectural space.

08, 09 Pakhalé's schematic and graphic orientation solution evolved from the architecture programme, leading to the signage system. The office levels are numbered as floors from ground floor up to the sixth floor. This is easy and logical for the users to understand. On the lab side there are five floors named as A, B, C, D and E, so creating a distinct nomenclature to avoid any confusion.

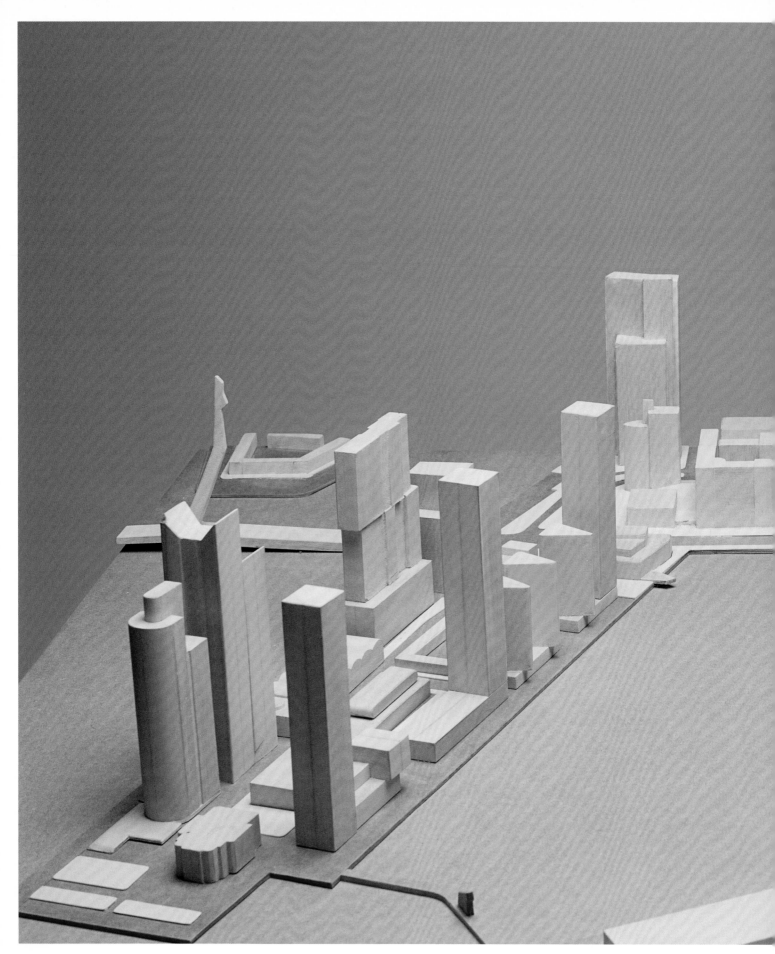

KOP CONNECT — The Kop van Zuid is a new neighbourhood in Rotterdam, located on the south bank of the Nieuwe Maas opposite the centre of the city. The transformation of this disused port area into an urban neighbourhood and its high-speed connections to European capitals will make Kop van Zuid an important destination. Some of the world's prominent architects, including Renzo Piano, Alvaro Siza, Francine Houben, Norman Foster and Rem Koolhaas, have created unique architecture on this waterfront. Didier Unglik of L'Etoile Properties invited Satyendra Pakhalé and Jouin Manku, Paris, to study the Rijnhaven area of Kop van Zuid to contribute to the overall concept of the project. Together with L'Etoile Properties and Jouin Manku, Pakhalé created a mixed-use programme for the House of Design, consisting of curated international design

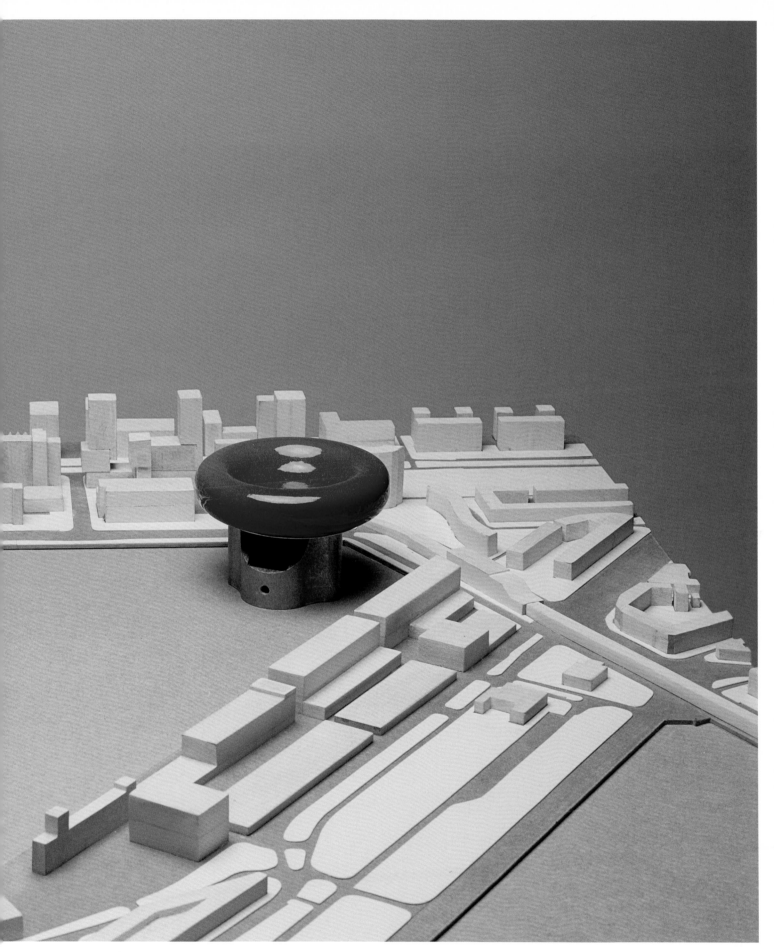

stores, waterfront public spaces, restaurants and cafés, terraced apartments, offices and facilities and a community learning centre for children with design at its core. Pakhalé further developed an architectural design concept, The Pearl of Kop van Zuid, with its programme under and above water level, will lend it a distinct identity.

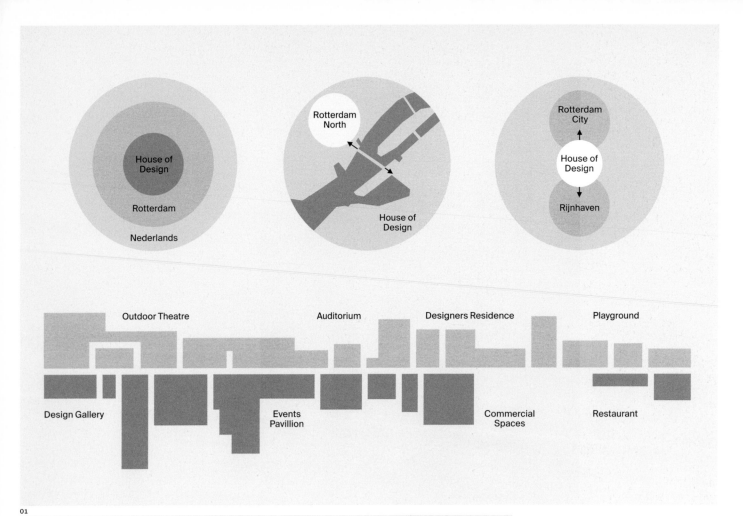

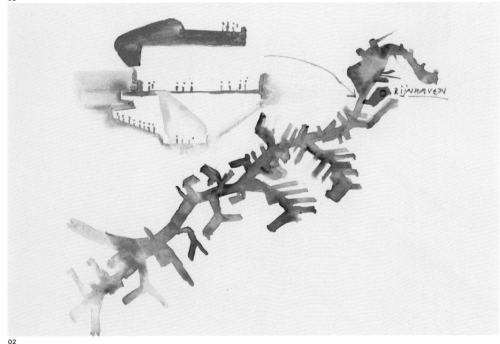

01, 02 Urban study showing how thanks to the high-speed trains passing through Rotterdam Central, Kop van Zuid will be directly connected to Brussels, Lille, Paris and London.
03, 04 Kop-Connect architectural concept sketch and model showing the 'Pearl' of Kop van Zuid seen from the Erasmusbrug Rotterdam.
05, 06 Watercolour sketches by Satyendra Pakhalé illustrating the concept of the 'Pearl' of Kop van Zuid, Rotterdam.

KOP CONNECT

A–F　Various models of the 'Pearl' of Kop van Zuid being studied at Pakhalé's studio.

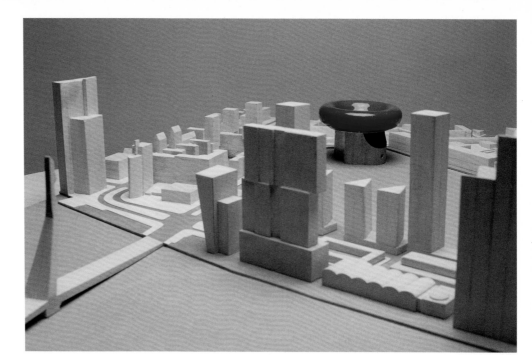

03

04

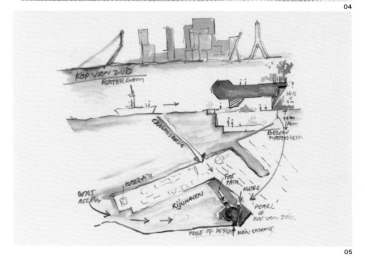

05

BRAND HARMONIZATION — Over 100 years old, the Swiss Franke Group comprises Franke Kitchen Systems, Foodservice Systems, Washroom Systems, Coffee Systems and Beverage Systems. Having manufacturing facilities in Europe, South and North America, Africa, Australia and Asia creates its own challenges as discrepancies in materials, product categories and shapes generate too many options for the Franke brand logo and its placement on the products. In particular, Franke Kitchen Systems with its product range of hoods, sinks, extractors, tops, stoves and ovens lacks a consistent brand logo. Massimo Vismara of Franke invited Satyendra Pakhalé to design and develop a new way to brand Franke products. The design problem at hand was twofold: the inconsistent manufacturing process (which had to be reduced to one or two

01

02

03

processes and materials); and the need to prevent the logo appearing too many times on a given product system. Pakhalé and his team researched all the Franke product types, the way the brand logo was applied and the type of manufacturing process used for production in order to simplify the logo and its application. Pakhalé designed a simple and elegant system solution that resolves the problem of multi-complex manufacturing and application of the diversity of logos on various Franke product lines. He solved the twofold issue and designed a contemporary Franke logo and Franke mark, what he calls the 'Franke Jewel', and so harmonized the brand.

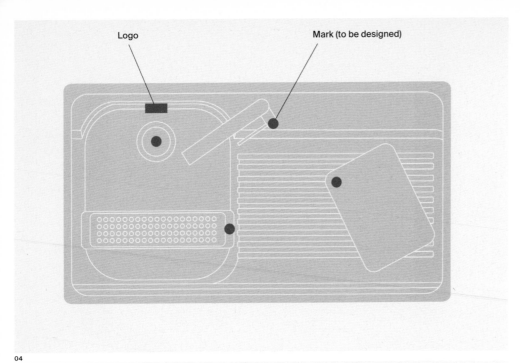

Logo   Mark (to be designed)

04

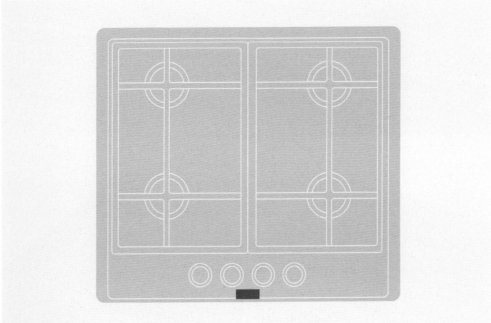

05

01–03 The Franke Logo on various materials such as wood, metal, plastics and Corian.
04, 05 Illustrations showing how the Franke logo and Franke mark can be applied to create a sophisticated image without being repeated on several adjoining products.
07, 08 Design sketch and design solutions for the Franke logo and the Franke mark by Pakhalé. These create a coherent image and simplify the logistic issues related to the manufacturing processes. By solving both the design challenges and re-designing the Franke logo with a contemporary language.

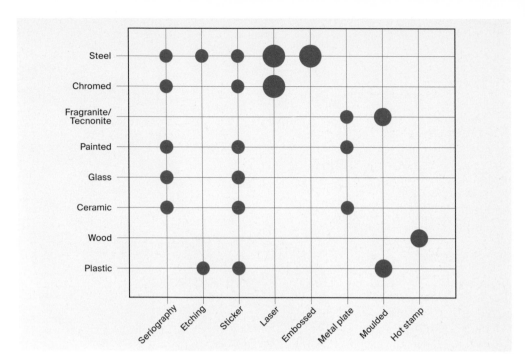

06

07

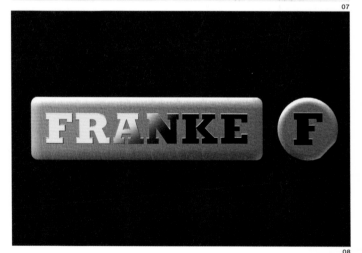

08

A–D   Franke management and product development team discussing the logo applications with Pakhalé.

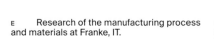

E   Research of the manufacturing process and materials at Franke, IT.

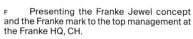

F   Presenting the Franke Jewel concept and the Franke mark to the top management at the Franke HQ, CH.

PANTHER — This monumental multi-chair was designed to celebrate the golden jubilee of Moroso, Italy. On the invitation of Patrizia Moroso, Pakhalé created a piece that entices the user to try out various postures – sitting, lounging, reclining – and therefore exudes playfulness. A typological innovation, Panther combines three sitting positions in a single, sinuous form that also evokes a leaping panther. 'We often neglect the basic necessities of life in the course of a hectic working day,' explains Pakhalé. 'Panther is intended to make us aware of our existence and to take time for contemplation and deep breathing.' The first edition of Panther was made in upholstered textile and the subsequent editions in fibreglass.

A

B

C

D

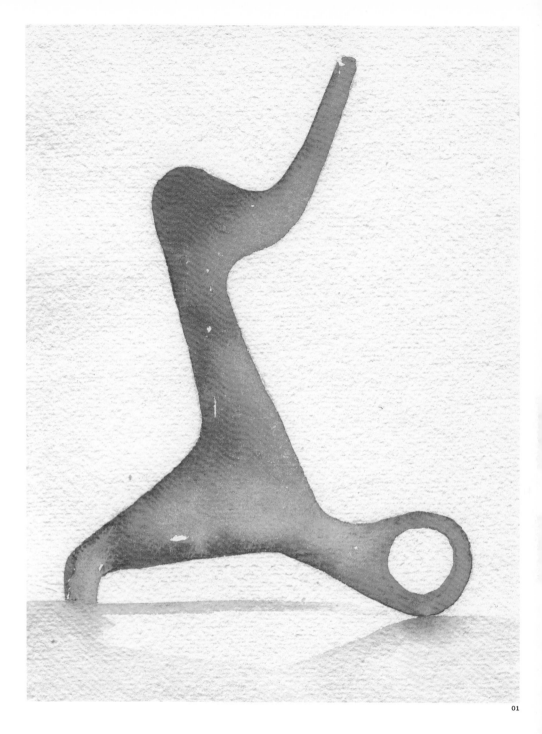

01

A, B   Panther scale 1:3 cast in bronze. Panther multi-chair exhibited at *Satyendra Pakhalé Design by Heart*, solo exhibition at Gallery Otto, Bologna, IT.

C, D   Panther mould in fibreglass. Giulio Castelli, Founder of Kartell, IT, and Sebastian Bergne, industrial designer, UK, on Panther at Gallery Otto, Bologna, IT.

01   Panther watercolour sketch by Pakhalé.

LIMITED EDITION

GRIP SATELLITE TABLE — Why reinvent the wheel when you can add a handle instead? Grip Satellite Table is created to make our lives easier in everyday scenarios. Pakhalé compares the table to a satellite that can orbit in a domestic or office setting and be moved from place to place – at work, by the sofa, indoors or outdoors. Pakhalé: 'We are all in a state of flux, responding to the contemporary nomadic state of our domestic and work locations. I created a side table which can be used in all sorts of scenarios – a spontaneous meeting, a coffee with a colleague or enjoy reading a book in the course of a busy day.' Grip Satellite Table is made of Corian, chosen for its hygienic properties, stability and durability.

A

B

C

01

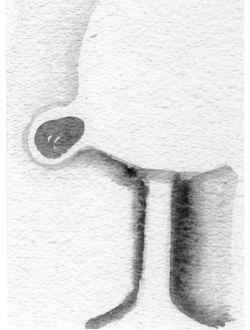

02

A   Checking the first working prototypes. Spontaneous meeting in the car park just before Pakhalé gave a keynote at Design Boost 2008, Malmö, SE.

B, C   Pakhalé explains a design detail to Anders Englund, design manager and founding partner of Offecct, Sweden. First prototypes.

01, 02   Grip Satellite table and a watercolour sketch by Pakhalé.

A DAILY PRACTICE

Satyendra Pakhalé is constantly sketching, using whatever materials are at hand – perhaps his favourite Apsara 6B graphite pencil, or the watercolour kit he made for himself. The Satyendra Pakhalé Archives contain several elaborately drawn portraits in pen and ink as well as several spontaneous studies made on restaurant paper mats and napkins. He started drawing as a child and has never stopped.

When he set up his studio, Pakhalé also began a daily practice of painting a watercolour on handmade cotton paper using just one brush. Within these self-imposed limits – basic tools, a paper size of 12.5 × 17.5 cm and a single truncated brush – the idea is to focus on the practice of 'thinking through abstraction'. In his watercolour sketches, we can follow a process of free exploration, watch the realm of 'poetic analogies' taking shape, and (sometimes) glimpse the form of a specific project emerging from them. The selected watercolours on the following pages illustrate Pakhalé's daily habit of letting go of the control of the rational mindset and surrendering instead to intuition and unconscious foresight.

01

01   13 July 2015, Watercolour on Pondicherry handmade cotton rag paper, 12.5 × 17.5 cm
02   13 January 2017, Indian ink on Pondicherry handmade cotton rag paper, 12.5 × 17.5 cm

02

A DAILY PRACTICE SATYENDRA PAKHALÉ

03

03   14 January 2015, Watercolour on Pondicherry handmade cotton rag paper, 12.5 × 17.5 cm
04   03 May 2013, Watercolour on Pondicherry handmade cotton rag paper, 12.5 × 17.5 cm

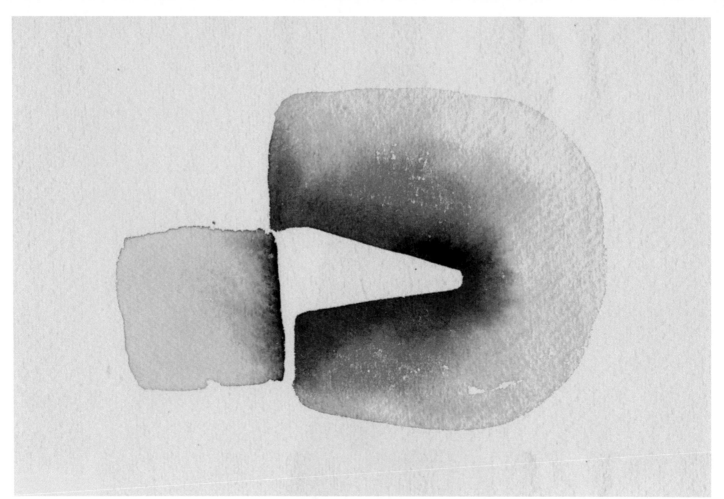

A DAILY PRACTICE

05

05   14 July 2015, Indian ink on handmade natural paper mottled with colour cotton fibres, 21 × 30.3 cm
06   15 July 2015, Watercolour on Pondicherry handmade cotton rag paper, 12.5 × 17.5 cm

A DAILY PRACTICE SATYENDRA PAKHALÉ

07

07   06 March 2005, Red ink on Pondicherry handmade cotton rag paper, 12.5 × 17.5 cm
08   16 August 2016, Watercolour on Pondicherry handmade cotton rag paper, 12.5 × 17.5 cm

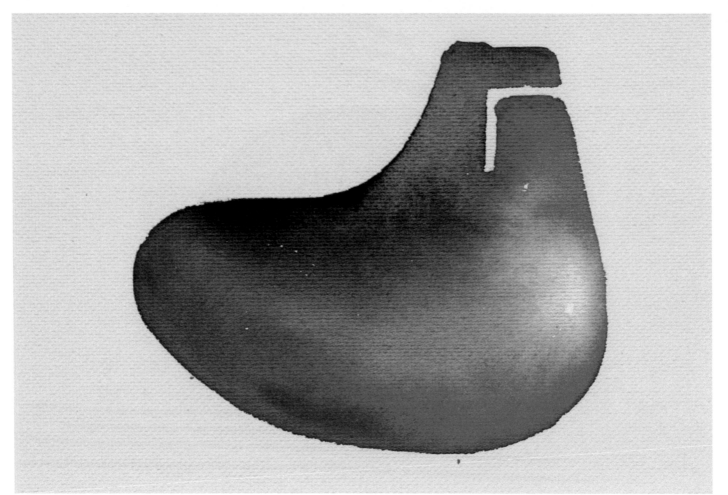

08

A DAILY PRACTICE

SATYENDRA PAKHALÉ

09

09   26 August 2011, Indian ink on recycled paper, 10.5 × 14.5 cm
10   06 July 2016, Watercolour on Pondicherry handmade cotton rag paper, 12.5 × 17.5 cm

A DAILY PRACTICE   SATYENDRA PAKHALÉ   410

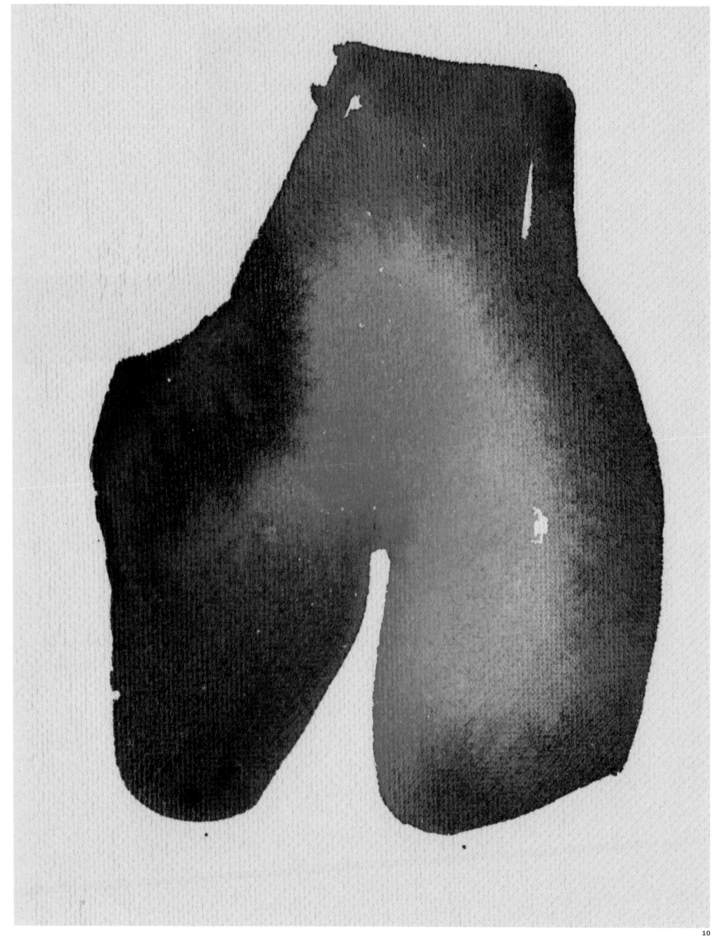

A DAILY PRACTICE

SATYENDRA PAKHALÉ

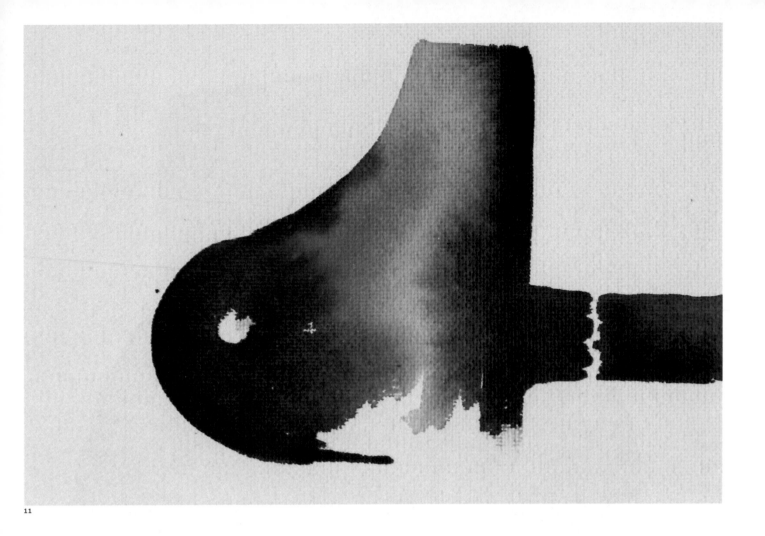

11

11   23 August 2016, Watercolour on Pondicherry handmade cotton rag paper, 12.5 × 17.5 cm
12   20 August 2017, Watercolour on Pondicherry handmade cotton rag paper, 12.5 × 17.5 cm

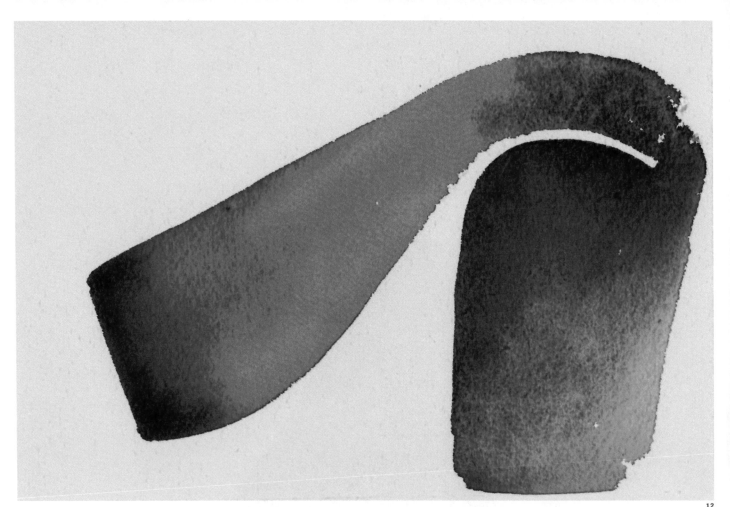

A DAILY PRACTICE

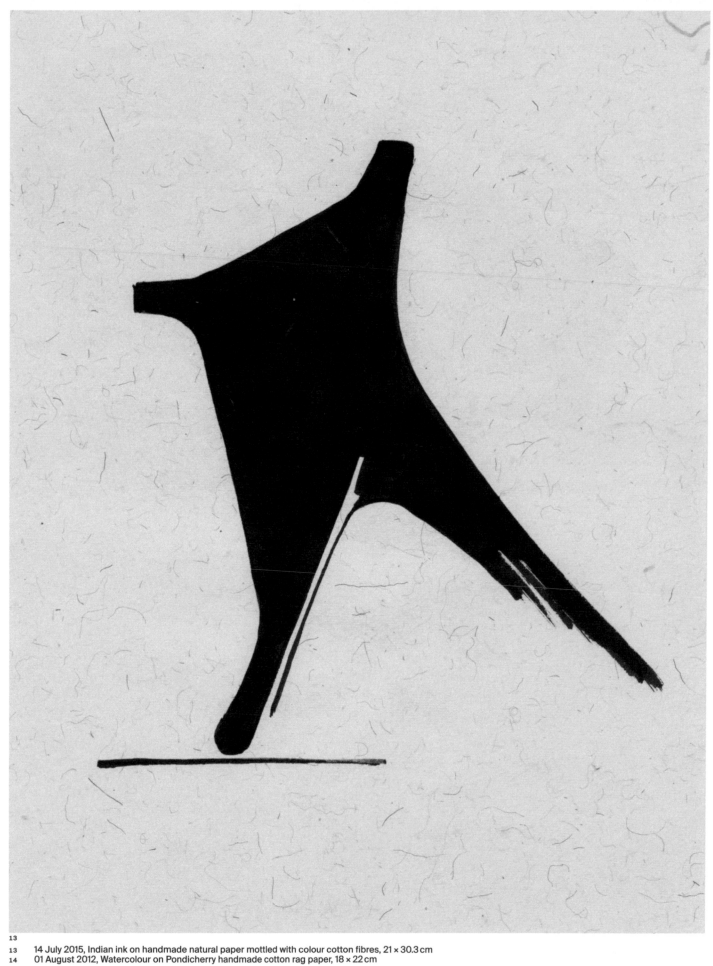

13

13 14 July 2015, Indian ink on handmade natural paper mottled with colour cotton fibres, 21 × 30.3 cm
14 01 August 2012, Watercolour on Pondicherry handmade cotton rag paper, 18 × 22 cm

14

A DAILY PRACTICE

CHRONOLOGY OF SELECTED WORKS

When I first met Satyendra Pakhalé, in 2001, he was spending a few months at the European Ceramic Work Centre (EKWC) in 's-Hertogenbosch, the Netherlands. Its director, my husband Koos de Jong, drew my attention to his work, and I was immediately intrigued. Assisted by the technical staff of the EKWC, Pakhalé was pushing the boundaries of ceramic design by developing chairs that are technically advanced while simultaneously relating to the language of craft. Although he never associated himself with the Droog Design platform that had been a strong force in the Netherlands since the mid-1990s, with this combination of high- and low-tech he definitely had something in common with several of the most important representatives of the Dutch design movement, including Marcel Wanders and Hella Jongerius. Pakhalé's ceramic chairs also reveal a symbolic language that hints at ritual offerings. With this, he was adding something profoundly intriguing and idiosyncratic to his designs.

As I had just started working at the Stedelijk Museum in Amsterdam as an industrial-design curator, I was looking for work by interesting young designers that could be shown in the museum. So I decided to organize the first solo museum exhibition of Pakhalé's work, called *From Projects to Products* in 2002. I have been following his career ever since.

From the beginning, Pakhalé has undertaken a wide range of projects with varied typologies and complexities. In the early years of his career, while at frog Design and subsequently at Philips Design, he worked mostly in the realm of high-tech industrial design. He produced innovative concepts for appliances, including the future-driven interior of a concept car in cooperation with Renault Design. Before training as an industrial designer in India and Switzerland, Pakhalé had trained as an engineer, which turned out to be of great advantage when working on such assignments. In the late 1990s, around the time he was establishing his own studio in Amsterdam, he developed a more personal design language by combining his sound technical knowledge with his ability to develop forms and meanings rooted in different cultures.

Influences of the social modernist legacy of Ulm, that came to him via Professor Sudhakar Nadkarni at the Industrial

Design Centre in Mumbai (who was himself trained by Dutch designer Hans Gugelot at the HfG in Ulm), of the culturally rich designs of Italian designer Ettore Sottsass Jr. (who used concepts of many compass points including India in his work), and of the internationalization of the design field – these all led to the multifaceted designer with a universal interest and human approach that Pakhalé is now. A true cultural nomad.

Over the years, he has created a remarkably broad oeuvre. It ranges from architectural design, interiors, exhibition concepts, appliances and table-top objects and furniture to toys – and from industrially manufactured pieces designed for the world's leading companies to one-offs and edition pieces for galleries. He works in almost every material you can think of: glass, ceramics, plastics, metals, leather and wood.

I detect great perseverance in his working method. Starting with research, it leads to sketches in pencil or watercolour, and then making models – either in his own studio, or having them 3D-printed. He can work for years on the development of a specific design before he is really happy with the result, meaning that he can have the pieces made by craftsmen around the world or develops the prototypes for the industrial pieces in cooperation with manufacturers' R&D departments. Typically, he does not let go when, for some reason, the piece cannot yet be produced.

All these qualities – his cultural sensibilities, perseverance, thorough research, technical insight, a great feeling for the symbolism of forms, and an ability to make use of inspirations from different backgrounds – are used by Pakhalé when teaching, too. With this profile he can inspire students to develop their own personal language. This has led to regular teaching posts, workshops and lectures at universities and tech conferences around the world. The Design Academy Eindhoven in the Netherlands invited him to devise and head the Master's programme in Design for Humanity and Sustainable Living from 2006 to 2010.

With a background rooted in different cultures, a multi-facetted way of working and cooperations around the world, Pakhalé is an interesting example of the very international design community of the past decades.

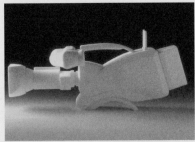

BTS-PROFESSIONAL-CAMERA — 1995,
Industrial Design, Philips Design, NL,
In production 1997, Die-cast aluminium,
35 × 26 × 17 cm

FRUITA — 1995, Industrial Design,
SP Archives, Slipcasting ceramic,
12 × 12 × 24 cm

3D PC FOR STUDENTS — 1995, Industrial
Design, Philips Design, NL, SP Archives,
Injection moulded plastics with aluminium
stand, 57 × 35 × 15 cm

FISH CHAIR — 1996, Industrial Design,
Commissioned by Cappellini, IT, In production
since 2005 Cappellini, IT, Rotomoulded
plastic, 55 × 87 × 72 cm

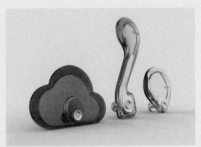

WATCH ME X - VISION ON MOVE — 1996,
Industrial Design, Philips Design, NL,
SP Archives, Injection moulded plastics with
metal sensors, Various

GARMENT PROJECT — 1996, Industrial Design, SP Archives, Wool, linen and cotton
tailored garments - Men's Shirt, Jacket and
Coat.

DIGITAL BUSINESS CARD — 1996, Industrial
Design, Philips Design, NL, SP Archives,
Injection moulded plastics, 6 × 9 × 0.25 cm

DIGAMAX — 1996, Industrial Design,
Commissioned by Verbatim, USA / Philips,
NL, SP Archives, Injection moulded plastics,
12.5 × 9.5 × 2 cm

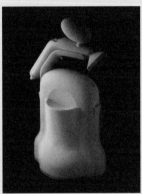

STEAM CLEANER PHILIPS — 1997, Industrial
Design, Philips Design, NL, SP Archives,
Injection moulded plastics, 19.5 × 12 × 29 cm

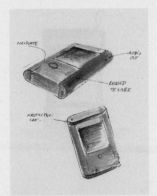

PHILIPS BG PORTABLE DIGITAL — 1997,
Industrial Design, Philips Design, NL,
SP Archives, Extruded and injection moulded
plastics, 8 × 12 × 1.5 cm

COPPER CHAIR — 1997, One-off, SP Archives,
Hand formed copper, 28 × 24 × 26 cm

PANGÉA CONCEPT CAR — 1997,
Transportation Design, Renault, France /
Philips Design, NL, Public Collection,
In production 1997, 458 × 182 × 208 cm,
196 × 182 × 208 cm

DIGITAL WALLET C-SAM — 1997, Industrial Design, Commissioned by C-SAM, USA, SP Archives, Injection moulded plastics, 12 × 9 × 1 cm

WINTER ASANA — 1997, Industrial Design, Commissioned by Habitat, UK, SP Archives, Upholstered with wooden structure inside, 82 × 89 × 97 cm

PINDOLA TABLE — 1997, Industrial Design, Commissioned by Zeritalia, IT, SP Archives, Industrial bent glass and aluminium, 140 × 86 × 75 cm

ANANDA TOTEMS — 1998, Industrial Design, SP Archives, Solid wood with flocked surface, Various

PANNA SPECTACLES — 1998, Industrial Design, Commissioned by Cottet, FR, SP Archives, Die-cast aluminium magnesium alloy, 15 × 15 × 5 cm

B.M. OBJECTS 1ST GENERATION — 1998, One-off, Public Collection, SP Archives, Bell metal lost wax casting process, Various

URBAN SCOOTER — 1999, Transportation Design, SP Archives, Injection moulded plastics and aluminium frame, 98 × 72 × 42 cm

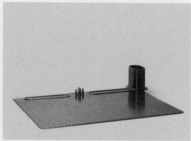

DESK MAT — 1999, Industrial Design, Commissioned by Magis, IT, Public Collection, SP Archives, Injection moulded plastic, 67 × 48 × 10 cm

B.M. HORSE — 2000, Limited Edition, ammann // gallery, DE, Public Collection, In production since 2007, Bell metal lost wax casting process, 52 × 80 × 95 cm

COPPER VASE — 2000, One-off, SP Archives, Hand formed copper, ⌀ 38 × 42 cm

H-OFF-MANN DESK — 2000, Industrial Design, Commissioned by For Example, IT, SP Archives, Industrial glass and wood, 130 × 65 × 75 cm

SURYA CALENDAR AND SUNDIAL — 2000, Industrial Design, SP Archives, Anodised formed aluminium and corian, ⌀ 20 × 6 cm

B.M. HORSE CHAISE — 2000, Limited Edition, ammann // gallery, DE, Private Collection, In production since 2008, Bell metal lost wax casting process, 137 × 59 × 82 cm

SQUARE WOODEN BOWLS — 2000, One-off, SP Archives, Solid carved tropical wood, 35 × 35 × 12 cm

S-SOFA — 2000, Industrial Design, Commissioned by Totem Design, USA, SP Archives, Upholstered with wooden structure and metal details, 196 × 86 × 82 cm

STEEL TRAY — 2000, Industrial Design, Commissioned by Alessi, IT, SP Archives, Deep drawn stainless steel, ∅ 67 × 3.8 cm

UTARAN — 2001, One-off, Private Collection, Autoclave embedded B.M. Objects in PMMA, 16 × 16 × 28 cm

FLOWER OFFERING CHAIR — 2001, Limited Edition, ammann // gallery, DE, Public Collection, In production since 2007, Slip casted ceramic, 69 × 65 × 85 cm

MINI FLOWER OFFERING CHAIR — 2001, Industrial Design, In production since 2009 Bosa Ceramiche, IT, Slip casted ceramic, 23 × 20 × 28 cm

GLOBE LAMP — 2001, Industrial Design, SP Archives, Wood, Mild steel, Molded globe, ∅ 56 × 105 cm

CERAMIC HORSE — 2001, One-off, SP Archives, High fired ceramic with special glazes, 52 × 80 × 95 cm

STAR HORSE — 2001, One-off, SP Archives, Flock surface with star constellation, 52 × 80 × 95 cm

EKWC - PLAYING WITH CLAY — 2001, One-off, SP Archives, High fired ceramic with special glazes, Various

KID CERAMIC CHAIR — 2001, One-off, SP Archives, High fired ceramic with special glazes, 32 × 38 × 56 cm

TAVA DINE, COFFEE DINE — 2001, Industrial Design, Commissioned by For Example, IT, SP Archives, Bent glass and wood, Various

POTTERY CHAIR — 2001, One-off, SP Archives, High fired hand thrown ceramics with terra sigillata surface finishing, 47.5 × 80 × 79 cm

BIRD CHAISE — 2001, One-off, Public Collection, Upholstered aluminium tubular structure, 167 × 46 × 92 cm

CANDLE HOLDER — 2002, Industrial Design, Commissioned by Alessi, IT, Private Collection, SP Archives, Deep drawn stainless steel, ⌀ 16 × 4.5 cm

STEELWAVE VASE — 2002, Industrial Design, Commissioned by Alessi, IT, Private Collection, SP Archives, Deep drawn stainless steel, ⌀ 22 × 30 cm

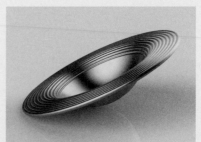

SATURN — 2002, Industrial Design, Commissioned by Alessi, IT, SP Archives, Deep drawn stainless steel, ⌀ 52 × 8 cm

KALPA VASE & BOWL — 2002, Industrial Design, Commissioned by Cor Unum Ceramics, NL, Public Collection, In production since 2002, Slip casted ceramic, 60 × 60 × 16 cm

AKASMA CENTREPIECE — 2002, Industrial Design, Commissioned by RSVP, IT, Public Collection, In production from 2002 to 2008, Industrial bent glass, Various

TAN-TABLE — 2002, Industrial Design, SP Archives, Industrial glass, rotomoulded plastic and aluminium

LAGORI - POST COMPUTER GAME — 2002, Industrial Design, Commissioned by Magis, IT, Public Collection, Injection moulded and blow moulded plastic, ⌀ 16 × 56 cm

PANTHER — 2002, Limited Edition, Commissioned by Moroso, IT, 2002, ammann // gallery, DE, 2007, Public Collection, In production since 2007, Upholstery with wooden structure, fibreglass, 147 × 58 × 196 cm

FLIP CHAIR — 2002, Industrial Design, SP Archives, Injection moulded polycarbonate, 98 × 60 × 80 cm

B.M. HORSE SIDE TABLE — 2002, Limited Edition, SP Archives, Bell metal lost wax casting process, ⌀ 40 × 42 cm, ⌀ 77 × 33 cm

SPICEBOX — 2002, Industrial Design, Commissioned by Alessi IT, SP Archives, Deep drawn steel, ⌀ 17.5 × 5 cm

FROM PROJECTS TO PRODUCTS — 2002, Solo Exhibition Design, Curated by Ingeborg de Roode, NL, Stedelijk Museum Amsterdam, NL

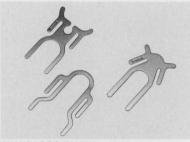

ANANDA BOOKMARKS — 2003, Industrial Design, Commissioned by DeVecchi, IT, SP Archives, Silver, Various

KID STOOL — 2003, Industrial Design, Commissioned by Magis, IT, SP Archives, Injection moulded plastic, ⌀ 60 × 58 cm

KID STEP — 2003, Industrial Design, Commissioned by Magis, IT, SP Archives, Plywood, injection moulded plastics, 46 × 36 × 35 cm

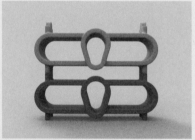

KID SHELF SYSTEM — 2003, Industrial Design, Commissioned by Magis, IT, SP Archives, Expanded polypropylene, 120 × 25 × 51 cm

ACHALA BASKETS — 2003, Industrial Design, Commissioned by C-lection, NL, SP Archives, Slip casted ceramic / Thermoformed Corian, Various

KID COMPUTER DESK CHAIR — 2003, Industrial Design, Commissioned by Magis, IT, SP Archives, Injection moulded plastic, 44 × 44 × 50 cm

SALT PEPPER BOTTLES — 2003, Industrial Design, Commissioned by Alessi, IT, SP Archives, Formed stainless steel and glass, ⌀ 8 × 17 cm

POUF — 2003, Industrial Design, SP Archives, Rotomoulded plastic, 36 × 34 × 58 cm

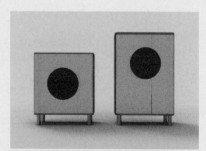

GLASS WARDROBE — 2003, Industrial Design, Commissioned by Zeritalia, IT, SP Archives, Industrial bent glass, 90 × 47 × 135 cm

BENT GLASS / PLYWOOD VASES AND TRAY
— 2003, Industrial Design, SP Archives,
Industrial bent glass / Plywood, Various

HIGH CHAIR — 2003, Industrial Design,
SP Archives, Expanded polypropylene,
50 × 74 × 77 cm

CITRUS PRESS — 2003, Industrial Design,
Commissioned by Alessi, IT, SP Archives,
Deep drawn stainless steel and slip casted
ceramic, Ø 16 × 12.5 cm

NUT CRACKER — 2003, Industrial Design,
SP Archives, Zamac-aluminium-zinc alloy,
3 × 3 × 19 cm

DOORHANDLE EXTRUSION — 2003,
Industrial Design, Commissioned by Erreti, IT,
SP Archives, Extruded aluminium,
14 × 7 × 5 cm

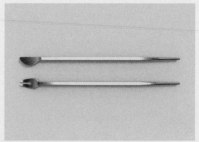

CHOPSTICKS — 2003, Industrial Design,
SP Archives, Forged Stainless steel,
1.5 × 0.5 × 30 cm

LOOP O2 MOBILE PHONE — 2003, Industrial
Design, Commissioned by O2, UK,
SP Archives, Metal forming and injection
moulded plastic, 5 × 2 × 8.5 cm

TOTEM CARPETS — 2003, Industrial Design,
Private Collection, SP Archives, Hand tuffted
carpets, Various

KID MULTI CHAIR — 2003, Industrial Design,
Commissioned by Magis, IT, SP Archives
Expanded polypropylene

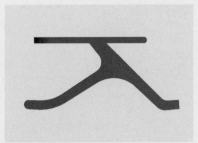

BIRD TABLE & CHAISE LONGUE — 2003,
Industrial Design, SP Archives, Rotomoulded
plastic, 167 × 44 × 81 cm

ROTO CHAIR — 2003, Industrial Design,
SP Archives, Rotomoulded plastic,
44 × 45 × 75.5 cm

AMSTERDAMMERTJE — 2003, One Off,
Commissioned by EKWC, NL, Public
Collection, SP Archives, High fired hand
thrown ceramics with glazed surface,
Ø 40 × 49 cm

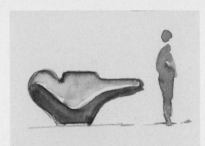

LC HAND CHAIR — 2003, Industrial Design, SP Archives, Upholstered with wooden structure and metal details, 80 × 97 × 75 cm

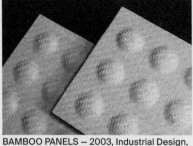

BAMBOO PANELS — 2003, Industrial Design, Commissioned by Government of Philippines, PHL, SP Archives, Hand-woven bamboo mat pressed on plyboo, 50 × 50 × 2.5 cm

KATAVA — 2003, Limited Edition, Commissioned by Erreti, IT, Private Collection, SP Archives, Aluminium sheet metal bent, 196 × 135 × 70 cm

PENDANT LAMP — 2003, Industrial Design, Commissioned by Established & Sons, UK, SP Archives, Deep drawn aluminium, 57 × 36 × 21 cm

CAN OPENER — 2003, Industrial Design, SP Archives, Injection moulded plastic with metal insert, 4 × 2 × 7.5 cm

DESIGN BY HEART - OTTO GALLERY — 2003, Solo Exhibition Design, Curated by Paola Antonelli, MoMA, New York, USA, Otto gallery Bologna, IT

ADD-ON RADIATOR — 2004, Industrial Design, Commissioned by TUBES Radiatori, IT, Public Collection, In production since 2004, Die-casted aluminium, 12 × 3 × 24 cm

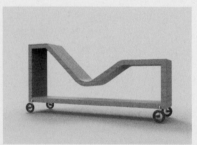

NAP CHAIR — 2004, Industrial Design, SP Archives, wood, 45 × 140 × 30 cm

PUZZLE CARPET — 2004, Industrial Design, Commissioned by Magis, IT, In production since 2005, Digitally printed PU, 36 × 36 × 1.5 cm

STEELWAVE FAMILY — 2004, Industrial Design, Commissioned by Alessi, IT, Private Collection, SP Archives, Deep drawn stainless steel, Various

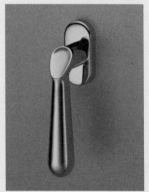

AMISA DOORHANDLE — 2004, Industrial Design, Commissioned by Colombo Design, IT, In production since 2004 to 2014, Die-casted brass, 13.5 × 10.5 × 5 cm

KID WALKER — 2004, Industrial Design, SP Archives, Wood and injection co-moulded wheel, 446 × 517 × 446 cm

KID WARDROBE — 2004, Industrial Design, Commissioned by Magis, IT, SP Archives, Plywood with gas injection moulded hinges and latches, 95 × 45 × 125 cm

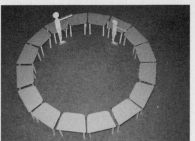

KID MULTI-TABLE — 2004, Industrial Design, Commissioned by Magis, IT, SP Archives, Injection moulded plastic with aluminim legs, 75 × 50 × 50 cm

BOWL SINGLE HANDLE — 2004, Industrial Design, Commissioned by Danese, IT, SP Archives, Ceramic slip casting, cork, 32 × 28.5 × 12.5 cm

DESKTOP LANDSCAPE — 2004, Industrial Design, Commissioned by De Vecchi, IT, SP Archives, Pneumatic formed metal, Various

AGMA TOY TROLLEY — 2004, Industrial Design, Commissioned by Magis, IT, SP Archives, Rotomoulded plastic and injection co-moulding, 70 × 49 × 63 cm

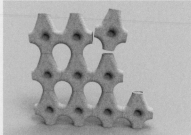

ARCHI ELEMENT — 2004, Industrial Design, SP Archives, Reinforced pre cast concrete, 48 × 12 × 58 cm

STEEL AND PLASTICS — 2004, Industrial Design, Commissioned by Tupperware, USA / BE, SP Archives, Composite metal plastic, 36 × 26 × 4 cm

PECOCK FAMILY — 2004, One Off, SP Archives, Paper Mache, Various

CELL PHONE — 2004, Industrial Design, SP Archives, Injection moulded plastic, Various

GARDEN LAMP — 2005, Industrial Design, Commissioned by Serralunga, IT, SP Archives, Rotomoulded plastic, 60 × 35 × 187 cm

KID TRONO — 2005, Industrial Design, Commissioned by Magis, IT, SP Archives, Rotomoulded plastic, 63 × 52 × 92 cm

TRAY TROLLEY — 2005, Industrial Design, Commissioned by Cappellini, IT, SP Archives, Reaction Injection Moulded PU with metal structure, 546 × 547 × 733 cm

LITTLE PANTHER — 2005, Industrial Design,
SP Archives, Injection moulded policarbonate
with wiremesh insert, 64.5 × 70 × 75 cm

ROYAL DIWANE — 2005, Industrial Design,
SP Archives, Rotomoulded plastic,
88.5 × 87 × 67 cm

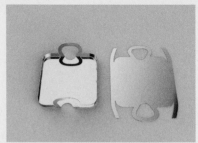

OFFICE TRAY — 2005, Industrial Design,
Commissioned by Danese, IT, SP Archives,
Laser cut and bent steel, 38.5 × 27 × 8 cm

MULTI-SENSORIAL SPEAKERS — 2005,
Industrial Design, SP Archives,
79 × 54.5 × 173 cm

FOUNTAIN PEN — 2005, Industrial Design,
SP Archives, Fabricated in metal and resin,
Ø 2.5 × 14.5 cm

KITCHEN TAPS — 2005, Industrial Design,
Commissioned by Nobili, IT, SP Archives,
Die-cast brass, 27 × 4.5 × 20 cm

UNIVERSAL FREEDOM TOWER 2031 — 2005,
Architecture, Commissioned by Domus
Magazine, IT, SP Archives, Pyongyang, DPRK

FISH TABLE — 2005, Industrial Design,
Commissioned by Cappellini, IT, SP Archives,
Rotomoulded plastic, 40 × 32 × 54.5 cm

Q-WATCH — 2005, Industrial Design,
Commissioned by CRAFT, FR, SP Archives,
Injection co-moulded technical ceramic,
Ø 4 × 0.8 cm

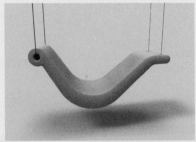

KID ROCKING CHAIR / SWING — 2005,
Industrial Design, Commissioned by Magis,
IT, SP Archives, Rotomoulded plastic,
100 × 42 × 42.5 cm

SANITATION - WC - BIDET - SINK — 2005,
Industrial Design, Commissioned by Flaminia,
IT, SP Archives, Ceramic slip casting, Various

OVEN TO TABLE VERSION 2 — 2005,
Industrial Design, SP Archives, Bent steel rod
with silicon handle detail, 35 × 18 × 13 cm

YMCA CHAIR — 2005, Industrial Design,
SP Archives, Wood, aluminium details,
65 × 73 × 84.5 cm

MEANDER TEXTILE — 2006, Industrial
Design, Commissioned by Vaeveriet, SE,
In production since 2006, Wool textile

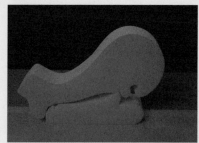

CITYSCAPE - LIMOGES PORCELAINE — 2006,
One-off, Commissioned by CRAFT, FR,
SP Archives, Slip casted porcelain, Various

VESPA REDESIGN — 2006, Industrial Design,
Commissioned by Made Magazine, IT,
SP Archives, 148 × 120 × 68 cm

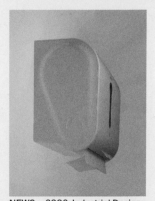

SQUARE MEAL — 2006, Industrial Design,
Commissioned by Design Biennal Saint-
Étienne, FR, In production since 2006,
Ceramic slip casting, 28.5 × 24 × 36 cm

SHELTER — 2006, Architecture, SP Archives,
Milan, IT, 481 × 297 × 519 cm

ALAYA CERAMIC BASKET — 2006, Industrial
Design, Commissioned by Bosa, IT,
In production since 2006, Ceramic slip
casting, Various

NEWS — 2006, Industrial Design,
Commissioned by Tork, SCA, SE, SP Archives,
Injection moulded plastic, Various

HORSE LAMP — 2006, One-off, SP Archives,
Bell metal lost wax casting process,
24 × 10 × 12 cm

PAK CHAIR — 2006, Industrial Design,
Commissioned by Magis, IT, SP Archives,
Spot-welded steel rod, 48 × 54 × 84 cm

DUST BIN — 2006, Industrial Design,
SP Archives, Injection moulded plastic,
27.5 × 30.5 × 43 cm

HI-SEE CHAIR — 2006, Industrial Design,
Commissioned by OFFECCT, SE, SP Archives,
Upholstered reaction injection moulded PUR
foam, 81 × 83 × 122 cm 69 × 51 cm

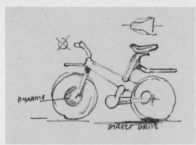

CITY BIKE — 2006, Industrial Design,
SP Archives, Various, 180 × 76 × 102 cm

DAILY BASKET BAG / PP — 2006, Industrial
Design, SP Archives, Injection moulded
plastic, 50 × 30 × 50 cm

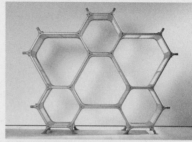

ALINATA SHELVING SYSTEM — 2007, Industrial
Design, Commissioned by Erreti, IT,
In production since 2007 to 2009, Extruded
aluminium with glass or plyboo panels,
180 × 37 × 130 cm

MINI ROLL CERAMIC CHAIR — 2007,
Industrial Design, Commissioned by Bosa, IT,
In production since 2008 Bosa, IT, Ceramic
slip casting, 20 × 25 × 27 cm

INSELLA FAMILY — 2007, Industrial Design,
SP Archives, Magnesium alloy die-cast,
Various

THERA CARPET — 2007, One-off,
Commissioned by I+I Carpet, IT, SP Archives,
Hand tuffted carpets, ⌀ 200 × 240 cm

MEANDER STACKABLE STOOL — 2007,
Industrial Design, Commissioned by Ann
Maes, Dutch Embassy Berlin, DE,
SP Archives, Upholstered moulded foam,
35 × 35 × 54 cm

BIRD NEST LAMP — 2007, Industrial Design,
SP Archives, Handblown Murano glass,
27 × 28 × 42 cm

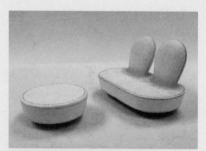

LIVING SOFA — 2007, Industrial Design,
Commissioned by Living Divani, IT,
SP Archives, Upholstered reaction injection
moulded PUR foam, 158 × 58 × 90 cm

SKELETON COPPER CHAIR — 2007, Limited
Edition, SP Archives, Copper sheet formed
and engineered, 78 × 53 × 46 cm

R-44-D HELICOPTER — 2007, Transportation
Design, SP Archives, 740 × 992 × 367 cm

ROLL CARBON CERAMIC CHAIR — 2007,
One-off, ammann // gallery, DE, Public
Collection, In production since 2008, Slip
casted ceramic with carbon fiber applied,
60 × 73 × 79 cm

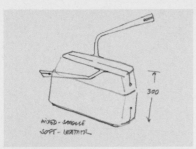

LEATHER BAG — 2007, One-off, SP Archives, Hand crafted saddle leather, 60 × 35 × 41 cm

PERSONAL SHOPPER — 2007, Solo Exhibition, Curated by Satyendra Pakhalé, NL, Ambiente, Messe Frankfurt, DE

HOME THEATER SYSTEM — 2007, Industrial Design, Commissioned by Sharp, JP, SP Archives, Various

O-LED DESK LAMP — 2007, Industrial Design, Commissioned by Yamagiwa, JP, SP Archives, Magnesium alloy die-casting, 20 × 27.5 × 45 cm

MIRROR FAMILY — 2007, Industrial Design, Commissioned by Magis, IT, SP Archives, Injection moulded plastics, Various

TOTEM CHAIR — 2008, Industrial Design, Commissioned by Magis, IT, SP Archives, Bent tubular aluminium and moulded seat in liquid wood, Various

GRIP SATELLITE TABLE — 2008, Industrial Design, Commissioned by OFFECCT, SE, SP Archives, Hydroformed metal and corian top, Ø 48 × 43.5 cm

KID DAY BED — 2008, Industrial Design, Commissioned by Magis, IT, SP Archives, Rotomoulded plastic with upholstered cushions, 80.5 × 140.5 × 51 cm

ISA MICRO CAR — 2008, Transportation Design, SP Archives, 290 × 154 × 189 cm

CUTLERY AND SPOONS — 2008, One-off, SP Archives, Hand forged aluminium cans, Various

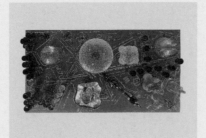

URBAN COMPATIBILITY — 2008, Exhibition Design, Commissioned by Iittala, FI, SP Archives, Various

LOOKING AT TOD'S — 2008, One-off, Commissioned by TOD's, IT, SP Archives, 39.5 × 136 × 180 cm

CHRONOLOGY OF SELECTED WORKS

SATYENDRA PAKHALÉ ORIGINS — 2008, Solo Exhibition, Curated by Gabrielle Ammann, DE, ammann // gallery, DE

B.M. HORSE STOOL — 2008, Limited Edition, ammann // gallery, DE, Public Collection, In production since 2008, Bell metal lost wax casting process, Ø 75 × 40 cm

CITY BOAT — 2008, Transportation Design, SP Archives, 319 × 193 × 100 cm

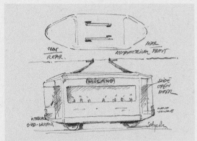

2015 SINGLE WAGON TRAM — 2008, Transportation Design, SP Archives, 1285 × 267 × 296 cm

ALU ROCKING CHAIR — 2008, Limited Edition, ammann // gallery, DE, In production since 2008, Casted aluminium, 48 × 80.5 × 83 cm

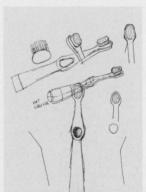

TOOTHBRUSH — 2008, Industrial Design, SP Archives, Co-injection moulded organic compound, 2 × 1.5 × 20 cm

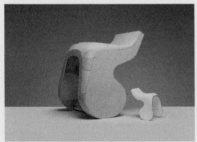

SADDLE CHAIR STOOL — 2008, Industrial Design, SP Archives, Die-cast magnesium alloy, 48 × 39.5 × 52.5 cm

KITCHEN KNIVES — 2008, Industrial Design, SP Archives, Forged iron, 3 × 2 × 25 cm

HÄSTENS DREAM BEDROOM — 2008, Solo Exhibition, Commissioned by Hästens, SE, Curated by Satyendra Pakhalé, NL, SP Archives

ALU TUBE CHAIR — 2008, Industrial Design, SP Archives, Aluminium tube, 73 × 82.5 × 92 cm

B.M. OBJECTS 2ND GENERATION — 2008, One-off, Public Collection, Bell metal lost wax casting process, Various

SATELLITE CHAIR — 2009, Industrial Design, SP Archives, Solid wood, 47 × 32 × 75.5 cm

WATCH AND CLOCK — 2009, Industrial Design, Commissioned by A. Manzoni & Fils, CH, SP Archives, CNC machined steel, 0.8 × 4 × 4.5 cm

KOP - CONNECT — 2009, Architecture, Commissioned by L'Etoile Properties, Paris, FR, SP Archives, Kop van Zuid, Rijnhaven, Rotterdam, NL

KUBU — 2009, Limited Edition, ammann // gallery, DE, Private collection, In production since 2009, CNC & hand sculpted wood, 186 × 60 × 87 cm

CHITTA - NECK PILLOW — 2009, Industrial Design, Commissioned by Experimenta, PT, SP Archives, Slip casted ceramic and cork base, 26 × 8 × 10 cm

METAL TRAY AND BOWL — 2009, Industrial Design, Commissioned by Skitch, IT, SP Archives, Cold forming metal with tubular structure, 52 × 59 × 66 cm

URBAN DESIGN — 2009, Architecture, Commissioned by Real Estate MIPIM, FR, SP Archives, La Défense, Paris, FR

WIREMESH FAMILY — 2009, Industrial Design, Commissioned by Magis, IT, SP Archives, Extruded aluminium frame, die-casted aluminium legs, moulded wiremesh, 46.5 × 40.5 × 83.5 cm

DESIGNERS VS. CHANEL NO.5 — 2009, Limited Edition, Commissioned by Al-Sabah Art & Design, KW, Private collection, 3D Printed Bronze, 4 × 15 × 18 cm

INPROGRESS - SOCIAL FICTION — 2010, Exhibition Design, Commissioned by Grand-Hornu, BE, Curated by Nestor Perkal, FR

CONVERSATION SOFA — 2010, Industrial Design, Commissioned by Hästens, SE, SP Archives, Upholstered hand crafted sofa with horse hair, wool and twin spring system, 63.5 × 120 × 90 cm

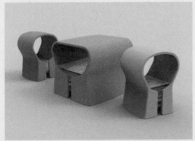

IN-BETWEEN — 2010, Industrial Design, Commissioned by OFFECCT, SE, SP Archives, Moulded pulp container, 35 × 58.5 × 52 cm

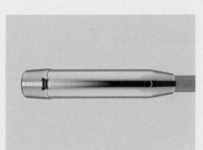

PENCIL HOLDER / SHARPENER — 2010, Industrial Design, SP Archives, CNC machined metal, ⌀ 20 × 1.5 cm

ECO FISH CHAIR — 2010, Limited Edition,
Commissioned by Walt Disney Signature,
USA, In production 2010, Rotomoulded in
recycled plastics, 55 × 87 × 72 cm

MOONBIKE — 2010, Transportation Design,
SP Archives, 129.5 × 60 × 106 cm

HUMIDIFIER — 2010, Industrial Design,
Commissioned by TUBES Radiatori, IT,
SP Archives, Slip casted ceramic,
Ø 19 × 5.5 cm

GLASS CHAIR — 2010, Industrial Design,
Commissioned by FIAM, IT, SP Archives, Bent
glass, 58 × 58.5 × 75.5 cm

STORAGE UNIT FIBO-NA — 2011, Industrial
Design, SP Archives, Bent wood, Various

STILL LIFE — 2011, Industrial Design,
Commissioned by TUBES Radiatori, IT,
SP Archives, Sheet metal forming, Various

MY PRIVATE SKY — 2011, One-off,
SP Archives, Moulded fibreglass

NEKA - NON ELECTRIC KITCHEN APPLIANCE —
2011, Industrial Design, SP Archives, Deep
drawing steel and injection moulded plastic,
Various

MOONWAKA — 2011, Transportation Design,
Commissioned by Moonlife Foundation, NL,
SP Archives, 16.5 × 131.5 cm

ENDLESS ALCANTARA — 2011, One-off,
Curated by Domitilla Dardi, MAXXI Museum,
Rome, IT, Laser-cut Alcantara stripes,
wooden structure with high polished
aluminium, 187 × 295 × 290 cm

SOUND PANELS — 2011, Industrial Design,
Commissioned by OFFECCT, SE, SP Archives,
Pressed technical textile, 6 × 234 × 234 cm

PEACOCK — 2011, One-off, SP Archives,
Casted bronze, 17.5 × 16 × 28 cm

VIRCHOW 16 — 2011, Architecture, Commissioned by Novartis, CH, SP Archives, Fabrikstrasse 6, Novartis Campus, Basel, CH

SPOUT OBJECT FAMILY — 2011, Industrial Design, SP Archives, Metal electrolysis, Various

CHAISE SINAN — 2011, Industrial Design, SP Archives, Leather upholstered with solid wood structure, 196 × 48 × 50 cm

BLACK WHITE SWAN — 2012, Limited Edition, ammann // gallery, DE, Private Collection, In production since 2012, Sculpted marble, 58 × 65.8 × 85.5 cm

REINVENT THE TOILET — 2012, Industrial Design, Commissioned by Gates Foundation, USA, SP Archives

DESIGN TECHNOLOGY — 2012, Exhibition Design, Commissioned by Marva Griffin, founder of Salone Satellite, IT

B.M. HORSE LO TABLE — 2012, Limited Edition, ammann // gallery, DE, Private Collection, In production since 2012, Bell metal lost wax casting process, 75 × 75 × 40 cm

FUTURE IS NOW — 2012, Centenary concept kitchen, Commissioned by Franke, CH, 250 × 250 × 250 cm

DR. AMBEDKAR NATIONAL CENTRE FOR SOCIAL JUSTICE — 2012, Architecture, Commissioned by Government of India, IN, 10, Janpath Road, New Delhi, IN

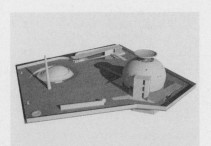

DR. AMBEDKAR NATIONAL MEMORIAL — 2012-2014, Architecture, Commissioned by Government of India, IN, 26, Alipur Road, New Delhi, IN

FRIDA PITCHER-VASE — 2012, Industrial Design, Commissioned by Cor Unum, NL, In production since 2019, Slip casted ceramic, glazed inside with tropical colours, Various

SWAN DINING CHAIR — 2012, Industrial Design, SP Archives, Injection moulded shell with tubular legs, 72.5 × 40.5 cm

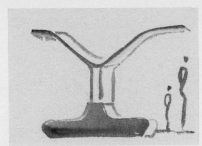

INTERNI SOLAR SHELTER — 2012, Exhibition Design, Commissioned by Interni, IT, SP Archives

B.M. HORSE HI TABLE — 2012, Limited Edition, ammann // gallery, DE, Private Collection, In production since 2012, Bell metal lost wax casting process, 60 × 90 × 83 cm

TIGER CARPET — 2012, Industrial Design, Commissioned by I+I, IT, SP Archives, Hand tafted wool, 240 × 220 cm

SADDLE FAMILY — 2012, Industrial Design, SP Archives, Hand crafted saddle leather with wooden structure, 86 × 75 × 96.5 cm

SAFARI TOY CAR — 2012, Industrial Design, Commissioned by TobeUs, IT, In production since 2012, TobeUs, IT, Solid wood, 16 × 7.5 cm

BRAND HARMONIZATION — 2013, Industrial Design, Commissioned by Franke, CH, SP Archives, 0.07 × 4.5 × 1 cm

KANGERI NOMADIC RADIATOR — 2013, Industrial Design, Commissioned by TUBES Radiatori, IT, SP Archives, Deep drawn aluminium and oak handle, 58.5 × 51.5 × 35 cm

ROTOMOULDED CHAIR — 2013, Industrial Design, SP Archives, Rotomoulded plastic, 64.5 × 53 × 75 cm

15 YEARS OBJECT — 2013, Industrial Design, SP Archives, CNC machined solid wood, 18 × 13.5 cm

STEELWAVE WATCH — 2013, Industrial Design, Commissioned by Alessi, IT, SP Archives, Deep drawing steel, ø 42 × 23.5 cm

OLIVE WOODEN SPOON — 2013, One-off, SP Archives, Hand carved olive wood, 20 × 6 cm

ALU DIE CAST CHAIR — 2013, Industrial Design, SP Archives, Die-cast aluminium, 56 × 20 × 46.5 cm

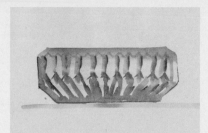

3D WEAVING FURNITURE — 2013, Industrial Design, Commissioned by De Padova, IT, SP Archives, Robotic 3d weaving, 120 × 85 × 38 cm

SP40 - REDSIGN CLASSIC P40 — 2014, Industrial Design, Commissioned by Tecno, IT, SP Archives, Die-cast aluminium, upholstered, 145 × 57 × 51 cm

B.M. HER SEAT — 2014, Limited Edition, SP Archives, Bell metal lost wax casting process, ⌀ 45 × 85 cm

ASSAYA CENTENARY ARMCHAIR — 2014, Industrial Design, Commissioned by Poltrona Frau, IT, In production since 2014, Hand crafted saddle leather, 80 × 90 × 50 cm

DESIGN AT FAIRCHILD — 2014, Exhibition Design, Curated by Cristina Grajales, New York, USA, supported by ammann // gallery and Giulio Cappellini, IT, Fairchild Tropical Botanic Garden, Miami, USA

AIRPORT MULTI-SEATING SYSTEM — 2014, Industrial Design, SP Archives, Wood, metal, moulded seat with die-cast aluminium structure, Various

LDC REDESIGN OF CLASSIC LES ARCS CHAIR — 2014, Industrial Design, Commissioned by Cassina, IT, SP Archives, Die-cast frame and formed saddle leather, 80 × 53.5 × 84 cm

MURANO GLASS LIGHT — 2014, Industrial Design, SP Archives, Handblown Murano glass, ⌀ 20 × 7 cm

B.M. VASE LARGE — 2014, Limited Edition, SP Archives, Bell metal lost wax casting process, ⌀ 140 × 95 cm

SALAKA — 2014, Limited Edition, Private collection, in production since 2014, Handblown Murano glass, ⌀ 53 × 40 cm

BATHROOM TAPS — 2014, Industrial Design, Commissioned by Boffi, IT, SP Archives, Die-cast brass, Various

FISH CHAIR VIOLA — 2014, Limited Edition, Cappellini, IT, In production 2014, Rotomoulded plastics in voilet colour, 55 × 87 × 72 cm

AQUAGRANDE PANI — 2015, Exhibition
Design, Commissioned by Flaminia, IT,
SP Archives, 100 × 55 × 22 cm

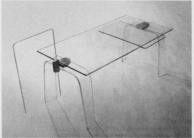

KAYO EXTENSIBLE TABLE — 2015, Industrial
Design, Commissioned by FIAM, IT,
In production since 2015, FIAM, IT, Bent glass,
200 × 90 × 80 cm

TEA FOR TWO TEAPOT — 2015, Industrial
Design, SP Archives, Slip casting ceramics
with metal infuser, 23.5 × 18 cm

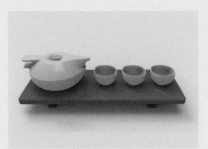

JINGDEZHEN TEA SET — 2015, Industrial
Design, SP Archives, Porcelain, 17 × 13.5 × 72 cm

STACKING TEAPOT — 2015, Industrial Design,
SP Archives, Slip casting ceramics,
18.5 × 23 × 27 cm

EAT-N-DRINK BIRD FEEDER — 2015,
Industrial Design, SP Archives, Handblown
Murano glass, Ø 16 × 26 cm

PARDUS — 2015, Industrial Design,
SP Archives, Moulded fibreglass,
84 × 73 × 39 cm

FLOWER S-VASE — 2015, Industrial Design,
SP Archives, Formed copper and marble
base, Ø 15 × 24 cm

MOKA SYNSET — 2015, Industrial Design,
SP Archives, Deep drawn stainless steel with
oak handle, Ø 9 × 17 cm

SINGULARITY TOYS — 2015, Industrial
Design, Commissioned by Naef Spiele, CH,
SP Archives, CNC machined wood, Various

UNIVERSAL CONTAINER FAMILY — 2015,
Industrial Design, SP Archives, Deep drawn
stainless steel, Various

CARVING THE SENSES — 2016, Exhibition
Design, Global Art Affairs, Venice Biennale, IT,
SP Archives, 163.5 × 138.5 × 280 cm

SARA — 2016, Industrial Design, SP Archives, Various

ORI-MIRROR — 2017, Industrial Design, Commissioned by FIAM, IT, SP Archives, Industrial bent glass, 186 × 155 × 17 cm

COC- MIXED-USE INNOVATION SPACE HOUTHAVENS AMSTERDAM — 2017, Architecture, Commissioned by Heren2, NL, SP Archives, Danzigerkade 69, Amsterdam, NL

B.M. OBJECTS 3RD GENERATION — 2018, Limited Edition, Private Collection, In production since 2018, Bell metal lost wax casting process, Various

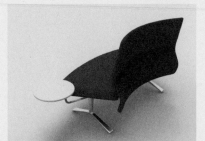

MEWA MODULAR SYSTEM — 2018, Industrial Design, Commissioned by Vaghi, IT, SP Archives, Die-cast aluminium and upholstered seat, Various

SP PERPETUAL COLLECTION — 2018, Industrial Design, Commissioned by Calyah, DK, SP Archives, Andhra Granite and Tropical wood, Various

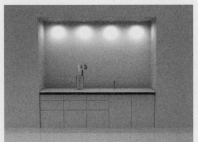

KITCHEN CONCEPT — 2018, Industrial Design, Commissioned by Franke, CH, SP Archives, Ceramics, quartz and fireproof wood, Various

BE-YO-LIGHT — 2018, Limited Edition, Commissioned by TraditioNow, CN, Private Collection, SP Archives, Gold foil application, 31.5 × 49.6 × 63 cm

SATYENDRA PAKHALÉ

1998 till now
Founder and principal designer Satyendra Pakhalé Associates, Amsterdam, the Netherlands

2006–2010
Head of the Department of the Master in Design for Humanity and Sustainable Living, Design Academy Eindhoven, the Netherlands

1995–1998
Senior Product Designer, Philips Design, Eindhoven, the Netherlands

1992–1993
Junior Product Designer, frog design, Altensteig, Germany

1992–1994
Product Design, Art Center College of Design (Europe), La Tour-de-Peilz, Switzerland

1989–1991
Master of Design, IDC - Industrial Design Center, IIT-B - Indian Institute of Technology Bombay, Powai, India

1985–1989
Bachelor of Engineering, VNIT - Visvesvaraya National Institute of Technology, Nagpur, India

1967
Born in India.

Multi-facetted designer Satyendra Pakhalé established his practice in 1998 in Amsterdam, the Netherlands, and is active internationally in the fields of industrial design, transportation design and architecture. He trained as a designer at the IIT-B (Indian Institute of Technology), Bombay, and later at the Art Center College of Design Europe, Switzerland. After his first working experience at frog Design, he was part of the pioneering new business creation team at Philips Design in the mid-1990s, conceiving some of the first product ideas for new digital communication technologies and transportation design.

Pakhalé has lectured worldwide, for example at CeBIT Germany, Casa Brasil and Future Design Days Sweden. In 2008 he was selected as one of L'Uomo Vogue's eighty most influential people in design and architecture worldwide. The Design Academy Eindhoven (the Netherlands) invited him to devise and head the Master's programme, Design for Humanity and Sustainable Living, from 2006 to 2010. He was advisor to the Ambassadors' Board of Brainport Design & Technology (Eindhoven) and has been active as a design and cultural policy contributor to cultural institutions.

Through numerous innovative design projects for leading clients, Pakhalé has developed a worldwide reputation for designing diverse product typologies, pushing the limits of technology and materials. His ongoing curiosity and cultural pluralism has led to limited-edition pieces and one-offs besides industrial design and architecture projects. His clients include Alcantara, Alessi, Cappellini, Franke, Fiam, Hästens, Moon Life Foundation, Poltrona Frau, Novartis and Tod's. He has won several international awards, such as the Bharat Samman 2013 and NRI Award 2012. The Indian Institute of Technology Bombay awarded him the IIT-B - Distinguished Alumnus Award 2013. His works are in permanent collections at major museums worldwide, including the Victoria and Albert Museum (London), Stedelijk Museum (Amsterdam), Montreal Museum of Fine Arts and the Centre Pompidou (Paris).

BIBLIOGRAPHY (SELECTED)

2018
— Giovanna Castiglioni, Carlo Castiglioni, Chiara Alessi, Domitilla Dardi and Calvi Brambilla, *100x100 Achille*, Maurizio Corraini, Italy
— Kimberlie Birks, *Design for Children*, Phaidon, United Kingdom

2017
— Beppe Finessi, *SaloneSatellite - 20 Years of New Creativity*, Corraini Edizioni, Italy

2016
— Global Art Affairs i.c.w. European Cultural Centre, *Time Space Existence*, Global Art Affairs Foundation, Italy
— Chris Meplon, *Ceci n'est pas une copie*, Design between Innovation and Imitation, CID Grand-Hornu, Lannoo Publishers, Belgium
— Alberto Alessi, Francesca Appiani, Maya Dvash, *Alessi IN-possible*, Silvana Editoriale, Italy

2015
— Mateo Kries, Jolanthe Kugler, *The Bauhaus #itsalldesign*, Bundeskunsthalle, Vitra Design Museum, Germany
— Aldo Cibic, *Looking ahead, The evolution of the art of making, 9 stories from Veneto: digital – not only digital*, 56th Venice Art Biennale, Marsilio Editori, Italy
— Rebecca Proctor, *The Sustainable Design Book*, Laurence King, United Kingdom

2014
— Rebecca Proctor, *1000 New Eco Designs*, Laurence King, United Kingdom

2013
— Jennifer Hudson, *The Design Book, 1000 New Designs for the Home and Where to Find Them*, Laurence King, United Kingdom

2012
— Duncan Hooson and Anthony Quinn, *The Workshop Guide to Ceramics*, Thames & Hudson, United Kingdom

2011
— Paul Rodgers and Alex Milton, *Product Design*, Laurence King, United Kingdom
— Pau Opra, *Design for Kids*, Links Books, Spain
— Karine Mazeau, *Design mobilier*, Eyrolles, France

2010
— Nestor Perkal, Jeanne Quéheillard, *In Progress*, Mongrafik éditions, France
— Charlotte and Peter Fiell, *Tools for Living*, Fiell, United Kingdom
— Jennifer Hudson, *1000 New Designs 2*, Laurence King, United Kingdom
— Francesca Serrazanetti, Matteo Schubert, *The Hand of the Designer*, Fondo Ambiente Italiano & Moleskine, Italy
— Michael Alpert, *The Haystack Reader – Collected Essays on Craft, 1991-2009*, University of Maine Press & Haystack Mountain School of Crafts, Orono & Deer Isle, USA

2009
— R. Craig Miller, *European Design, Shaping the New Century*, Merrell, USA
— Sophie Lovell, *Limited Edition Prototypes, One-Offs and Design Art Furniture*, Birkhäuser, Switzerland

2008
— Jennifer Hudson, *Process - 50 Product designs from concept to manufacture*, Laurence King, United Kingdom
— Robert Klanten, Sven Ehmann, Andrej Kupetz, Shonquis Moreno & Adeline Mollard, *DESIRE The Shape of Things to Come*, Gestalten, Germany
— Sabrina Sciama, Elisa Facchetti, *Box Circa 40_2, Foreign designers around 40 years old*, Edizioni Fiera Milano, Italy

2007
— Charlotte and Peter Fiell, *Design Now!*, TASCHEN, Germany
— Koos Eissen and Roselien Steur, *Sketching*, BIS Publishers, the Netherlands
— Raymond Guidot et Nestor Perkal, *L'expérience de la céramique, CRAFT Centre de recherche sur les arts du feu et de la terre Limoges*, Bernard Chauveau Éditeur, France
— Sophie Lovell, *Furnish - Furniture and Interior Design for the 21st Century*, Die Gestalten Verlag, Germany
— Patricia Urquiola, *The International Design Yearbook 2007*, Laurence King, United Kingdom
— Beppe Finessi, *Avverati a Dream Comes True*, Skira, Italy

2006
— Elsa Francès, *Biennale Internationale Design Saint-Étienne, Le livre*, Editions Cité Du Design, France
— Martine Aubry, Caroline Naphegyi, *Bombay L' Album Maximum City*, Terrail/Edigroup, Lille3000, France
— Geurt Imanse, Jan van Adrichem, *Aanwinsten/ Acquisitions, 1993–2003*, Stedelijk Museum Amsterdam, the Netherlands
— Jennifer Hudson, *1000 New Designs and where to find them – A 21st Century Sourcebook*, Laurence King, United Kingdom
— Oscar Ascensio, *Design Design, Meubels @ Lampes*, Linea Editorial, Spain
— Mel Byars, *50 New Chairs*, Rotovision, United Kingdom
— Laurel Saville and Brooke Stoddard, *Design Secrets: Furniture*, Rockport Publishers, USA

2005
— Anton Reijnders, *The Ceramic Process – A Manual and Source Inspiration for Ceramic Art and Design European Ceramic Work Centre*, A & C Black Publishers, United Kingdom, University of Pennsylvania Press, USA
— Alastair Fuad-Luke, *The Eco-Design Handbook*, Thames & Hudson, United Kingdom

2004
— Mel Byars, *The Design Encyclopedia*, The Museum of Modern Art, New York, USA
— B. Martin Pedersen, Laetitia Wolff, Michael Porciello, *Product Design 3*, Graphis, USA
— Nestor Perkal, *Objects of desire, a collection of contemporary vases*, CID Grand-Hornu, Diffusion Editions, Belgium
— Tom Dixon, *The International Design Yearbook 2004*, Laurence King, United Kingdom

2003
— Chris Lefteri, *Ceramics, Materials for inspirational design*, Rotovision, United Kingdom

— Timo de Rijk, *Designers in Netherlands – een eeuw productvormgeving*, Ludion Amsterdam, the Netherlands

2002
— Editors of Phaidon Press, *Spoon book, 10 x 10 Designers*, Phaidon, United Kingdom
— Renny Ramakers, *Less + More, Droog Design in Context*, 010 Publishers Rotterdam, the Netherlands
— Daniel Rozensztroch, *Cintres Hangers*, Le Passage, France

2001
— Michele De Lucchi, *The International Design Yearbook 2001*, Laurence King, United Kingdom

2000
— Paola Antonelli, Giulio Cappellini, Vanni Pasca, *Beyond European Design, Abitare il Tempo – Experimentation and Research Exhibitions*, Edizioni Grafiche Zanni, Italy

1998
— Stefano Marzano, *Creating Value by Design - Thoughts & Facts*, Philips Design, BIS Publishers, the Netherlands
— Jean Pierre Rioux, *Renault*, Éditions Hazan, France

EXHIBITIONS (SELECTED)

2018
— *Made in Holland: 400 years a global brand*, Princessehof Ceramic Museum Leeuwarden, the Netherlands
— *SaloneSatellite Permanent Collection*, Legno Arredo ITS Rosario Messina Foundation Study Centre, Lentate sul Seveso, Italy

2017
— *Ceci n'est pas une copie*, Centre d'innovation et de design, Grand-Hornu, Belgium
— *Alessi IN-possible*, La Triennale di Milano, Italy
— *SaloneSatellite. 20 Years of New Creativity*, Fabbrica del Vapore, Milan, Italy
— *Ghost Memory – what a joy! 30° Ghost Anniversary*, Milan Fair, Italy
— *The value of design*, Red Dot awarded products, Cité du Design Saint-Étienne, France

2016
— *Time Space Existence*, Venice Architecture Biennale, Global Art Affairs, Palazzo Michiel, Venice, Italy
— *Houselife*, Museum of Decorative Arts and Design, Bordeaux, France

2015
— *Looking ahead. 9 stories from Veneto: digital – not only digital*, Venice Art Biennale, Italy
— *Das Bauhaus #itsalldesign*, Vitra Design Museum, Weil am Rhein, Germany
— *Wirkkala Revisited*, Design Museum Helsinki, Finland
— *Alessi IN-possible*, Design Museum Holon, Israel

2014
— *Design at Fairchild*, Fairchild Tropical Botanic Garden, Coral Gables Miami, USA
— *Sydney Indesign*, Habitus Home Exhibition, Sydney, Australia
— *Modular system - Add-On Radiator*, Paris Designer's Days, France
— *100% Tobeus: 100 Designers for 100 New Toy Cars*, Canada National Design Museum, Toronto, Canada

— *Cappellini 2000-2012*, ICFF New York, USA
— *Industry City*, New York, USA
— *Tom Vack. Vanity of Object*, Die Neue Sammlung, The Design Museum, Munich, Germany
— *Modularity - Add-On Radiator*, Malta Design Week, Fort St Elmo Valletta, Malta

2013
— *Outset Design Fund*, Victoria & Albert Museum, London, United Kingdom
— *Meet Design Around the World*, Triennale di Milano, Italy

2012
— *International Design for Children*, The Dowse Art Museum, Lower Hutt, New Zealand
— *Design & Technology - 15th Anniversary SaloneSatellite*, Milan Design Week, Italy

2011
— *Daily Future*, Moon Life Concept Store, Moon Life Foundation, Amsterdam, the Netherlands
— *Can you imagine? Alcantara, power of a material*, MAXXI Museum, Rome, Italy

2010
— *Meeting of Minds*, Hästens Flagship, Stockholm, Sweden
— *10 Years of Via Milano*, Oude Kerk Amsterdam, the Netherlands
— *In Progress*, CID Grand-Hornu, Belgium

2009
— *Design Lounge*, ammann // gallery, Cologne Fine Art & Antiques, Cologne, Germany
— *The Clue Design*, Gwanju Design Biennale, South Korea
— *Satyendra Pakhalé – Architecture & Design*, MIPIM Le marché international des professionnels de l'immobilier, Cannes, France

2008
— *Satyendra Pakhalé – OriginS*, solo exhibition, ammann // gallery, Cologne, Germany
— *Urban Compatibility littala*, Design Boost, Malmö, Sweden

2007
— *Personal Shopper. We can't afford to buy CHEAP things*, Ambiente Frankfurt Fair, Germany
— *Satyendra Pakhalé – Selected design works*, Design Boost, Stockholm, Sweden

2006
— *Bombay Maximum City*, Co-Curation & Design, Lille3000 - European Cultural Capital, Lille, France
— *Bamboo architectural elements, Transformation: Nature & Beyond*, Material ConneXion Flagship, New York, USA

2005
— *Satyendra Pakhalé – three projects*, Future Design Days, Stockholm, Sweden
— *Ole Palsby Retrospective*, The Danish Museum of Art and Design, Copenhagen, Denmark

2003
— *Satyendra Pakhalé - Design by Heart*, solo exhibition, OTTO Gallery, Bologna, Italy
— *un:Usual – Satyendra Pakhalé*, Entrata Libera, Milan, Italy

2002
— *From Projects to Products*, solo exhibition, Stedelijk Museum Amsterdam, the Netherlands
— *Panther Off-Scale – 50 Projects*, Moroso Golden Jubilee, Milan, Italy

2001
— *Work 'n' Play by Satyendra Pakhalé*, SaloneSatellite, Milan, Italy
— *World Wide Design*, Atelier Renault, Paris, France

2000
— *Design works*, group exhibition, Gallery Arte e Industria, Parma, Italy

1999
— *Beyond European Design*, Abitare il Tempo, Verona, Italy
— *Young designers in Milano*, Alterpoint Milano, Italy

1998
— *Vision on move*, Evoluon Philips, Eindhoven, the Netherlands

1997
— *Pangéa Concept Car*, Geneva International Motor Show, Switzerland

ART FAIRS (SELECTED)

Limited editions presented by ammann // gallery
— Collective Design Fair, New York, USA, 2014, 2015, 2017
— Cologne Fine Art & Antiques, Germany, 2008
— Design Miami/ Basel, Switzerland, 2007-2014, 2018
— Design Miami/ Basel, Miami Beach, USA, 2012-2014
— Pavilion of Art & Design, London, United Kingdom, 2010-2013, 2017, 2018
— Pavilion of Art & Design Paris, France, 2011-2013
— The Salon Art + Design New York, USA, 2017, 2018

PUBLICATIONS (SELECTED)

ARGENTINA
Studio Magazine

AUSTRALIA
Cool Hunting Green, Pol Oxygen, Habitus Living, Belle Magazine

AUSTRIA
IMMO Kurier, Form Art - Die Presse, H.O.M.E.

BELGIUM
Designers Weekend, Promateria, GAEL, Brussels Economic, Elle Décoration, DAMn, TLmag

BRASIL
KAZA, ARC Design, Valor Econômico, iDeia, Jornal do Estado de Minas Gerais

CHINA
Elle Décor, Prime, Modern Deco, Colorfulness China, Ceramics Design, Architecture Update, Cutting Edge

FRANCE
Beaux Arts, Intramuros, Architectural Digest, Yooko, Elle Décoration, Vogue, L'Automobile, inView, Jalouse, Numéro, L'Express Mag, Marie Claire, IDEAT, Artravel, Côté rénovation, Tendances, À vivre, Les Echos, L'Oeil

GERMANY
Form, Design Report, Wohnen, Architectural Digest, H.O.M.E., Elle Décoration, Creative Face Magazine, A&W, Raum und Wohnen, Art Aurea, L'Officiel Hommes, Casa Deco, Köln Internetzeitung, GG Magazine, Süddeutsche Zeitung Magazin

INDIA
Home Review, The MAN, CW Interiors, Home Trends, Elle

Décor, Elle, Index Media, Living etc, Platform, India Today Home, Casaviva, Vogue, Financial Chronicle, Creative Gaga, The Telegraph, Architectural Digest, Economic Times, Mint, The Hindustan Times, The Hindu, Blackbook, Home & Design, Express Computer, The Sunday Standard, Good Homes, Architecture Update, DDN, NRI Achiever

IRELAND
Sunday Times

ITALY
Domus, Interni, Abitare, Ottagono, Il Sole 24 Ore, La Repubblica, Business, Corriere della Sera, Ventiquattro, La Repubblica delle Donne, Design Italia, MADE 05, Costruire, DDN Design Diffusion News, Grazia Casa, Casaviva, Elle, Decore Living, DDB Magazine, L'expresso, MODO, Casa da Abitare, Brava Casa, BOX, Donna Moderna, Glamour, Mood, Carnet Arte, Case & Country, DONNA, HOME, Gulliver Magic, Agenda, ANNA, Artravel, Auto and Design, Casa D, Area, Spazio CASA, Style Magazine, Capital Living, GRAZIA, Il Giornale Dell'Arredamento Yachts Italia, Casa Vogue, Vanity Fair, L'Uomo Vogue, Forum, Flair, Ville & Casali, Casa & Design, CasAmica, FLAMagazine, atcasa, Platform

JAPAN
AXIS, Loro Magazine, Mono, Hanatsubaki, Flashfilm

THE NETHERLANDS
Frame, Items, Het Parool, KLM Holland Herald, Elsevier, Dutch Design Digest, Amsterdam Index, Volkskrant, IM Identity Matters, Design NL, Eigen Huis & Interieur, Capitalogue, Residence, SALT Magazine, India Nu, Nieuw in Nederland, Villa d'Arte, Beter Wonen, Elle Wonen, Wonen.nl, Art-nl, Elegance, Intermediair, De Gruyter Fabriek, Daily Future, Dutch Daily, Woth Magazine, Audi Magazine

RUSSIA
Mezonin, Monitor, Elle Decor, Tatlin, Harper's Bazar, LE Magazine, Hi Home

SINGAPORE
Surface Asia, Dwell Asia, Square Rooms

SOUTH AFRICA
Design Indaba, VISI Design & Architecture

SOUTH KOREA
Archiworld, Casa Living, Elle Décor, Casa, Esquire, MetaTrend

SWEDEN
Plaza, FORM, Forum, RUM Architecture-Design, David Carlson Report, Designboost, Leva & Bo, The Fair Review

SWITZERLAND
Tendance Deco, Wohnrevue, Wohnen, DuPont Magazine, Dein Einfamilien Haus, Raum und Wohnen

UNITED KINGDOM
Financial Times, Wallpaper, Blueprint, The Guardian, BBC World Service, Of Indian Origin, New Design Magazine, Questia, Square Mag, Frieze

UNITED STATES OF AMERICA
ID Magazine, MATTER, Dwell, Eyesin, Interior Design Magazine, Metropolis, Surface, DOT, Travel + Leisure, The New York Times Home, Modern Magazine

MUSEUM COLLECTIONS (SELECTED)
— Victoria and Albert Museum, United Kingdom
— The Centre Pompidou, France
— Stedelijk Museum Amsterdam, the Netherlands
— M+ Museum of Visual Culture, Hong Kong
— MAKK Museum für Angewandte Kunst Köln, Germany
— Montreal Museum of Fine Arts, Canada
— Die Neue Sammlung – The Design Museum, Germany
— Fonds National d'Art Contemporain, France
— Design Museum Den Bosch, the Netherlands
— Musée départemental d'art contemporain de Rochechouart, France

AWARDS (SELECTED)
— Green GOOD DESIGN Award, Athenaeum Museum of Architecture and Design, USA, 2016
— Red Dot Awards, Germany, 2008, 2016
— Distinguished Alumnus Award, Indian Institute of Technology Bombay, India, 2013
— Bharat Samman, Non Resident Indian Institute, United Kingdom, 2013
— Non Resident Indian Institute Award, United Kingdom, 2012
— International Design Award, LA Interiors, USA, 2007
— Editor's Choice Award, ICFF, USA, 2003
— National Design Grant, Foundation for Fine Art, Architecture and Design, the Netherlands, 2002
— Atelier Grant, Sofa Stichting, the Netherlands, 2001
— International Exhibition Grant Mondriaan Stichting, the Netherlands, 2001
— National Design Grant, Foundation for Fine Art, Architecture and Design, the Netherlands, 1999
— International Design Distinction Awards, International Design Magazine, USA, 1994, 1998, 1999
— Design Distinction, New Notable Product Design II, USA, 1995
— GOLDSTAR Design Award, LG Corporation, South Korea, 1993
— First Prize, Full Scholarship Art Center College of Design (Europe), Switzerland, 1992
— Janus De L'Etudiant, l'Institut Français du Design, France, 1991

LECTURES (SELECTED)
— *Between Memory and Oblivion - Between Tradition and Innovation*, keynote TraditioNow Chinese Handicrafts, Masters in Residence, Nanjing University of Arts, Nanjing, China, 2018
— *Thoughts on Design in Blockchain*, WeWork, Shanghai, China, 2018
— *Four Architectural Design Projects* - the Netherlands, Switzerland and India, Vos & Partners Developers, Rotterdam, the Netherlands, 2018
— *Culture of Innovation, The new frontiers of the design radiator: aesthetics and functionality at the service of energy efficiency*, Tubes Workshop, Venice Architecture Biennale, Italy, 2016
— *Design in Social Context - exploring design as a global agent for social development*, Design Museum Dharavi, Spring House Amsterdam, the Netherlands, 2016
— *Sensorial Design*, keynote, Archiscuola conference at

Central House of Architects, Moscow, Russia, 2016
— *Culture of Creation - Evoking Senses, Colloquium on Perception and Experience*, Museum Andersen, Rome, Italy, 2016
— *Sensorial Design*, Istituto Europeo di Design, Rome, Italy, 2016
— *Empowering Through Design - Design in Culture of Manufacturing*, India Design Forum during Make in India Week, Mumbai, 2016
— *Design as a singular practice*, The Hong Kong Polytechnic University School of Design, Hong Kong, 2014
— *Design Opportunities for one of the largest Rail Networks* – India, Brazil & China, Railway & Mass Transit Interiors, Technology and Design Expo, Cologne, Germany, 2013
— *Future Digital Lifestyles looking at the Past*, keynote at CeBIT Global Conferences Design for Digital Lifestyles, CeBIT Hannover, Germany, 2013
— *Challenges in Industrial Sectors in India and Abroad*, Non Resident Indian Institute Seminar, New Delhi, India, 2013
— *Design as Universal Poetry*, International Seminar on Creative Economy and Design, Belo Horizonte, Minas Gerais, Brazil, 2012
— *Curiosities*, Indian Institute of Technology Bombay, Industrial Design Centre, Bombay, India, 2012
— *Industrial Design with Cultural Content*, Munich Creative Business Week, Die Neue Sammlung – The Design Museum, Munich, Germany, 2012
— *Industrial Design as a Cultural Catalyst*, KAIST Korea Advanced Institute of Science and Technology, Daejeon, South Korea, 2011
— *Urbanization or Migration: The Role of Culture in Indian and German Transitional Medium-Sized Cities*, Staatliche Kunstsammlungen Dresden, Germany, 2011
— *Cultural connections! Innovation as core of design*, Hong Kong Design Institute, Hong Kong, 2011
— *Designing Public Space – Ceremonial & Memorial*, keynote at Human Cities, Istanbul, Turkey, 2010
— *Industrial Iconography*, Design Boost Sweden Made in Arnhem, the Netherlands, 2010
— *Design for Life – Myth or Reality?*, Mini DesignBoost, Arkitekturmuseet Stockholm, Sweden, 2010
— *Innovation is the other term for Design – not just a competitive necessity*, Casa Brasil, Sindmóveis International Seminar, Bento Gonçalves, Brazil, 2009
— *You Can't Afford to Buy CHEAP Things* - Notes on Sustainable Design, Ambiente, International Frankfurt Fair, Germany, 2009
— *Notion of Progress*, White Lady's Lecture Series, Design Academy Eindhoven, the Netherlands, 2008
— *Humanity and more*, Master Programme Lecture Series, Design for Humanity and Sustainable Living, Design Academy Eindhoven, the Netherlands, 2008
— *Making It Real*, The Art of Life and Design Seminar, Aalto University – School of Arts, Design and Architecture, Helsinki, Finland, 2008
— *Design is a process*, keynote at After Stockholm Event, Oslo, Norway, 2008

— *Consumption or Creation!* Design Lecture Series, University of Economics Izmir, Turkey, 2008
— *Innovation, does it really matter?*, Design Day Focus Industry, Louisiana Museum of Modern Art, Humlebæk, Denmark, 2007
— *Global City: Human City: a Socio-Cultural Perspective*, Human Cities, Sustainable Environmental Design Colloquium, Brussels, Belgium, 2007
— *Innovation: Design Economics*, Design Indaba, Cape Town, South Africa, 2006
— *Shift or shiftless: Making Things*, Future Design Days, Stockholm, Sweden, 2005
— *Hands and more*, retreat symposium, Haystack Mountain School of Crafts, Deer Isle, Maine, USA, 2004
— *Lightness*, Fashion Institute Technology and Design, New York City, USA, 2002
— *My love affair with ceramics*, Department of Ceramics, Hogeschool voor de Kunsten, 's-Hertogenbosch, the Netherlands, 2002

JURY (SELECTED)
— iF Design Talent Award 2018/02, iF Design World Guide Taipei, Taiwan, 2018
— Design Plus Awards, Special Edition Ethical Style, Ambiente, Frankfurt, Germany, 2017
— Designer's Saturday Awards, Oslo, Norway, 2011
— China's Most Successful Design Awards, Shanghai, China, 2011
— Red Dot Design Awards, Essen, Germany, 2010
— Tokyo Design & Art Environment Awards, Tokyo, Japan, 2010
— Machina Design Awards, Warsaw, Poland, 2009
— SaloneSatellite, Fondazione Cosmit, Milan, Italy, 2009
— Design for Europe, International Competition, Biennale INTERIEUR, Kortrijk, Belgium, 2006
— Forum AID Award, Nordic Architecture and Design, Stockholm, Sweden, 2006
— Transformation Tupperware International Competition, New York, USA, 2005

TEACHING (SELECTED)

HEAD OF THE DEPARTMENT 2006–2010, Design Academy Eindhoven, Design for Humanity and Sustainable Living, Eindhoven, the Netherlands

GUEST FACULTY 2001–2014
— School of Design, Hong Kong Polytechnic University, Hong Kong
— Industrial Design Department, KAIST Korea Advanced Institute of Science and Technology, South Korea
— Hong Kong Design Institute, Hong Kong
— Les Ateliers, ENSCI Ecole Nationale Superieure de Creation Industrielle, France
— Man and Living Department, Design Academy Eindhoven, the Netherlands
— Man and Activity Department, Design Academy Eindhoven, the Netherlands
— Ceramics Department, Haute Ecole d'Arts Appliqués Geneva, Switzerland
— China project, Ceramics Department, Hogeschool Den Bosch, the Netherlands

CLIENTS (SELECTED)
— Alcantara, Italy
— Alessi, Italy
— Al Sabah Gallery, Kuwait
— Bosa, Italy
— Calyah, Denmark
— Cappellini, Italy
— Cassina, Italy
— Colombo Design, Italy
— CorUnum, the Nethelrands
— CRAFT, France
— C-Sam, USA
— C-Lection, the Netherlands
— De Vecchi, Italy
— Erreti, Italy
— Fiam, Italy
— Flaminia, Italy
— Franke, Switzerland
— Hästens, Sweden
— Iittala, Finland
— Lille3000, France
— L'Etoile Properties, France
— Magis, Italy
— Material ConneXion, USA
— Messe Frankfurt, Germany
— Moon Life Foundation, the Netherlands
— Moroso, Italy
— Novartis, Switzerland
— Offecct, Sweden
— Poltrona Frau, Italy
— RSVP, Italy
— SCA, Sweden
— Tecno, Italy
— TOD's, Italy
— TraditioNow, China
— Tubes, Italy
— Vaghi, Italy
— Väveriet - Ludvig Svensson, Sweden

ALBERTO ALESSI — Took over the management of Alessi Spa in 1970. Since then, the third-generation Managing Director of the company has successfully explored the frontiers of design and technology, positioning the company as a design leader and partnering with many world-class designers, offering products from fundamental household and trade items to innovative yet practical and stylish product ranges. His risk management skills are sought by prominent technology and design-led organizations around the world. He believes that more and more people are buying objects for intellectual and spiritual nourishment. Alessi is a member of the Academic Board of the UIAH, Aalto University of Technology, Helsinki and sits on the honorary committee of the Design Museum, London. He is a senior fellow of the Royal College of Art, London; honorary professor of the Hochschule der Bildenden Künste, Saarbrücken; doctor Honoris Causa of the UIAH of Helsinki; doctor of Fine Arts at the Miami University of Oxford, Ohio; and has an honorary doctorate degree from the University of Central England, Birmingham. In 1998, he received the Design Award for Lifetime Achievement from the Brooklyn Museum of Art.

GABRIELLE AMMANN — A globally respected gallerist and one of the leading tastemakers within the collectible design market, Gabrielle Ammann founded ammann//gallery in Cologne in 2006. With a degree in interior architecture and a deep knowledge of art, Ammann cultivates a cutting-edge programme devoted to the intersections between art, architecture and design. Ammann has been working since the 1980s with some of the most important artists and designers in the world like Ron Arad, Zaha Hadid, Marc Newson and Studio Alchimia. Simultaneously, she has nurtured a new generation of designers like Studio Nucleo, Satyendra Pakhalé and Rolf Sachs, who produce works with innovative approaches to exploring materials, form and space. Alongside the gallery programme, Ammann partners with curators to realize museum exhibitions and is a published author.

PAOLA ANTONELLI — The Senior Curator at The Museum of Modern Art in the Department of Architecture & Design is also MoMA's founding Director of Research & Development. She has curated numerous shows, lectured worldwide, and has served on several international architecture and design juries. She has taught at the University of California, Los Angeles; the Harvard Graduate School of Design; and the MFA programmes of the School of Visual Arts in New York. With a Master's in Architecture from the Polytechnic of Milan, Paola Antonelli has also earned Honorary Doctorates from the Royal College of Art and Kingston University, London, and the Art Center College of Design, Pasadena. She earned the 'Design Mind' Smithsonian Institution's National Design Award in 2006 and in 2007 was named one of the twenty-five most incisive design visionaries by *Time magazine*. In 2011 she was inducted in the Art Directors Club Hall of Fame and in 2015 she received the AIGA Medal.

JACQUES BARSAC — A prolific writer, and award-winning documentary film-maker with an insatiable curiosity for art and history (UNESCO award for *Le Corbusier* in 1990), Barsac is the director of numerous art and history documentaries that have won several prizes at international festivals: *Charlotte Perriand*, *Le Corbusier*, *Jean Cocteau*, and *The Roman Face*, *Winston Churchill*, *The Year One Thousand*, *Clovis*, and *The Eagle and the Sphinx*. He received the Academy of Architecture Publications Silver Medal and the Department of Equipment's Architecture Promotion Trophy for his film *Le Corbusier*. A pioneer of new audiovisual technologies, he was also president of a society of authors. He lived close to Charlotte Perriand for fifteen years and was 'the wall that sent the ball' when she wrote her autobiography, *A Life of Creation*. He is the author of several books about Charlotte Perriand.

GIULIO CAPPELLINI — The architect and designer Giulio Cappellini is the Art Director of Cappellini, which has been part of the Poltrona Frau Group since 2004. Cappellini's collections are 'known for tapping new trends and far-flung talents', and have included works by Erwan and Ronan Bouroullec, Tom Dixon, Alessandro Mendini, Jasper Morrison, Marc Newson, Satyendra Pakhalé, Inga Sempé and many more. After graduating in architecture, Giulio Cappellini worked as a designer and art director both in the family business and for other internationally famous design brands. Over the years, his work as a designer has proposed a personal reading of contemporary design, both for the Cappellini brand, and as art director of other important design brands. *Time magazine* lists Cappellini among the top ten trend setters in fashion and design. His lectures at the Milan Polytechnic always generate great international interest.

ARIC CHEN — The Curator at Large at M+, the new museum for visual culture in Hong Kong, where from 2012-2018 he served as the museum's first Lead Curator for Design and Architecture, was responsible for building its design and architecture collection and curatorial program. Currently based in Shanghai, Chen is also Professor of Practice at the College of Design & Innovation at Tongji University. He previously served as the inaugural Creative Director of Beijing Design Week and has organized and contributed to numerous biennials, museum exhibitions and other projects all over the world. He is the author of *Brazil Modern* (Monacelli, 2016) and his writings have been widely published in leading publications such as *The New York Times*, *Monocle*, *Architectural Record*, and *PIN-UP* among them.

CRISTIANO CROSETTA — Chief Executive Officer and partner of TUBES Radiatori in Resana, north of Venice. TUBES runs the entire production cycle of both the historic Basics and Extras collections as well as the more recent Elements design collection. TUBES was established in 1994 on the strength of its founders' thirty years of experience in the heating and plumbing sector, and Crosetta took on the role of commercial director, managing the entire Italian sales network and, from 1996, its foreign distribution too. In 2014 he was appointed CEO of TUBES, taking over the management of the company with the aim of making it increasingly competitive and successful. TUBES has partnered up with leading international architects and designers for several years, enabling it to consolidate the radiator as a star feature and break away from its secondary, strictly technical image. Crosetta has been a speaker at several trade fairs and design events such as Design of Wellness and Energy Efficiency In Design Radiators.

MARVA GRIFFIN WILSHIRE — Venezuelan by birth but Milanese by adoption, since entering the world of design and furniture in the 1970s, Marva Griffin Wilshire founded Salone Satellite, an initiative of the Salone Internazionale del Mobile, and has curated it since the first edition in 1998. She is the driving force behind this showcase for young talent, which over the past twenty years has given an early platform to some of the design industry's biggest names. She has been a member of the Philip Johnson Architecture & Design Committee at the Museum of Modern Art (MoMA) in New York since 2001. She was named Expo 2015 WE-Women Ambassador for the Universal Exposition held in Milan in 2015 and was appointed Ambassador of Italian Design by the Ministry of Foreign Affairs in 2016. For over twenty years she was International Press Director for the Milan Furniture Fair. Recently, Griffin was awarded an Ambrogino d'Oro Gold Medal, Milan's highest honour.

VITTORIO LIVI — The founding director of FIAM Italia, Vittorio Livi has always been passionate about glass. His first company, Fullet, produced decorated glasses for the furniture industry. Artiglass, Curvovetro, Cromoglass and Vellutart followed. In 1973, while he was setting up all these companies, he established FIAM Italia, the first company able to produce curved-glass furniture items by well-known international designers such as Ron Arad, Cini Boeri, Daniel Libeskind, Doriana and Massimiliano Fuksas, Giorgetto Giugiaro, Makio Hasuike, Vico Magistretti, Enzo Mari, Satyendra Pakhalé, Philippe Starck and others. FIAM Italia is now the world leader in its field, with global distribution and products in twenty-five international museum collections. In 1992 he bought the crumbling Villa Miralfiore, Pesaro, which dates back to 1260, and restored it with its original Italian-style garden. Part of Villa Miralfiore is a glass museum with works by artists including Enrico Baj, Vasco Bendini, Eugenio Carmi, Gianni Colombo, Danny Lane, Umberto Mariani, Bruno Munari, Arnaldo Pomodoro, Walter Valentini, Oscar Piattella and Luigi Veronesi.

STEFANO MARZANO — Served as Chief Design Officer and CEO of Philips Design at Royal Philips International between 1991 and 2011. Thereafter he was Chief Design Officer of Electrolux and a member of the Electrolux Group management team from January 2012 until he retired at the end of 2013. Marzano holds a doctorate in architecture from the Milan Polytechnic and honorary doctorates in design from the University Sapienza in Rome and the PolyU of Hong Kong. Until 1998 he was a professor at the Domus Academy in Milan and a member of the academy's strategic board. From 1999 to 2001 and from 2017 to 2019 he was a professor of the Milan Polytechnic. Marzano is the founding member of the European Design Leadership Board. He is founding dean and advisory board member of THNK School of Creative Leadership, Amsterdam. He was a co-founder and chairman of the advisory board of the Faculty of Design at Eindhoven University of Technology. Marzano is the author and editor of several books on design and innovation. In 2005, *Business Week* named him one of the world's thirty-eight 'Best Leaders'.

JUHANI PALLASMAA — One of the world's most distinguished architects and architectural-design thinkers, Juhani Pallasmaa's previous positions include: Member of the Jury of the Pritzker Architecture Prize, Rector of the Institute of Industrial Arts, Helsinki; Director of the Museum of Finnish Architecture, Helsinki; and Professor and Dean of the Faculty of Architecture, Aalto University of Technology, Helsinki. He has also held visiting professorships at several universities internationally. Pallasmaa is author or editor of several books, among others the classic *The Eye of the Skin: Architecture and the Senses*.

TIZIANA PROIETTI — An architect with a Ph.D. in Architectural Design, Tiziana Proietti gained her doctorate at the Sapienza University of Rome in collaboration with the University of Technology TU Delft in 2013 and is currently Professor at the University of Oklahoma, USA. Her research activity explores human perception in architectural spaces with a special focus on the relationship between the senses and the cognitive value of proportion. After a decade of studies on proportion in architecture, Proietti is currently developing her research by connecting neuroscience and architecture in collaboration with the Salk Institute in San Diego and the SPaCE Lab at the University of Southern California.

INGEBORG DE ROODE — The Curator of industrial design at the Stedelijk Museum Amsterdam since 2001, Ingeborg de Roode studied Art History in Leiden and started her museum career as a curator at the Dutch Textile Museum in Tilburg. From 2009 to 2012 she chaired the Modernism Today initiative, which organized lectures and symposia. She has published on design in *Het Financieele Dagblad*, various magazines, catalogues and other publications. She has organized many exhibitions, including, *Designs for Children: Furniture / Playgrounds by Aldo van Eyck* (2002), and *Nest: Designs for the Interior* (2005). In 2010 De Roode was commissioned by the Via Milano Foundation to organize the exhibition *10 years of Via Milano: New Dutch Design* at the Oude Kerk in Amsterdam. Her most recent exhibitions for the Stedelijk Museum include *Marcel Wanders: Pinned Up. 25 years of design* (2014). *Living in the Amsterdam School* (2016), *Solution or Utopia? Designs for refugees* (2017), *and Studio Drift. Coded Nature* (2018).

WERA SELENOWA — Having gained wide experience in management and organization, specifically in the arts and in start-up companies, Wera Selenowa joined Satyendra Pakhalé Associates as Managing Director in 2010. Prior to this position, she worked in Zurich as head of administration for three start-up companies in the areas of e-publishing, pharmaceutical medicine and investment and completed her International Executive MBA in General Management at the University of Salzburg Business School. Following her passion for the arts, design and economics, she graduated in arts management in Germany while gaining work experience in the USA, Germany and Switzerland, so setting the stage for further international activities. Born in Moscow, she grew up in Zurich, Switzerland.

WALTER M. SPINK — Professor Emeritus of Indian Art at the University of Michigan, Ann Arbor, USA; Walter M. Spink is the world's leading authority of Ajanta, a UNESCO World Heritage site. Spink has returned to this site regularly with zeal and dedication. He has enabled hundreds of students, not only from the University of Michigan, but also from institutions around the world, and particularly those in India, to participate in his site seminar. Spink has published widely on Indian Art in general, and on Ajanta and related sites in particular.

RENÉ SPITZ — Having studied History, German Literature and Communications in Munich and Cologne, René Spitz gained his Ph.D. in 1997 with a thesis on the political history of the Ulm School of Design from 1953-68 (published with the support of the Alfried Krupp von Bohlen und Halbach Foundation, Essen). Since then he has regularly published academic and journalistic contributions on design history and current developments in design, and has taught design criticism, theory and history at the University of Wuppertal and elsewhere. His current research project is on the concept of design. Since 2001, he and Martin Rendel have curated exhibitions during the Cologne Furniture Fair, including on Konstantin Grcic, Ross Lovegrove, Greg Lynn, Tokujin Yoshioka, Ronan and Erwan Bouroullec, Andrea Branzi, Stefan Ytterborn and others). The rendel & spitz agency has won many international design awards. Since 2004 Spitz has been a member and chair of the IFG advisory board.

Our special thanks for their generous sponsorship go to our partners with whom we have worked on numerous inspiring projects over the years. We truly appreciate your continuous support, thanks to which we were able to realize this monograph.

ALESSI, Italy

AMMANN//GALLERY, Germany

calyah

CALYAH, Denmark

CITIZEN M HOTELS, the Netherlands

L'Etoile Properties

PARIS · LONDON · HAMBURG · AMSTERDAM · MADRID · SEOUL · LUXEMBOURG

L'ETOILE PROPERTIES, France

OFFECCT

OFFECCT, Sweden

POLTRONA FRAU, Italy

TUBES

TUBES RADIATORI, Italy

VAGHI, Italy

CONCEPT
Satyendra Pakhalé, Tiziana Proietti

AUTHORS
Alberto Alessi, Gabrielle Ammann, Paola Antonelli, Jacques Barsac, Giulio Cappellini, Aric Chen, Cristiano Crosetta, Marva Griffin Wilshire, Vittorio Livi, Stefano Marzano, Juhani Pallasmaa, Tiziana Proietti, Ingeborg de Roode, Wera Selenowa, Walter M. Spink, René Spitz

EDITOR
Jane Szita

GRAPHIC DESIGN
Mainstudio, Amsterdam
(Edwin van Gelder and Florian Schimanski)

TRANSLATION
Bronwen Saunders, Walter van der Star

PROOF-READING
Bronwen Saunders

PHOTOGRAPHY
Nicole Marnati

LITHOGRAPHY
Beeldproductie, Egbert de Haas

PRINTING
Unicum, Tilburg, the Netherlands

PAPER
Munken Print White 100 g/m²
Magno Volume 115 g/m²
Rainbow Grey 120 g/m²

TYPEFACE
Suisse Int'l

Mr. Satyendra Pakhalé, designer is the sole author of the design works published in this monograph. All works are protected by intellectual property rights law. The designer is the inventor and author of the designs and claims the right to maintain and preserve its wholeness and entirety.

nai010 publishers is an internationally orientated publisher specialized in developing, producing and distributing books in the fields of architecture, urbanism, art and design.
www.nai010.com

nai010 books are available internationally at selected bookstores and from the following distribution partners:
North, Central and South America — Artbook | D.A.P., New York, USA, dap@dapinc.com

Rest of the world — Idea Books, Amsterdam, the Netherlands, idea@ideabooks.nl

For general questions, please contact nai010 publishers directly at sales@nai010.com or visit our website www.nai010.com for further information.

Printed and bound in the Netherlands

ISBN 978-94-6208-514-5

NUR 656
BISAC DES000000

PHOTOCREDITS
Claudio Amadei, Italy 130, 133
Ammann Gallery, Germany 104, 114, 115, 160–163, 277, 334, 335
Corné Bastiaansen, the Netherlands 92, 100–102
Henrik Berg, Sweden 66, 67, 69
Francesca Bottazzin, Italy 354–356
Cap Design, Italy 29–31, 279
Colombo Design, Italy 76
Michele Durazzi, Italy 346–348, 350, 351, 360–362, 366, 367
Erreti, Italy 234, 235
Frans Feijen, the Netherlands 39–44
Steven A. Heller, USA 19
Danny Hollander, the Netherlands 15, 258, 259
Karkel / AChP, USA 343
Celia D. Luna, USA 151
Emanuele Macciò, Italy 330
Federico Marin, Italy 172–175
Nicole Marnati, Italy 26, 27, 29, 58–61, 72–75, 77, 90, 91, 94, 95, 103, 106–110, 128, 129, 193–199, 162, 164–167, 188, 189, 201, 204, 205, 218, 219, 232, 233, 236–238, 250, 251, 253, 264, 265, 268–270, 282, 283, 285–287, 288, 289, 296, 297, 302, 317, 323, 332, 333, 373, 378–381, 388, 389, 391, 398, 399
Satyendra Pakhalé, the Netherlands 36–38, 87, 114, 117, 148, 149, 151, 181, 183, 205, 307, 309, 311
Lena Palmé, Sweden 239
Andrea Passuello, Italy 202, 203
Michael Penck, Australia 83, 84
Rolf Petersen, USA 21
Philips & Renault Design, Europe 115, 245, 260–263
Poltrona Frau, Italy 220, 222, 223
Jussi Puikkonen, Finland 375
Tiziano Rossi, Italy 96, 97, 122–124, 127, 186, 187
RSVP, Italy 111
Satyendra Pakhalé Associates, the Netherlands 21, 23, 28, 29, 31–35, 42–47, 51, 62–65, 68, 69, 70–73, 75, 78, 79, 93, 98, 99, 103, 105, 111, 115, 117, 125, 126, 129–143, 147, 148, 149, 151, 154–157, 159, 162, 163, 165, 168–171, 174, 175 181, 183, 192, 193, 199, 200, 205–207, 215, 221, 223–231, 234, 235, 239 247, 252–257, 266, 267, 270, 271, 276, 277, 279, 284, 287, 288, 290–295, 298, 299, 311, 358, 359, 300, 301, 307, 309, 317, 318, 322, 324, 325, 326–329, 334, 335, 349, 358, 359, 363–365, 371, 373, 375, 380, 382–387, 391, 392, 393, 395–397, 399
Kevin Standage, United Kingdom 148
Leonardo Talarico, Italy 352–356
Tubes, Italy 55, 314–320
Nico Tucci, Italy 190, 191, 193
Tom Vack, Germany 321

SPECIAL THANKS
Abdelkader Abdi, David Adjaye, Alberto Alessi, Danilo Alliata, Yashadatta Alone, Ivano Ambrosini, Gabrielle Ammann, Malin Andersson, Ben and Linda Andrea, Surya Andrea, Paola Antonelli, Francesca Appiani, Ron Arad, Roberto Archetti, Masayo Ave, Paolo Avvanzini, Roberta Avvanzini, Shin Azumi, Isabelle Clotilde Bagdasarianz-Küng, Gijs Bakker, Uwe Bahnsen, Stefano Barbazza, Gloria Barcellini, Rachael Barraclough, Jacques Barsac, Patrizia Beltrami, Uno Bento, Adriano Berengo, Marco Berengo, Boris Berlin, Nuno Bernardo, Erna Beumers, George Beylerian, Ayse Birsel, Hélène Binet, Maria Angelica Bitetti, Maria Blaisse, Christian Blaser, Luisa Bocchietto, Andrea Boragno, Massimo Bortott, Bosa Family, Kristine Bowne, Alessandro Bozzini, Damian Bradfield, Matteo Brioni, Anne-Marie Buemann, Anne Marie Button, Fernando and Humberto Campana, Giulio Cappellini, Gianmaria Caravaglia, Anna Castelli Fererri, Giovanna Castiglioni, Rattan Chadha, Wai Chang, Natalie Chatterjee, Mark Chau, Aric Chen, Min Chen, Vivian Cheng, Marie Chevalier, Pradeep Chotkan, Francesco Cianfarani, Aldo Cibic, Felix Claus, Alessandro Colla, Michele Colombo, Nicola Coropulis, Maurizio Costa, Marie Coudron, Crosetta Family, Simona Cusini, Torkil Dantzer, Domitilla Dardi, Liz Davis, Jacob de Baan, Carlotta de Bevilacqua, Cees de Bont, Kos de Jong, Reinier den Boer, Eva de Klerk, Tammo De Ligny, Fabrizio De Lucia, Eames Demetrios, Reinier den Boer, Maddalena De Padova, Luca De Padova, Ingeborg de Roode, Cok de Roy, Maranke de Vos, Fariba Derakshani, Farrokh Derakshani, Varghese Devassy, Tjeerd de Vries, Peter Diamandis, Marcus Diebel, Menno Dieperink, Berend Dijk, Lisa Dinges, Robert Dirig, Sebastian Doermann, Natascha Drabbe, Dorothy Dunn, Michele Durazzi, Lidewij Edelkoort, Ian Ellison, Hans-Peter Engeler, Anders Englund, Maria Helena Estrada, Teresa Estrela, Hartmut Esslinger, Rosa Maria Falvo, Rolf Fehlbaum, Beatrice Felis, Fulvio Ferrari, Silvia Ferrari, Georgina Ferrer, Brigitte Fitoussi, Giuseppina Flor, Stefano Fornari, Perry Forsberg, Monica Förster, Marion Fouré, Alicia Framis, Rasmus Frankel, Galina Fürer, Ashvin and Nadine Gatha, Simona Giacomelli, Elisa Giovannoni, Stefano Giovannoni, Colin Giroth, Ernesto Gismondi, Adem Gokcinar, Mireia Gordi i Vila, Annika Gregianin, Chiara Gregotti, Anouk Groen, Marva Griffin Wilshire, Guus Gugelot, Valerie Guillaume, Giulia Guzzini, Zaha Hadid, Willem Haitsma, Claire and Gabor Halmos, Bente Vita Hansen, Frank Heijlighen, Marie-Louise Hellgren, Petra Hesse, Matthew Higgins, Jutta Hinterleitner, Petra Hölscher, Constanze Hosp, Florian Hufnagl, Mariana Idiarte, Madhukar Ingole, James Irvine, Nora Janning, Waldick Jatoba, Eun Ji Woo, Charles O. Job, Wolfgang Johnson, Marie-Laure Jousset, Jonathan J. Kamp, Moriko Kira, Robert Kloos, Raghu Koli, Denisa Kollarova, Sabrina Koning-Woud, Harri Koskinen, Eero Kovisto, Dorota Koziara, Diana Krabbendam, Huub Kuijpers, Dingeman Kuilman, Robin Kuipers, Charlotte Landsheer, Patrick Le Quément, Stefan Lechner, Jonathan Leendertse, Yoann Legaignoux, Benny Leong, Dimitri Liaos, Christina Schiøtt Liaos, Joris Link, Daniele Livi, Vittorio Livi, Birgit Lohmann, Jerry, Jordi and Ryan Lopies, Alberto Lovato, Ross Lovegrove, Renato Luzi, John Maeda, Ann Maes, Pierangelo Maffiodo, Vico Magistretti, Nigel Majakari, Francesca Francone Madreya, Riccarda Mandrini, Raffaella Mangiarotti, Fiorenza, Andrea and Massimo Mapelli, Enzo Mari, Karmelina Martina, Diego Martinelli, Mauro Martinuzzi, Stefano Marzano, Lorenzo Marzoli, Karola Matschke, Alberto Meda, Ambra Medda, Rahul Mehrotra, Fulvia Mendini, Alessandro Mendini, Chris Meplon, Jelena Milutinovic, Barbara Minetto, Radboud Molijn, Claus Mølgaard, Carl Moroder, Patrizia Moroso, Jasper Morrison, Tomoko Mukiyama, Pradnya Murti, Ton Musch, Kim Myung Suk, Sudhakar Nadkarni, Ravi Nafde, Sascha Naji, Ki-Young Nam, Tek-Jin Nam, Cristina Nardi, Nicolette Naumann, Yukiko Nezu, Sandra Nielen, Frans van Nieuwenborg, Daniel Nikol, Fabio Novembre, Hiroe Okubo, Kirsten Ørskov, Olga Ortiz Sanchez, Leïla Othman, Toni Paci, Pakhale Family, Juhani Pallasmaa, Tim and Yuki Pallis, Nenne Palmé, Ole Palsby, Vanni Pasca, Alberto Pasquale, Divia Patel, Oscar Peña, Michael Penck, Alberto Perazza, Eugenio Perazza, Enrico Perin, Nestor Perkal, Pernette Perriand-Barsac, Thu Phan, Warner Philips, Anna Pierleoni, Lars Pihl, Ilaria Pilatte, Francesco Pilotto, Sam Pitroda, Mia Pizzi, Marie Pok, Michael Polachowski, Ludovica and Roberto Palomba, Laura Polinoro, Jos Poodt, Fabio Prestini, Tiziana Proietti, Uli Prutscher, Jussi Puikkonen, Thomas Quilliou, Heike Rabe, Sandra Rabenou, Renny Ramakers, Apolinario Ramos, Pravin Ramteke, A.G. Rao, Thomas Rathgeber, Emma Reigans, Els Reijnders, Paola Restelli, Giulia Riccucci, Rene Rietmeyer, Hans Robertus, Joppe Rog, Alberto Rogato, Claudia Rolim, Thea Roolfs, Marialaura Rossiello, Corinna Rösner, Jos Rutten, Jan Ryde, Valentina Salvi, D. N. Sandanshiv, Emma Sandsjö, Andrea Sanson, Anne Marie Sargueil, Laura Sarvilinna, Céline Savoye, Folke Schlueter, Herbert Schmid, Erich Schmid, Jana Scholze, Bibi Seck, Magda Seifert, Wera Selenowa, Alceo Serafini, Ges and Karmen Sheldrake, Kaita Shinagawa, Sindri Sighvatsson, Halina Sikora, Nagsen Sonare, Tuuli Sotamaa, Marcia R. A. Sookha, Ettore Sottsass Jr., Dick Spierenburg, Gregorio Spini, Walter M. Spink, René Spitz, Mirko Splendiani, Benoit Steenackers, Sebastian Steinmetz, Hannes and Lulu Stephensen, Peter Strang, Hyeon-Jeong Suk, Barbara Summa, Ilkka Suppanen, Mads Nicolas Surel, Ratan Tata, Christoph E.G. ten Houte de Lange, Bastien Tercinier, Mariko Terrada, Kurt Tingdal, Angela Thomas, Norman Trapman, Elena Domela Nieuwenhuis Trisotto, Robin Uleman, Didier Unglik, Tom Vack, Ester Pirotta Vack, Christel Vaenerberg, Elisabetta, Luigi and Matteo Vaghi, Robbie van Bakel, Kitty van Boven, Ferdinand van den Berg, Peter van den Hoogen, Dimitri van der Brugh, Mariska van der Burgt, Els van der Plas, Joanna van der Zanden, Cock van Driel, Adrian van Hooydonk, Pim van Lingen, Frans van Nieuwenborg, Miranda van Oostrom, Bryan van Schooten, Tim van Slooten, Allard van Son, Eelco van Welie, Diederik Veelo, Willemijn Verloop, Marcel Vermeulen, Patrick Virginia, Massimo Vismara, Antoinette Vonder Mühll, Jannes and Monique Vos, Ching Wan, Heidi Weber, Nicholas Fox Weber, Irma Werndly, Laetitia Wolff, Kyung Won Chung, Nhi Wong, Woody K. T. Yao, Fabio Zanchetta, Simone Zanchetta

COLOPHON